I0819360

THE ROMAN WORLD WAR

The Roman World War

FROM THE IDES OF MARCH TO CLEOPATRA'S SUICIDE

GIUSTO TRAINA

TRANSLATED BY
MALCOLM DeBEVOISE

PRINCETON UNIVERSITY PRESS
PRINCETON & OXFORD

Published by Princeton University Press

41 William Street, Princeton, New Jersey 08540
99 Banbury Road, Oxford OX2 6JX

press.princeton.edu

GPSR Authorized Representative: Easy Access System Europe—Mustamäe tee 50, 10621 Tallinn, Estonia, gpsr.requests@easproject.com

ISBN 978-0-691-25787-7
ISBN (e-book): 978-0-691-28732-4
ISBN (Web PDF) 978-0-691-25789-1

British Library Cataloging-in-Publication Data is available

Editorial: Ben Tate and Josh Drake
Production Editorial: Jill Harris
Jacket Design: Karl Spurzem
Production: Danielle Amatucci
Publicity: Alyssa Sanford and Charlotte Coyne
Copyeditor: Irina du Quenoy

Jacket image: Ancient stone relief of Roman warship.

This book has been composed in Arno

Printed in the United States of America

10 9 8 7 6 5 4 3 2 1

CONTENTS

List of Figures and Maps vii

Preface: The End of the Roman Republic: Civil War or World War? ix

Introduction: Caesar's Last Campaign 1

PART I. THE WORLD AFTER THE IDES OF MARCH

1 Apollo vs. Dionysus 21

2 Western Warlords 37

3 The Wars of the Tyrannicides 52

4 Avenging Caesar 68

PART II. JOYS AND SORROWS OF THE TRIUMVIRS

5 Between Concord and Discord 83

6 The Advent of a Golden Age 100

7 The *Imperium* Strikes Back 114

8 *Mare Nostrum* 125

PART III. THE END OF A REPUBLIC

9 Antony's Eastern Campaign 139

10 End of the Young Pompey, Wars of the Young Caesar 153

11 The Inimitable Life of Alexandria 167

12 The Oath of All Italy 177

Translator's Note 189

Notes 191

Select Bibliography 209

Index 221

FIGURES AND MAPS

Figures

2.1. *Aureus* of Sextus Pompey 43

3.1. Fragment of the base of the statue of Brutus 55

4.1. Denarius struck in honor of I. Mussidius Longus 69

5.1. Denarius struck in honor of Cn. Domitius Ahenobarbus Imperator 88

5.2. Depiction of Cleopatra and Ptolemy XV Caesar 95

7.1. Silver drachma of Artawazd II 116

7.2. Silver denarius bearing the image of Quintus Labienus 118

8.1. Depiction of Antiochus of Commagene and Vahagn 129

9.1. Coin struck in honor of Antony and Cleopatra, 34 BCE 143

9.2. Drachma bearing the image of Phraates IV 145

Maps

1. Caesar's civil wars 4
2. Roman Syria 58
3. The Philippi Campaign 75
4. The Mediterranean during the Triumviral Period 110
5. The Parthian Empire 115

6. The campaign against Sextus Pompey 133
7. Octavian's Illyrian War 159
8. The Donations of Alexandria 174
9. The Battle of Actium 181
10. The Roman world under Augustus 186

PREFACE

The End of the Roman Republic: Civil War or World War?

IN ROMAN memory, the last years of the Republic occupied the better part of a century marked by civil wars: Sulla versus Marius, Caesar versus Pompey, Octavian versus Antony—all of them long and bloody. An obscure schoolmaster named Lucius Ampelius, in a summary of these wars composed for the benefit of his young student Macrinus (whom some scholars have identified as the future praetorian prefect, then emperor [217–18 CE]), described the last one as having been conducted by "Caesar Augustus against several generals": in the first place Caesar's murderers, Brutus and Cassius, but also Sextus Pompey and Mark Antony.[1] Plainly this was no ordinary conflict. It was a great war that lasted fourteen years, from the assassination of Caesar in 44 BCE until the definitive defeat of Antony and Cleopatra by Octavian in 30—a short but very intense period that we might call, paraphrasing the title of John Reed's book on the Russian Revolution, "Fourteen Years That Shook the World."[2]

Looking at the matter in this way, as schoolboys under the Principate were taught to do, the wars of the late Republic appeared to be so many settlings of accounts among Romans, factional conflict interrupted from time to time by the need to fight against barbarians and rebels. The final victory of Octavian, who in 27 took the name Augustus and brought forth the Principate from the Republic, put an end to the civil wars.[3] Yet the situation was much more complicated than people in Ampelius's time were accustomed to suppose. The events of the late Republic cannot properly be characterized as a concatenation of civil wars, because their implications were worldwide. To speak of them in this manner may seem anachronistic, for the term "world war" was not used before the nineteenth century; the ancients, however, had no trouble telling the difference between ordinary and extraordinary wars.[4] Appian, for example, an Alexandrian Greek active in the second century CE who was acutely sensitive to the situation of non-Roman peoples, clearly showed that the Roman civil wars set in motion a sequence of events amounting to nothing less than a global conflict.

The Romans themselves were keenly aware, at least from the middle of the first century before our era, that their internecine conflicts had acquired an international dimension, from Spain in the west to the Parthian Empire in the east. The historian Florus—a native of Roman Africa and therefore personally acquainted with the far-reaching extent of Roman dominion—describes the combat between Caesar and Pompey as one that could not "justly be called merely a civil war, nor a war between allies, nor yet a foreign war; it was rather a war with all these characteristics and something worse than a war."[5] Nor can the events of the late Republic be properly interpreted without taking into account its most important military campaign: the great expedition to the Balkans, and thence to the East, initially undertaken by Caesar and interrupted by his assassination. Octavian and Mark Antony were unable to fully realize Caesar's ambition in the years that followed.

In the traditional historical perspective, centered on Rome and Italy, neighboring peoples had a more or less close view of the Roman civil wars, but only as bystanders. North Africans, Hispanics, Celts, Greeks, Thracians, and Armenians looked on from the front rows of this vast theater, the nearest spectators of a tragic drama on which their fate depended. In distant Mesopotamia, seated in the back rows, the Parthians likewise observed the vicissitudes of their rivals, who from time to time suspended hostilities to conclude or renew more or less durable alliances that occasionally allowed them to eliminate the weakest friendly rulers seeking to increase their power at the expense of Rome.

Modern scholarship has not departed very far from this perspective. The argument developed by Ronald Syme in *The Roman Revolution* (1939), one of the finest books on ancient history ever written, focusing on Roman power and considering non-Roman peoples as little more than incidental casualties of internal warfare, remains influential still today.[6] Commenting on the Parthian victories of 40 BCE, Syme seeks to reassure his readers, saying that "the domination of the nomads was transient."[7] And although he is rather sympathetic to Antony, he cannot help but conclude that Antony and Cleopatra "were a pretext in the strife for power . . . merely pawns in the game of destiny."[8]

It goes without saying that Symes, a proud New Zealander and British citizen, could hardly have been expected to take a postcolonial view of the matter. As we enter the second quarter-century of the new millennium, however, the dominant view of ancient history is still the one elaborated in the nineteenth and twentieth centuries. The study of non-Greeks and non-Romans in particular has changed dramatically since the 1980s, it is true, in large part owing to the writings of Edward Said.[9] Even so, only a few maverick scholars are trying to change the way in which Greeks and Romans and their interaction with other peoples are conceived; the history of Rome is still mostly treated as a history of the Romans, in which their foreign subjects and enemies remain in the background, no matter how foreign, how "barbarian" they were.[10] A more inclusive history of antiquity is badly needed. No matter how glorious its past, the study of ancient history cannot avoid contemplating novel geopolitical perspectives and historiographical methods.

Nevertheless there are encouraging signs of a growing openness to new ideas. Kristina Sessa has called for a truly global approach to Late Antiquity aimed at "keeping Late Antiquity weird."[11] This is rather easier for scholars in her branch of the field: The written evidence that has come down to us from the last century of the Republic is less multilingual. The events of this period are nonetheless sufficiently well attested, in some cases by extra-classical sources, that we can begin to imagine making the age of the civil wars seem weirder than it is now widely believed to have been.[12]

The idea for the present work came to me some years ago as the result of a conversation with Anthony Rowley, the history editor at Éditions Fayard in Paris, who had enjoyed my "one-year book," *428 A.D.*[13] Rowley suggested that it might be fruitful to apply to ancient history the methodology of "connected histories" introduced by Sanjay Subrahmanyam in a seminal article published in 1997.[14] Doing this took me some time, but I was able to persevere in the wake of Rowley's untimely death with the encouragement of his successor, Sophie Hogg, who patiently put up with my delays and then, even more patiently, helped me see my way through to the end of the final draft, facilitated by the lockdown that forced me to stay home and write.

A further step was taken with the appearance of the Italian edition, which came out almost a year later, in 2023. In addition to my very capable editors Giovanni Carletti and Caterina Coriani, I owe thanks to Imma Eramo, who translated the book from the French while taking care to verify its factual accuracy on many points. Most of the additions and corrections made to the Italian edition have been incorporated here.

At Princeton I am grateful to Ben Tate, the acquiring editor, for his unstinting support, and to Malcolm DeBevoise for his fine translation and his painstaking review of all the citations in the notes. I also thank the press's anonymous referees for their helpful comments. It would be impossible to mention all the friends, colleagues, and students who helped me to improve the text, correct errors, and locate bibliographical and iconographical references. I would like at least to acknowledge the kind assistance of Pierangelo Buongiorno, Luciano Canfora, Franco Cardini, Francesco Carriere, Omar Coloru, Roberto Cristofoli, Michèle Coltelloni-Trannoy, Paolo Liverani, Samuele Rocca, Daniele Salvoldi, Federico Santangelo, and Anne Vial-Logeay.

The end of the Roman republic is one of the best documented periods of Antiquity. Without claiming to have written a genuinely comprehensive history, since most of our sources reflect more the Roman point of view than that of other peoples, I have nonetheless tried to strike a new balance, elevating these peoples above the secondary role to which they have been consigned until now and highlighting, alongside the main interpreters of this world tragedy, the role of several minor Roman characters and, above all, a cast of non-Romans less well known than Cleopatra, yet no less involved in the Great Game between Rome, Parthia, and the nations in between, as well as the civil conflicts in other parts of the *imperium Romanum*, foremost among them the Moor Bogud, the Dacian Burebista, the Thracian Sadalas, the Cilician Tarcondimotus, and the Armenian Artawazd II. Yes, Artawazd, not "Artavasdes"—let's refer to him as his own subjects did. A small detail, perhaps, but a step in the right direction.

THE ROMAN WORLD WAR

INTRODUCTION

Caesar's Last Campaign

THE VIOLENT death of Julius Caesar abruptly cancelled all his plans, beginning with the eastern campaign. The dictator was to have left Rome on 18 March 44 to rejoin his legions, which had already crossed the Adriatic. Three days earlier—the Ides of March, according to the Roman calendar—he was fatally stabbed by a group of conspirators. The historian Nicolaus of Damascus noted the striking contrast between Caesar's inert remains and the grandeur of his campaigns, real or imagined: "The corpse was still lying where Caesar fell, covered ignominiously in the blood of the man who had marched as far west as Britain and the Ocean and who was planning to march east against the realms of the Parthians and the Indians so that, when they were subjugated, sovereignty over all land and sea would be combined into one empire—this man's corpse was lying there, then, no one having had the courage to stay and carry it off."[1]

Nicolaus's *Life of Augustus*, written shortly after the death of the *princeps* in 14 CE, is the earliest account that has come down to us of Caesar's determination to march eastward for the purpose of resuming hostilities against the Parthian Empire, which extended from Mesopotamia to Central Asia. In 54–53, the Parthians had repulsed the attempted invasion of Mesopotamia by a great army led by the ambitious Marcus Licinius Crassus; some forty thousand men, legionaries and auxiliaries were annihilated by cavalry and allied forces on 9 June 53, on the plain of Carrhae (modern Harran, in Turkey, near the Syrian border). Crassus had foreseen neither the enemy's reaction nor its tactical superiority. A few days after the massacre of his men he died, rather stupidly, in a skirmish. It is said that his head was brought to the king at the end of a banquet, a macabre scene described by Plutarch.[2] Several surviving legionaries were captured. The Parthians had taken possession of the military standards of seven legions as well, a mortal blow to the prestige of Rome in the East and the height of its humiliation there.

In the aftermath of Carrhae, the Parthians and their Arab allies repeatedly raided the Roman province of Syria and, in 51, arrived at the gates of Antioch, confident that the quality of their forces and the restlessness of the local population under Roman domination would enable them to prevail.[3] The civil war between Pompey and Caesar delayed the Roman response. Legionary soldiers stationed in Syria, commanded by Gaius Cassius Longinus (later one of Caesar's assassins), finally managed to contain the invasion, but defensive capabilities needed nonetheless to be reinforced if Roman authority were to be restored. In 50, when Caesar was still in Gaul, the Senate ordered him to commit two of his legions to the war against the Parthians. Pompey, now preparing for war, took advantage of this turn of events to undermine his rival by making sure that Caesar's troops remained in Italy, at his own service.[4] In sparing the Parthians the costs of a new war, Pompey assured himself of the support of the Parthian king, Orodes II. Indeed, when Caesar attacked, "the Parthians took the Pompeian side both because of their accord with Pompey in the Mithridatic War and also because of the killing of Crassus, whose son [Marcus Licinius Crassus Junior, a veteran of the Gallic campaigns like his brother Publius, who died at Carrhae] they had heard had sided with Caesar, and they had no doubt that he would avenge his father if Caesar prevailed."[5]

In the campaign that was to culminate in a decisive battle against Caesar at Pharsalus on 9 August 48, Pompey tried to enlist the active participation of the Parthians, but to no avail; Orodes, it was said, demanded Syria in exchange.[6] After his defeat, Pompey allegedly hesitated to take refuge with the king, notwithstanding that Orodes appeared for the moment to be the best placed to receive Pompey and the remnants of his army and to protect them in their weakened condition, so that they might regroup and set off again in larger numbers.[7] According to

Cassius Dio, no doubt relying on a source favorable to Pompey, this was a baseless rumor: The Parthians could not be trusted, because they had imprisoned Pompey's ambassador, and Pompey was forced to decide whether to take refuge in Egypt or in Africa.[8] However this may be, Pompey was killed in Egypt a few months after his defeat at Pharsalus.

Nothing any longer stood in the way of war against the Parthians, though Caesar's legionaries were exhausted from long years of fighting at home and abroad. In the summer of 47 he went to Syria and then to Cilicia, for the purpose of restoring order in those parts of the East under Roman control. A good number of Pompey's former allies asked for forgiveness. The dictator's shrewdness in granting clemency, on payment of a tribute, won their allegiance.[9] In Syria Caesar received the kings, sovereigns, and rulers whose states bordered Syria and Cilicia and the other Roman provinces, more or less powerful allies who were then incorporated into the *imperium Romanum*.[10] In the less urbanized regions of Anatolia, the Romans did not exercise direct control but practiced what might be called an imperialist form of hegemony dedicated to establishing a balance among competing political interests and to collecting taxes. The title of king was respected in the East; even the least formidable monarchs possessed a religious charisma that guaranteed the loyalty of their subjects and the obedience of nobles. It was altogether in Rome's interest to respect these traditions while at the same time supporting local rulers, even if from time to time it was convenient to impose ones of its own choosing. Furthermore, Caesar could count on the support of Antioch, a major city, and on that of the Jews, thanks to his excellent relations with John Hyrcanus II, high priest of the Temple of Jerusalem.

Nevertheless Caesar, who in the meantime had moved from Syria to neighboring Cilicia, could not stay long in the East. He had hoped to be able to begin preparing a campaign against the Parthians, but he still had to conclude the civil war against Pompey's sons and allies, in Africa to begin with and then in Spain. In the meantime, during his long absence from Rome, riots had broken out; he had to get back home as quickly as possible. Having sorted out the situation in Syria (which had been bled white by the Pompeian governor, Quintus Caecilius Metellus

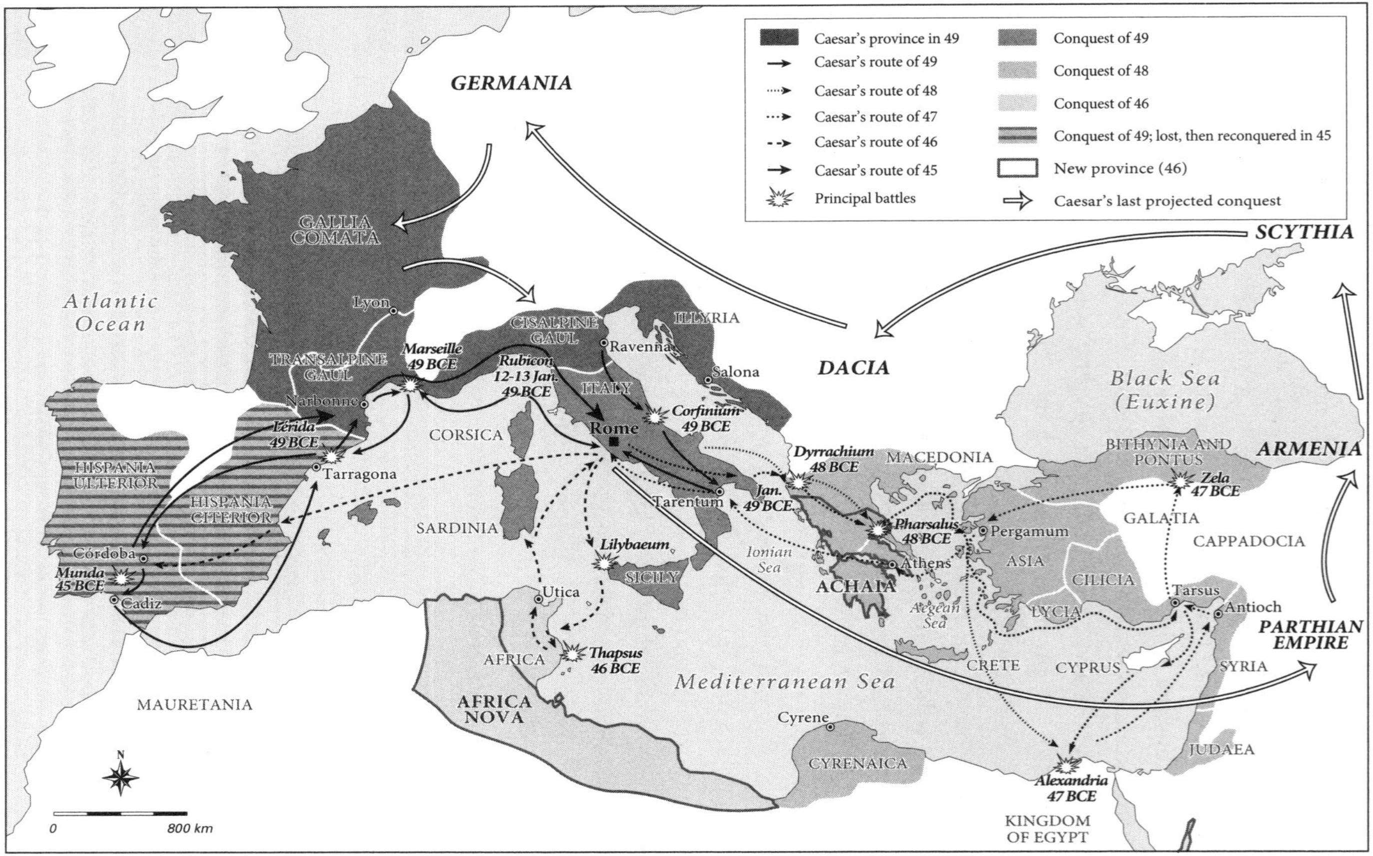

MAP 1. Caesar's civil wars

Scipio), he entrusted the province to his cousin Sextus Iulius Caesar, probably his designated successor.[11] On his way back to Italy, at Zela in Pontic Cappadocia (as it should be called, rather than "Pontus"), Caesar easily defeated ("veni, vidi, vici") Pharnaces II, son of Mithradates VI Eupator and ruler of the Cimmerian Bosporus, who was trying to recover the North Anatolian regions that once belonged to his dynasty. Later, in a speech delivered in early 43 and reported by Cassius Dio, Cicero accused Mark Antony of having fomented the uprisings four years earlier. "He was chiefly responsible," Cicero allegedly said, "for the fact that the whole region of Pontus and Parthia was not subdued at that time immediately after the victory over Pharnaces. Owing to Antony's misdeeds, Caesar was obliged to come back here at once, before he could settle matters abroad, as [otherwise] he would have been able to do."[12] He was mainly concerned, then, with Rome's strategic position in the East—something of far greater consequence than mere propaganda or a grandiose desire to imitate Alexander the Great. This was grand strategy at its best.

The Romans were not unaware of Caesar's ambitions. These were confirmed in the summer of 46 when he celebrated a series of spectacular triumphs, dedicating four ceremonies to his victories in the four parts of the world: Gaul, Africa, Pontus, and Egypt. Chariots weighed down with booty and prisoners were paraded before the people. Conquered territories were personified, with paintings and gilded statuary portraying the Rhine, the Rhône, and the Ocean as captives.[13] Among the prisoners were a few more or less high-ranking figures, among them the orphaned prince Juba, son of the king of Numidia, who had been allied with Pompey; Arsinoë, Cleopatra's younger sister and queen of Egypt from 48 to 47; and above all, Vercingetorix, the Gallic chieftain who dared to defy Caesar and who had been brought to Rome following his defeat at Alesia in 52. By reason of their youth, Juba and Arsinoë were spared. Juba received a Roman education and a few years later was appointed king of Mauretania by Augustus; Arsinoë, as we will see, took refuge in Asia Minor. No pity was shown to Vercingetorix, strangled shortly after the ceremony. Other less prestigious prisoners were sent to their death in the arena.

In this way Caesar managed to thoroughly reinterpret the traditional Roman triumph, to the delight of the people but to the great dismay of his adversaries. He used these ostentatious and sensational ceremonies to advertise his military glory in a festive atmosphere, even permitting his soldiers to chant satirical couplets mocking the ambiguous sexuality of their commander. He also took posthumous revenge on Pompey, his long-standing rival, whose three triumphs in 61 had diminished his reputation. Nevertheless, if he stirred the imagination of the Roman people, he also created ill will among a number of senators—and all the more as the Spanish triumph he celebrated the following year, in October 45, was in fact a triumph over the Pompeians.[14] Care was taken in all these cases to present his victories as triumphs over foreign enemies, sidestepping the delicate question of civil discord.

Caesar spent lavishly on entertainments and stage plays performed "by actors of all languages." In an artificial basin dug near his gardens and filled with water, an ancient naval battle pitting "Tyrian" against "Egyptian" fleets was reenacted.[15] The Circus Maximus was the scene of a pitched battle involving a thousand men, sixty horsemen, and forty elephants.[16] Spectacles of this kind were meant to make the people forget the clashes between Roman armies. The display of strange animals, symbolizing Rome's hold over the barbarian world and the wild creatures that populated it, emphasized the greatness of the games' sponsor, particularly in the case of previously unknown species. Caesar's Egyptian triumph introduced a "spotted dromedary" (*kamēlopardalis*, probably a giraffe)—a final revenge on Pompey, who, in the entertainments he hosted during his second consulate in 55, had brought to Rome a rhinoceros and other exotic beasts.[17]

In the meantime the situation on the eastern frontier was far from being stabilized. A veteran of Pompey's campaigns, the knight Quintus Caecilius Bassus, spread the false report that Caesar had been killed in Africa and that the Pompeians had made him governor of Syria.[18] A mutiny ensued in which Sextus Caesar met his death. Claiming for himself the rank of praetor, Bassus took command of the troops in Syria, establishing his base of operations in the wealthy city of Apamea. Quintus Cornificius, the governor of Cilicia (known also as a poet of the "neoteric" tendency), was ordered to put down the rebellion, but Bassus was able to obtain the support of local tribal chieftains ("phylarchs") and vigorously resisted; the Parthians, taking advantage of his momentary absence from Syria, once again seized control of the province. Sallust, in the first letter to Caesar attributed to him, presciently warned that the only possible cause of the fall of Rome would be the recurrence of internal wars that, by killing so many of its citizens, would open the way to foreign potentates and barbarians.[19] The very next year Orodes threw his support in favor of Bassus's resistance, sending his son Pacorus at the head of a large army.[20] The campaign against the Parthians became crucial. Caesar, having at last vanquished the Pompeians and brought the civil wars to an end, could now at last prepare for his return to the East.

The Roman people craved further conquests and spoils, and the aristocracy, for its part, did not object to another expedition. It was necessary, they said, to defend the provinces, to avenge Crassus and the honor of Rome, and to subjugate a kingdom that aspired to be a rival empire. At this time Crassus's military abilities had not yet been called into question, as they were to be later, the unfortunate general being caricatured as a rich man consumed by ambition and devoid of strategic talent. To be sure, critics such as Cicero disparaged the Roman *imperatores,* more or less openly, for their dreams of glory. Nevertheless, when the Senate issued its decree authorizing the eastern campaign, there was no opposition. Cassius Dio, writing about the events of early 44, said that "a longing came over all the Romans alike to avenge Crassus and those who had perished with him, and they felt some hope of subjugating the Parthians then, if ever. [The senators] unanimously voted the command of the war to Caesar, and made ample provision for it."[21]

Nicolaus of Damascus did not exaggerate when he spoke of a campaign against the "kingdoms of the Parthians and the Indians"; an Indo-Scythian kingdom did in fact exist on the eastern border of the Parthian Empire. Crassus himself was precisely the sort of figure on whom Cicero had heaped scorn, imagining that his oriental conquests would far surpass those of his predecessors Lucullus and Pompey in the event, as he confidently supposed, that his armies succeeded in reaching "Bactria, India, and the Outer Sea."[22] Nicolaus, a shrewd analyst of the geopolitical situation in the East, could hardly have been unaware that the new campaign he mentioned called to mind the exploits of Alexander, whom Caesar and several other generals of the Republic took as their model.

The king of Macedon, by putting an end to the Achaemenid Empire while uniting Europe and Asia under a single sovereign, haunted the imagination of young Roman aristocrats brought up on accounts of his adventures who marveled at the daring Alexander displayed during his Indian campaign. In 62 a Celtic king of the Boii brought "Indian" slaves captured in the North Sea and offered them to Quintus Caecilius Metellus, proconsul of Cisalpine Gaul.[23] For Cornelius Nepos, who relates this anecdote, it was proof that one could sail along the coast of the "Outer Sea" (the Ocean) from Frisia to distant India. The identity of these captives has been the object of a great deal of speculation, including the fanciful suggestion that they were Eskimos from North America or Greenland. There is nothing surprising about this; after all, more than one author was unable to tell India apart from Ethiopia.

To be sure, there were those in Rome who said that Alexander had distinguished himself on the battlefield only against Orientals, unskilled in the art of war, and could hardly have defeated either Roman legions or the fierce barbarians of northern and southeastern Europe. Roman conquests extended over a great arc that encompassed lands in the both the West and the East where he had never set foot. The myth of Alexander nonetheless had lost none of its power. Around 69, when he was a little more than thirty years old and posted to Spain as quaestor, Caesar went to Gades (modern-day Cádiz), an ancient colony bordering the Atlantic, westernmost extremity of what the Greeks called the *oikoumenē*, the inhabited world. Allied to Rome, Gades depended mainly on the sea for its livelihood and "fitted out the most and largest merchant-vessels;" its fishermen, according to Strabo, ventured forth as far as the shores of Mauretania.[24] Visiting the temple of Hercules Gaditanus (the Punic divinity Melqart), and seeing there a statue of Alexander, "he heaved a sigh, and as if out of patience in having as yet done nothing noteworthy at a time of life when Alexander had already brought the world to his feet, he straightaway asked for his discharge, to grasp the first opportunity for greater enterprises in Rome."[25]

It hardly matters that Caesar invented this story after the fact; it is no less revelatory for that. Gades was located near the Columns of Hercules, which is to say at the end of the world in the West; the statue of Alexander symbolized the desire to reunite the *oikoumenē*, from Spain to India. For the same reason, in 55 and 54, Caesar attempted to conquer Britain. The expedition met with little success, but it caused a sensation in Rome; it was said that he had gone there in the hope of finding pearls.[26] Possibly he was inspired by Pompey, who had displayed an enormous quantity of oriental pearls during his triumph in 61, as a result of which they became a fashionable accessory among the upper class; but the accounts of Alexander's conquests had certainly influenced him as well.[27] It also needs to be kept in mind that Caesar visited the Temple of Hercules in Gades not as a tourist, but for the purpose of asking the priests of the sanctuary about a troubling experience, having dreamt that he had slept with his mother. This type of dream was not unusual among the ancients; what is more, it was thought to be a favorable omen.[28] The priests set the young Roman's mind at rest, reassuring him that his destiny was to conquer the Earth, "our common parent."[29]

Later, in the spring of 47, after having helped Cleopatra win a dynastic war for the throne of Egypt, Caesar accompanied her on a tour of the Nile (she was pregnant with his child at this time), at the head of a fleet of four hundred ships. According to Suetonius, he meant to go as far as the borders of "Ethiopia" (sub-Saharan Africa), which is to say the first cataract, but his army had refused to follow him.[30] There is no reason to doubt the veracity of this account. The plan of his eastern campaign is telling in this regard.

A few weeks before his assassination, Caesar's enemies spread disturbing rumors. The details varied, but all of them accused the dictator of intending to make himself king. Some whispered that Caesar sought to found a kingdom and establish his capital at Ilium, the site of ancient Troy.[31] According to the most common version, however, this kingdom was to be centered in Egypt, for it was at Alexandria that the queen had given birth to his son Ptolemy XV, whom Alexandrians called Caesarion ("little Caesar" in Greek). After Caesar's murder in March 44, Cleopatra returned to Egypt and, following the death by poisoning of her brother and husband Ptolemy XIV, she publicly recognized her child as Caesar's; in Rome, Mark Antony declared to the Senate that Caesar had himself recognized the boy (though Caesar's will contradicts this).[32] Cleopatra seems to have stayed in Rome on two occasions, in 46 and then in 44; if so, she would have been there on the fateful day, the Ides of March, when Caesar was cut down and then, according to Cicero, took flight at once.[33] Caesar's liaison with the Egyptian queen was not the only one of its kind. He would soon be authorized, it was said, to take as many wives as he wished, in order to guarantee a male line of descent; his affairs included Eunoë, wife of his ally Bogud, king of Mauretania.[34] But Egypt was a still more important conquest, for its riches were to play a fundamental role in supporting the campaign against Parthia.

Caesar had nonetheless not forgotten Rome. Unlike his rival Pompey, who had launched a massive building program whose principal landmarks served mainly to emphasize his exalted status as a triumphant general, Caesar devoted himself to public works of civic utility. Additionally, he drafted bills providing for the enlargement of the city, endowing it with new facilities and embellishing it with spectacular monuments. Still more farsightedly, he drew up plans for draining the Pontine Marshes to the south of Rome; for digging a canal that would run as far as Fucine Lake in the center of the Peninsula; and for constructing a road that would connect the Adriatic Sea with the Tiber, crossing over the Apennines. If Rome were to be transformed into the center of a unified world, it would be necessary to create a road network linking the capital to the rest of the empire, not only for the purpose of improving communications but also in order to ensure that an expanding city would have an adequate supply of provisions. Similarly, the partial emptying of Fucine Lake and the draining of the wetlands through which the Apennine route passed would allow Caesar not only to put large tracts of land under cultivation but also, since the marshes were places of refuge for brigands, to offer traders and travelers greater protection.

Caesar's oriental expedition had more than the conquest of a rival empire in view. Writing a few years after Nicolaus of Damascus, Velleius Paterculus tells us that Caesar contemplated at least two major campaigns. Velleius mentions this important detail in his summary of the early life of Octavian, the future Augustus. Octavian, then nineteen years old, was waiting for Caesar in Epirus, at the Greek city of Apollonia (modern-day Pojan, in Albania), where he had been sent in advance of accompanying Caesar in the wars against the Dacians and the Parthians.[35] We will soon become acquainted with Octavian. For the moment let us concentrate on those aspects of Caesar's campaign that amount neither to a repetition of Crassus's campaign nor to a mere readjustment of eastern borders. Instead, we are given to consider a grand strategy consisting of two elements, a Balkan campaign in the first instance, and a second campaign in the East—which is to say a war against the king of the Dacians, Burebista, to begin with, and then another one against Orodes. Appian describes the expeditionary force in some detail, saying that sixteen infantry units and ten thousand cavalry were already stationed on the other side of the Ionian Sea.[36] Later, apparently having realized that this was not an army large enough to accomplish its purpose, he says that it included six legions in addition to "all the other archers and light-armed troops stationed with them, a large force of cavalry, and a full supply of all the corresponding equipment."[37]

Several sources mention Orodes, but they are silent in connection with Burebista, even though for forty years he dominated the geopolitics of the Balkans. With Burebista, the Dacians entered into history. As part of a large ethnic group, the Thracians, of which they constituted the northern branch, they were related to the Getae, who by the fourth century BCE had created a network of diplomatic and commercial relations with the neighboring communities. In Burebista's time, the Getae and the Dacians seem to have formed a single *ethnos*. Pompeius Trogus, in a digression on the history of the Balkans, recounts the occupation of this territory by the Celts, their subsequent withdrawal to Gaul, the origins of the Pannonians, and the "progress of the Dacians thanks to the King Burobustes."[38]

Strabo gives a brief portrait of Burebista, mentioning the "great power" that he had managed to acquire in the space of only a few years, having subjugated the neighboring Celtic and Germanic peoples.[39] His state, divided into four regions, pursued an aggressive foreign policy marked by incursions into the Balkans, proceeding southward into Macedonia and Illyria and northward into the Celtic strongholds of the Boii and the Taurisci. The king had established his residence at Sarmizegetusa Regia, a city noted for its Hellenistic architecture and situated in the heart of a region rich in gold and salt deposits.

During this period, the federated peoples under Burebista were able to raise an army of two hundred thousand men.[40] The sovereign had profited from Roman victories in the East, which weakened the Greek cities on the Black Sea and eliminated the powerful king of Pontic Cappadocia, Mithradates VI Eupator. Nevertheless the Romans had not succeeded in imposing their control over the western sector of the Black Sea. In 61 the proconsul of Macedonia, Gaius Antonius (nicknamed Hybrida, uncle of Mark Antony), had been attacked by the Bastarnae, a Germanic tribe that may have been part of the coalition led by the Dacians/Getae.[41] Still today Romania celebrates Burebista's exploits; under the regime of Nicolae Ceaușescu, he was honored above all for having unified the country and assuring the continuity of the Romanian people down through the centuries.

The Romans considered the Dacians a threat, for their Celtic allies would constitute a formidable adversary in the event they were able to act in concert, as in the case of most of the peoples who lived beyond the Alps, and who accordingly were regarded as potentially dangerous—hence Caesar's visit to Illyria, as proconsul in 54, in the midst of the Gallic Wars. During this same period, he reinforced the Alpine arc with a network of fortifications, consolidating Roman control of a strategic line of defense as far to the east as Emona (modern-day Ljubljana), from which roads led on to the Nauportus and Sava River Valleys, held by the Taurisci confederation; additionally, with the founding of Salona and Narona, he took further steps to colonize the Adriatic. Strabo says that Caesar had prepared to make an expedition against Burebista when he reigned over the Getae.[42] According to a tradition passed on by the first historians of the Gothic nation (Cassiodorus and Jordanes, writing in the sixth century of our era), Burebista subjugated the "Goths"—probably peoples of the Eurasian steppe who had conducted raids on Germanic territories. In this account Burebista was said to have been stronger than Caesar, "the first to have claimed for himself command over all the Romans, who had conquered the entire world and who had subdued every kingdom . . . and [who] nonetheless, in spite of repeated attempts, was unable to subdue the Goths."[43]

Burebista's attitude toward the Romans was no different than that of Orodes. A Greek inscription found in Bulgaria memorializes Akorniōn, the royal ambassador who negotiated the alliance with Pompey in Macedonia.[44] Burebista may have been one of those "friendly" kings whose goodwill not only signified submission to the Roman people, but also implied a personal bond with Pompey himself.[45] In his speech at Caesar's funeral, Antony accused Pompey of "setting up a kingdom of his own" in Macedonia.[46] But neither Getae nor Dacians figure in the list of Pompey's troops at Pharsalus ("barbarians with disordered ranks and discordant tongues," in Lucan's phrase)—evidence that Burebista, like Orodes, had preferred neutrality.[47] The Thracians had furnished Pompey with auxiliary units, however, albeit in rather small, even token numbers: King Cotys IV, of the Astaean dynasty, sent five hundred horsemen under the command of his son Sadalas, while the homonymous Cotys VI, of the Sapaean dynasty, sent his son Rhascupolis (or Rhescuporis), who came from Macedonia with two hundred men; Sadalas was pardoned.[48] Caesar well knew that clemency was useful in dealing with kingdoms of lesser importance, but not with empires or with kingdoms aspiring to become empires. Moreover, in his address to the troops before the battle, he instructed them to concern themselves solely with the Italian forces, since their allies were only "prisoners from Syria and Phrygia and Lydia, always ready to flee or be someone's slave."[49] There was no need, then, to pay attention to their harassing tactics; after victory was achieved, however, it would be necessary to massacre them, to set an example.

The situation in the Balkans was critical, every bit as dangerous as the "powder keg" of the nineteenth and twentieth centuries. Pompey's surviving soldiers found shelter in Dacian communities, an embarrassment to Caesar's commanders, who had been pursuing them. In the meantime the Dalmatians had occupied sixty cities; Caesar's former lieutenant, Publius Vatinius, who in 45 had been granted proconsular authority, managed to reconquer twenty of them by the end of the year.[50] In the Cimmerian Bosporus, Caesar installed on the throne the powerful and "most friendly" Mithridates of Pergamum with responsibility for protecting the Roman provinces against the depredations of barbarians and enemy kings.[51] In this way he hoped to guarantee dynastic continuity, but in his absence the political balance of the region remained precarious.

The Balkan powder keg exploded in 45, when Mithridates was killed in battle by Asander, formerly ruler of the Bosporan kingdom, who had earlier vanquished Pharnaces. The Scythians and the Sarmatians, who seem to have formed part of the king's army, played an important role; Asander in any case now became the undisputed master of the Bosporus, subjecting the peoples of the hinterlands to his will.[52] Rome eventually recognized his royal title, but at the moment of Caesar's death he threatened to upset the geopolitical stability of the region around the Black Sea. At the same time, Suetonius tells us, it was necessary "to check the Dacians, who had poured into Pontus and Thrace."[53] This largely explains why Caesar wished to do battle with the Dacians before the Parthians and to march against Burebista. If he were to succeed where Crassus had failed, he would have to consolidate his existing alliances and create a network of new ones in southeastern Europe. This was no simple matter, for the hinterlands were unfamiliar territory and certain legends, such as that of the existence of a canal connecting the Adriatic with the Black Sea, were still current.[54]

None of these possible reasons for Caesar's campaign would appear to justify it as a *bellum iustum*, a legitimate—indeed, a legal—war. Appian gives a better idea of his motivations and, at least in the case of the Parthians, the actual cause of war: "[Caesar] began to devise a great campaign against the Getae and the Parthians. He intended to take the initiative in making plans against the Getae, a rough and war-loving neighbor, and to wreak vengeance on the Parthians for breaking their agreement with Crassus."[55] The only motive given for war against the Getae is their proximity to the Roman province of Macedonia; the threat posed by these barbarians required no further explanation. As for the Parthians, it was not the death of Crassus that justified war but the violation of certain pacts whose details are unknown to us. It may be that these were accords negotiated by Crassus and Mithradates III, the rival brother of Orodes II who had sought Rome's help and whom Orodes had had executed a year before the attempted Roman invasion and its tragic outcome at Carrhae.

Suetonius and Plutarch, writing at the time of the emperor Trajan's campaigns against the Dacians and the Parthians, provide additional information about the geopolitical context of the dictator's last campaign. Suetonius speaks of measures "for the protection and extension of the Empire." After mentioning the necessity of containing the Dacians, he adds that the campaign against the Parthians was to pass through Lesser Armenia and that Caesar did not wish to risk a battle with them until he had learned everything he needed to know about the strength of their forces and their preparations.[56] It was a fraught time. The assassination of Sextus Caesar had complicated the situation in Syria. Further to the east, Caesar's legions could not pass through Greater Armenia, for after Carrhae the young king Artawazd II, son of the great Tigran II (Tigranes in Greek and Latin), had broken all ties with Rome and sealed a matrimonial alliance with Parthia, his sister having married Orodes's son, the crown prince Pacorus. The only possible route went through the friendly kingdom of Cappadocia, governed by Ariobarzanes III, who had ruled over Lesser Armenia since 45 with Caesar's blessing.

Plutarch, for his part, is at pains to demonstrate Caesar's ambition (*philotimia*) and great accomplishment (*megalourghia*). Having defeated all his domestic enemies, Caesar now found himself in competition with himself, for "he planned and prepared to make an expedition against the Parthians; and after subduing these and marching around the Euxine by way of Hyrcania, the Caspian Sea, and the Caucasus, to invade Scythia; and after overrunning the countries bordering on Germany and Germany itself, to come back by way of Gaul to Italy, and so to complete the circuit of his empire, which would then be bounded on all sides by the ocean."[57]

Caesar, in other words, sought to give Roman conquest its fullest possible extent, for the territory of its empire was meant to coincide with the inhabited world. No doubt it was expected that this project would occupy Caesar and his legions for several or more years. A few weeks after Caesar's death, Cicero (who had no tender feelings for the dictator) said that he would never have come back from such a campaign.[58] After all, he was fifty-six years of age, worn out from long years of war and suffering from epilepsy. But this last visionary ambition was perfectly in accordance with the personality of a man "who seemed to be completely unconquerable [for] he was said never to have been defeated in the three hundred and two battles he [had] fought up to that time in Asia and in Europe."[59] Why Plutarch does not mention the preliminary campaign against the Getae is more perplexing, though the passage I have just quoted from *The Life of Caesar* does not contradict other sources. Nor can the circular itinerary it describes fail to recall the achievements of Alexander the Great.

In Rome and throughout Italy, Caesar assumed the extraordinary office of dictatorship. A few weeks before his assassination, having been given the title of "dictator in perpetuity"—the expression *dictatura perpetua* should probably be understood as signifying an open-ended dictatorship, rather than a dictatorship for life—he appointed Marcus Aemilius Lepidus for a second time as commander of the cavalry (*magister equitum*), in effect making Lepidus his right-hand man. The senatorial session of 15 March was intended to confirm Caesar's status in the provinces and, above all, to deliberate on an unprecedented matter. In February, the sacerdotal college of the quindecemviri (whose dean, Lucius Aurelius Cotta, was Caesar's maternal uncle) had been directed to consult the Sibylline Books, the obscure oracular responses conserved in the temple atop the Capitoline hill, the heart of Roman civic religion, dedicated to the divine triad of Jupiter, Juno, and Minerva. Cotta announced the finding of the priests, that only a king could conquer Parthia; in order to bring his eastern campaign to a successful conclusion, then, Caesar ought to acquiesce in this prediction and allow himself to be named king, in disregard of an ancient tradition.[60] The month before, in late January 44, the Senate had decided, again after deliberation, to grant Caesar not only divine honors but also the title *Divus Iulius*. All the more strongly, then, having refused the title of king, did the dictator refuse to be divinized in life.

No matter. The plot had already begun to take shape. One member of the conspiracy, Decimus Brutus (a distant cousin and former lieutenant of Caesar, who had appointed him governor of Cisalpine Gaul for the year 43), played a key role. He convinced the dictator not to postpone the Senate session on the Ides of March, arguing that it was a way of respecting the response of the Sibylline Books without contravening ancestral custom (*mos maiorum*). Caesar should therefore allow the senators to proclaim him king of the provinces beyond Italy, authorizing him to wear a diadem outside the Peninsula.[61]

What was being proposed was not a return to the monarchy of Romulus, of course, much less a monarchy of the Hellenistic type; even his most loyal supporters would not have countenanced that. And yet in agreeing to assume a perpetual dictatorship—a deliberately ambiguous formula—Caesar had broken a political taboo. In the eyes of his enemies, he had to be eliminated not only because he sought to establish a monarchy, but also because he envisaged an empire whose center would no longer be the city of Rome. There can be no question that these rumors exerted considerable pressure on the course of events, accelerating the plotters' timetable: A triumph in the East would lead to an irresistible increase in Caesar's prestige. The eastern campaign was forestalled by Caesar's death, of which it was one of the causes. In the meantime, he had assembled a very large and experienced army. Most of his soldiers were already stationed beyond the Adriatic, in the province of Macedonia, where they awaited the arrival of their general. Among these soldiers was Caesar's young heir, Octavian.

PART I

The World after the Ides of March

1

Apollo vs Dionysus

CAESAR'S DEATH also postponed his plan to make an updated survey of the world's geography. As a superior military strategist, he well knew the value of accurate information; one has only to recall the famous opening passage of *The Gallic War*, where Gaul is said to be divided into three parts. Anyone who wished to control the world could no longer be content with literary accounts, often obsolete if not actually mistaken, except for purposes of propaganda. In early 44 BCE, then, Caesar entrusted four Greek surveyors, selected for their erudition, with the task of composing a description of the known world: Nicodemus, Didymus, Theodotus, and Polyclitus. To each of them he assigned one of the four parts of the world, Nicodemus having responsibility for the East, Didymus for the West, Theodotus for the North, and Polyclitus for the South.[1]

The exploration of the world conducted by means of these expeditions departed from the conventional view due to Eratosthenes, accord ing to whom the earth was comprised of three continents, recalling Pompey's three triumphs: the first for his victories in Africa, in 79; the second for his victories in Spain, in 71; and the third, most spectacularly, for his victories in the East in 61, when it was emphasized that he was the first Roman general to have covered himself with glory on all three continents.[2] But Caesar, his great rival, with four conquests celebrated in 46 (Gaul, Pontus, Africa, Egypt), as well as another in Spain the following year, could well boast of having triumphed in four parts of the world. This quadripartite schema was found a century later in the first description of the world written in Latin, the *Chorographia* of Pomponius Mela, a Spaniard born near the Strait of Gibraltar.

The story of the four surveyors, which enjoyed a certain notoriety in the Middle Ages, has been a source of perplexity for modern scholars. Some regard it as a fictive account; others consider it to report nothing more than a series of minor cadastral missions. So well does it agree with Caesar's visionary spirit, however, that the possibility cannot be excluded that it has a basis in historical truth. It seems very probable that, as in the case of his other great undertakings, he saw the surveying of the four parts of the inhabited world (*oikoumenē*) as a coherent enterprise, notwithstanding that for the moment, as a practical matter, there was little chance it could be carried out in any truly comprehensive fashion beyond the territory consisting of Roman provinces and kingdoms allied with Rome. It is also perfectly consistent with the development of science in Rome during this period. Modern scholars, led astray by Greek traditions blaming Caesar for the destruction of Alexandria in 46, lost sight of the value that scholars of his time placed on scientific inquiry.

Not all Romans shared Caesar's curiosity. The great polymath Varro, in his treatise on agriculture, cast in the form of a dialogue (which he finished in 37 BCE at the age of eighty), was alert to the rather caricatural chauvinism of the time. The opening scene is set in Rome, in the exclusive district of Carinae where Pompey and Cicero lived. At the Temple of Tellus, Varro's father-in-law Gaius Fundanius, a senator, and the knights Gaius Agrius and Publius Agrasius (all three names harked back to agriculture) contemplate an image of Italy, not necessarily a map, painted on one of the temple walls. The date is probably about 54, when the building was being renovated under Cicero's supervision.[3] Varro's characters, citing Hellenistic geographical writings, observe that southern European lands are more favorable to cultivation than Asiatic and African territories, to say nothing of northern Europe, with its "permanent winters." From this it followed at once that Italy was a farmer's paradise.[4]

Varro regards this chauvinism, not unironically, as a sign of resilience. Italy had recently known its share of devastation, first from the Social

War of 91–89 and ancillary conflicts, then from the Third Servile War of 73–71, when the revolt led by Spartacus, a Thracian warrior reduced to slavery, held Roman forces at bay with an army of slaves and outcasts for almost two years. But one must not suppose that Varro had merely given voice to the simplistic prejudices of instinctive patriots who had never left Italy. However uneducated their notions of geography may seem, we are told that they had, in fact, traveled overseas. Agrasius asks his friends, "You have all traveled through many lands; have you seen any land more fully cultivated than Italy?" Agrius and Fundanius say that they have not, that no foreign land of which they have direct knowledge is more fruitful. This was the case of Varro himself, who, before devoting his old age to study, had served his country in Spain (under Pompey against Caesar) and on the Aegean Sea. He may have drawn upon these experiences in writing his geographical treatises, sadly lost, as well as upon information collected during campaigns led by Pompey in the East and by Caesar in Gaul, Britain, and Germany and transmitted either directly (in the form of Caesar's commentaries, for example) or through the writings of scholars with firsthand knowledge of the events they describe.

However this may be, Caesar was perfectly aware of the dangers posed by insufficient information. The chauvinism of the protagonists of Varro's dialogue reminds us of the weak point of Roman generals, who underestimated the military capabilities of their adversaries and remained ignorant of the physical environments in which they lived and of their customs. The tactical errors that ruined Crassus in 53 arose from an ineffective system of intelligence gathering that encouraged the belief that his enemies would be easily overcome. Caesar's scouts (*exploratores*) and spies (*speculatores*) may well have formed a reconnaissance network of exceptional quality, but that was not enough. Ambitious plans on a global scale required a thorough familiarity with all the relevant factors of warfare; Caesar's failure in Britain was in large part the result of inadequate preliminary research.

The question arises whether the surveyors appointed by Caesar (and their assistants) succeeded in collecting new information of military significance. According to ancient sources, they finally completed their mission under Augustus. They would therefore have been carrying out their work throughout the period of the last civil war, and then for some time afterward. To begin with, however, when Caesar succumbed to the plotters' blows, several months passed before any thought could be given to the surveyors' expeditions. On the Ides of March, the young Octavius was in Apollonia, in Illyria, on the other side of the Ionian Sea, where Caesar had sent him to pursue his studies.[5] For more than forty years, young Roman patricians were strongly advised to continue their education in Greece. In the first half of the 70s, Cicero and Caesar had gone to Rhodes to study under the great rhetorician Apollonius Molon. A generation later, Caesar's future assassin Gaius Cassius Longinus also studied at Rhodes; Brutus, the other charismatic leader of the conspiracy, went to Athens instead. Pompey, by contrast, confided the education of his children Gnaeus Jr. and Sextus to a teacher from the province of Asia, Aristodemus of Nysa.[6] Despite its illustrious past, which was proudly said to go back to the time of the Trojan War, Apollonia was certainly not a major cultural center; Cicero described it only as a "large and important city."[7] There were teachers there, of course, who did not fail to notice Octavius's talent, but he had arrived from Rome with his own tutor, the philosopher Apollodorus of Pergamum.[8] Two of his fellow students there, Quintus Salvidienus Rufus and Marcus Vipsanius Agrippa, went on to serve in his military campaigns shortly afterward.[9]

As a center of learning, Apollonia could hardly claim to compete with Athens, whose Roman students during this period included the poet Horace and Marcus Tullius Cicero, son of the great Cicero. Marcus junior had gone to Athens in March 45, at the age of twenty, to study with Cratippus of Pergamum, a philosopher of the Peripatetic school who had obtained Roman citizenship, granted by Caesar at the request of his friend and sponsor Cicero Senior.[10] Cicero also persuaded the Athenian authorities to invite Cratippus to remain in the city and give instruction there.[11] For a certain time, Marcus junior also attended the lectures of a professor of rhetoric named Gorgias, who turned out to be a master of debauchery. Cicero had high hopes for his only son, to whom he dedicated his treatise *On Duties*, finished in late 44. Marcus junior, though he dutifully devoted himself to the study of Greek, would have preferred a life of action; at a very young age, he had fought at Pharsalus on Pompey's side, and after Caesar's victory, he hoped to join the dictator's forces in Spain.[12] Cicero, at considerable personal expense, resolved to remove his bellicose offspring from the temptations of Roman militarism.

If Apollonia was not renowned as a center of learning, it did enjoy an important strategic position. Situated on marshlands lying between the Adriatic and Ionian Seas, the city was a staging point on the Via Egnatia, the great military road that connected the Adriatic and the Ionian Seas with Thessalonica, passing through a part of the Balkans where decisive battles had long taken place. In the war between Pompey and Caesar, the citizens of Apollonia had cast their lot with the Caesarian camp, thinking to strengthen the city's prestige by comparison with its rival Dyrrachium (now Durrës, in Albania). Modest though its claim to intellectual preeminence may have been, Apollonia was the ideal place for marshaling troops in transit from the Italian port of Brundisium (Brindisi). Octavius's studies were no more than an interlude while he awaited Caesar's arrival and the beginning of the expeditions against the Dacians and then the Parthians. He stayed in Apollonia for only three months.

On hearing the news of Caesar's assassination, Octavius went back to Rome. He could not have remained there very long, however, for the army that Caesar had sent to Macedonia had been in place since January under the command of the legate Marcus Acilius Caninus.[13] The proconsul of Macedonia was Quintus Hortensius, son of the great orator praised by Cicero, while Illyria was governed by Publius Vatinius, a veteran of the wars in Gaul and the war against Pompey, whom Caesar had put in charge of the operations against the Dalmatians, a group of Illyrian chiefdoms (though one cannot properly speak of a province of Illyricum during this period, military commands similar to proconsulships had nonetheless been set up there).[14] In the meantime, Vatinius was losing patience with his commander: In late January 44, writing to Cicero from his base at Narona, Vatinius expressed his displeasure at not being granted a triumph by Caesar, despite everything he had done in Dalmatia.[15]

During his stay in Apollonia, Octavius became curious about his horoscope, a rather popular form of astrological forecasting among Roman aristocrats. Just after the Ides of March, Cicero published his treatise *On Divination*, in which he criticized astrologists who claimed to know the future on the basis of the movements of the stars.[16] These savants supplemented the traditional *disciplina* of the Etruscans with various types of esoteric knowledge. All foreign astrologers during this period (including Egyptians) were referred to as Chaldean, meaning Babylonian, with the result that barbarian wisdom was now seen as an exotic mélange.

Horoscopes figured prominently in Octavius's childhood. At the time of his birth, Publius Nigidius Figulus, a senator and a foremost scholar who introduced Chaldean astrology to Rome, predicted that the child would one day rule the world. A few years later, during the campaign against the Bessi, his father Gaius Octavius, the governor of Macedonia in 60, consulted "barbarian oracles" in the "sacred grove of *Liber Pater*," perhaps the sanctuary of Perperikon in southern Bulgaria; it was in any case probably associated with the cult of Zagreus, identified by the Greeks with Dionysus.[17]

In the matter of his birth chart, Octavius, accompanied by Agrippa, went to the observatory of a local astrologer named Theogenes, who cast the charts of the two young men, presumably with the aid of an astrolabe. For Agrippa, a "great and almost incredible career" was predicted; but when Octavius's turn came, the astrologist prostrated himself before him.[18] Apparently, this story was concocted much later (perhaps around 11 BCE, when Augustus published his horoscope). Be that as it may, Apollonia was the starting point of his long journey to power. The news of Caesar's death was brought by a freedman sent by Octavius's mother, Atia.

Octavius and his friends were about to have dinner. A few of the city's prominent citizens, though they did not know exactly what had happened, nonetheless suspected that it was a matter of the greatest seriousness and went at once to Octavius's home.[19] They counseled him not to act precipitously, but rather to remain in Apollonia until the situation in Italy became more settled. Agrippa and Salvidienus, however, urged him to march on Rome at the head of an army of veterans at the earliest opportunity.[20] The discharge of so many soldiers from Caesar's campaigns, numbering in the tens of thousands, had created a social problem. Caesar had been careful not to found an undue number of military colonies, preferring to settle veterans throughout Italy and in the islands of the Tyrrhenian Sea (though he did establish the colony of Turris Libisonis [Porto Torres] in Sardinia); moreover, he had continued to recruit soldiers until 46.

Tensions came to a head following his final victory, and the crisis remained unresolved at the time of his death. During these same years, he had granted Roman citizenship to a certain number of foreign soldiers, from Spain and Gaul, with the aim of enlarging and fortifying the circle of Roman loyalties. In view of the mixed character of the population in places where veterans had been relocated, he sought to promote a certain uniformity in the administration of towns and cities by reconstituting municipal institutions.

Looking to appropriate the charisma of his adoptive father, Octavian (as he was now informally known, pursuant to the terms of Caesar's will) therefore set out to Italy, where he found men ready to follow him. He later mentioned this decision in the text known in modern scholarship as *Res Gestae divi Augusti*, which begins with a memorable statement of intent: "At the age of nineteen, on my own responsibility and at my own expense, I raised an army, by means of which I restored liberty to the republic, which had been oppressed by the tyranny of a faction."[21] Before resuming Caesar's projects, it was necessary not only to equip himself with a private army but also to be assured of a secure base of support at the heart of Roman power.

His days as a student were now over: he dismissed his tutor Apollodorus and gave up trying to master Greek.[22] In the meantime, Brutus and Cassius had obtained an "amnesty" (from the Greek *amnēstia* [forgetfulness]), promulgated by Mark Antony, one of the consuls that year, for the purpose of avoiding civil war. This measure, which Cicero claimed to have recommended in the first instance, drew upon an "ancient Athenian precedent." The restoration of democracy in 403 was understood to require all citizens to solemnly agree that "all recollection of disputes should be obliterated and forgotten for all time," which is to say that political reconciliation should be achieved by means of a general amnesty.[23]

Antony, of course, had proposed the measure in exchange for a series of self-serving resolutions. Under the threat of reaction from the people and veterans, the Senate was obliged to ratify all of Caesar's official acts since, in anticipation of a long absence from Rome, the dictator had already appointed magistrates, priests, provincial governors, and military commanders for the next five years. Antony could rely on the support of a great number of senators, particularly those who had been co-opted or rehabilitated by Caesar, to enlarge the assembly. From the beginning, Antony had no choice but to take the political context into account, recognizing that the "liberty" invoked by the conspirators henceforth mainly concerned the aristocratic class. Moreover, he had to find a way to maintain good relations with the army, which felt itself to be Caesar's orphan in a sense, having, by acclamation, awarded Caesar the title of *imperator* (victorious general) for the first time in 60. The authority of conservative senators was limited, however, by their fear of Antony's consular powers.

Brutus and Cassius were made to leave Rome. On 5 June 44 the Senate entrusted them with responsibility for supervising the city's grain supply. Cassius, formerly *praetor peregrinus* (charged with adjudicating disputes between aliens or between aliens and Roman citizens), was sent to Sicily; Brutus, who had to yield the office of *praetor urbanus* to Antony's brother Gaius Antonius, was sent to the province of Asia. Cassius, forty-three years of age when he raised his dagger against Caesar, was an experienced soldier. As quaestor in Crassus's army, he had survived the disaster of Carrhae, and for two years he had organized the defense of Syria, putting down an insurrection in Judaea, among others.[24] In 51 he repulsed the Parthians on their arrival at the gates of Antioch, with the young prince Pacorus at their head, crushing the army commanded by Osaces (Vasak) by employing a stratagem that Frontinus, in the last quarter of the first century CE, saw fit to include in his collection of exemplary military gambits.[25] Cicero, who as proconsul in the neighboring province of Cilicia at the time had conducted military operations on the border with Syria, tells us that Osaces was grievously wounded and died a few days later.[26] Cassius, seeing himself as a heroic warrior of the Republic, naturally regarded the prospect of working as a provincial grain inspector as an outrage.[27]

Brutus, two years younger than Cassius, did not share his martial spirit, but he had other talents. In 53 he had been quaestor in Cilicia, where he was known for a rather cavalier attitude toward financial transactions. In 48, at Pharsalus, he fought under Pompey and was subsequently pardoned by Caesar; the following year, he assisted Caesar in his diplomatic campaigns in the province of Asia, and the year after that, he governed Cisalpine Gaul. In August 45 Brutus and Cassius were both rewarded with provinces, Brutus being put in charge of Crete, with the title of proconsul, while Cassius was put in charge of Cyrenaica. Caesar felt great affection for him, and all the more as he had had an affair with his mother, Servilia, when Brutus was already an adolescent. As he was being stabbed, he asked Brutus (in Greek), "You too, son?"[28]

In sum, Octavian was not ready to inherit Caesar's mantle. Avenging his death remained the principal objective, but it was also necessary to neutralize potential rivals, beginning with Antony, who had managed to take advantage of the opportunity presented by the funeral ceremonies for Caesar, in which his great nephew, still in Apollonia, was unable to take part. This was of little importance, however, since in the meantime Caesar's will had been unsealed and the Romans informed of the fact that he had adopted Octavius, leaving him a large share of his patrimony. The situation was now dramatically different.

Antony's charisma depended, above all, on successfully managing Caesar's political legacy. The sudden appearance of a young heir on the scene upset all his calculations. Not only did Octavian lay claim to this legacy, he was also determined to diminish Antony's authority as consul. Antony tried to thwart or counteract Octavian's attempts, by means of spectacles and by spreading money around, to win popular favor. So long as he could delay testamentary disposition, the patrimony Octavian coveted would not pass to him. Furthermore, as though he intended to present himself as Caesar's legitimate successor, Antony retained possession of his personal and official documents.

Once again, the stars—in the event, a particular star—came to Octavian's aid. The young man who was now beginning to be called "Caesar" profited from a new celestial sign: the passage of an especially brilliant comet, called the Julian star (*sidus Iulium*), which was to play an important role in the propaganda of the following years. At Rome, the comet appeared between 23 and 25 July during the Ludi Victoriae Caesaris, private games decreed by Caesar in commemoration of his triumph at Pharsalus that his heir had hastened to transform into funeral games; so wondrous an event was undoubtedly welcomed for making it possible to erase the memory of the baleful prodigies that had punctuated the last months of the dictator's life.

In general, comets were considered to be unfavorable signs. Pliny the Elder held that they are "terrifying star[s] and not easily expiated."[29] In this particular case, however, the matter was more complicated. The *sidus Iulium*, represented more than once on Roman coins, was taken to symbolize Caesar's cosmic kingdom, following the example of Hellenistic kings; somewhat earlier, contrary to Iranian tradition, coins minted under Mithradates VI of Pontic Cappadocia and Tigran of Armenia had borne the image of comets.

With the opening of Caesar's will, Octavius's full name was Gaius Julius Caesar Octavianus; ancient authors usually call him Caesar. He disliked the second cognomen, which called attention to his origins; indeed, he never used it himself. Nevertheless I shall continue to call him Octavian, to avoid any confusion with Caesar himself. Antony had succeeded in controlling the situation, but, in spite of his desire to reestablish *concordia*, he created a climate of terror instead. The Romans, accustomed though they were to overbearing rulers, found the consul's arrogance excessive. There can be no doubt that he offended conservative sensibilities. Cicero, an adamant adversary, spoke of his "brutality" (*immanitas*).[30] Allegedly, when Antony was Caesar's *magister equitum*, he traveled around Italy in a Gaulish war chariot (*essedum*) alongside his mistress, the mime actress Volumnia Cytheris, a freedwoman.[31]

While Antony restructured the system of provincial appointments, ostentatiously affirming his own consular *imperium*, his armed escort was stationed near those places where the Senate met, in this way intimidating its members and influencing their voting. Directed by lieutenants of disreputable character, his guard was composed without exception of experienced centurions, including in its ranks a section of Ituraean archers, formidable warriors from a region between Lebanon and the Anti-Lebanon whom Cicero, shocked by their presence in the Forum, described as "the most barbarous men of all nations."[32]

Under the Republic this kind of military exoticism was not unusual; barbarian arms decorated the trophies and the homes of victorious commanders. But Antony's enthusiasm did not stop there. According to Cicero, during a banquet, he ordered the public slaves to flog one of his partisans, the senator Lucius Varius, with leather thongs.[33] Cicero considered this episode a manifestation of Antony's brutality toward his companions in dissipation (the punishment in this case was normally reserved for unworthy soldiers or slaves, or, in the extreme case, misbehaving pupils). A comparison of the relevant passages of the *Philippics* (fourteen vehement speeches that Cicero delivered against Antony, the first one on 2 September 44) with a fragment from Posidonius suggests that the practice was, if not common, at least not without precedent in the East.[34] According to Posidonius, a Parthian king's "friend" had no place at his table, being made instead to sit like a dog at the feet of the sovereign, who often had him whipped; the wretched courtier, drenched in his own blood, was then obliged to venerate his tormentor as a benefactor.[35] Posidonius was bound to consider this reprehensible, by contrast with the honors that Hellenistic kings bestowed on their friends; Roman readers, who hated the Parthians for obvious reasons, could not help but consider such treatment as proof of oriental despotism.

Varius's thrashing was very likely a reinterpretation of an ancient Iranian custom, or at least what was taken to be an ancient Iranian custom. In the late Republic, however, not all Romans recognized the allusion. The situation in which Varius—saddled with the eloquent Greek nickname Cotyla, meaning a cup or vessel—found himself was a sort of initiation ceremony associated with the drinking parties that Antony had made an emblem of his ideological program. This aspect of the matter needs to be taken seriously, as evidence of a deeper purpose, rather than minimized, by reducing Varius's degradation to the level of cruel inebriated jesting. Cicero, in portraying Antony's senatorial allies as undignified underlings and their master as a drunk addicted to unbridled debauchery, did just this. What Cicero failed to see, willfully or not, is that Antony's excesses were bound up with his fascination with the exotic, and that he was not alone among the Romans of his time in finding the exotic a source of fascination. Nor was Antony the only "orientalist" of among the statesmen of his generation, and for good reason: A representative of Rome who wished to govern effectively in the East had to apply rules of administration different from the ones sanctioned by Greco-Roman tradition. The Parthian threat having once again upset the equilibrium established by Pompey, it became necessary to devise a less unilateral relationship. Caesar had perfectly understood this, and Antony had no alternative but to continue his policy, by extending it.

Aristocratic entertainments were a fundamental element of late Republican society, bringing patrons and clients together in an atmosphere of shared tastes and culture. The considerable expense they involved, which a consul could sometimes cover by drawing upon public funds, increased their popularity. Friends and freeloaders filled up the "public" part of Antony's home, the reception hall, where the mistress of the house, his wife Fulvia (widow in turn of politicians like Publius Clodius Pulcher and Gaius Scribonius Curio), exerted her own very substantial influence. Important matters of state were not infrequently decided on such occasions. Through Fulvia's intercession, to name one prominent example, ambassadors from Galatia, at a cost of some millions of sesterces, obtained restitution of the possessions of their king, Deiotarus (possibly Deiotarix), tetrarch of the chiefdom of the Tolistobogii. Accused by another Galatian prince of having hatched a plot to kill Caesar, Deiotarus was made to stand trial in Rome, where Cicero, who knew him from the time of his proconsulship in Cilicia in 51–50, pleaded in his defense. Though Deiotarus was not found guilty, Caesar deprived him of Lesser Armenia and a part of Galatia, confiding them respectively to Ariobarzanes III of Cappadocia and Mithridates of Pergamum. Antony reestablished Deiotarus's power, citing the authority of Caesar's own maps, which he had kept for himself, and may have falsified, on the pretext that a *lex Iulia* authorized Deiotarus to reoccupy his territories.

In exchange, the consul received a colossal sum that allowed him to repay his outstanding debts. Cicero objected that the transaction had been brokered by Fulvia and tried to discredit the king on the ground that he was determined to occupy these territories militarily.[36]

Antony was well acquainted with the East and well understood the central place of Galatia in Roman foreign policy. Deiotarus had made significant improvements with regard to the governance and security of the region. Seeking, not without difficulty, to replace the tribal system of the Celts of Asia by a Hellenistic monarchy, he drew inspiration from exemplars of Greek culture, particularly in connection with architecture, as well as the military model of Rome (thirty cohorts of his army were armed in the Roman fashion).[37] In 54, when Crassus and his army passed through Galatia, the general found the king occupied with the construction of a new city (perhaps mistaken for the fortress of Peium, which housed the royal treasury). Deiotarus could not be accused of indulging a superficial taste for Hellenism: Diophanes of Nicaea dedicated to him his abridgment in six volumes of the Greek translation of the manual on agriculture composed in the Punic language by Mago of Carthage; and Cicero, during the trial, made a point of praising his abilities as an administrator, describing him as an "excellent family man, and industrious farmer and stock raiser"—in other words, a providential man for the kingdom.[38]

It was under these favorable circumstances that Antony sought to augment his military resources by seizing control of the army billeted in Macedonia, sent by Caesar, not far from Apollonia. Its six legions and various auxiliaries formed a quite respectable expeditionary force. Among the large number of auxiliaries, Appian mentions light infantry, archers (indispensable for parrying Parthian thrusts), and warriors from the Gymnesian Islands, today the Balearics, renowned for their ability to launch projectiles with a sling.[39] It was said that the Dacians, before they learned of Caesar's death, were laying waste to Macedonia.

Command of the Roman troops had been confided to Publius Cornelius Dolabella, Cicero's former son-in-law and a rival of Mark Antony. The two consuls who assumed office at the beginning of the year 44 were Caesar and Antony; in anticipation of Caesar's departure for the

East, Dolabella was named suffect consul in his place. Antony, fearing the veterans who made up Octavian's personal army, planned to reassign the Macedonian forces to Italy on the pretext that the Parthians, at least for the moment, posed no threat. He asked the Senate to use them for the purpose of bringing barbarians in the Balkans to heel; the Senate took its time, dispatching a commission to Macedonia to assess the situation. Antony finally obtained command of the army for the year 43, while exchanging the governorship of Macedonia for that of Cisalpine Gaul.[40]

Macedonia was entrusted to his younger brother Gaius Antonius, who set out for the province in late 44, probably a few weeks before the end of his term as urban praetor. In the meantime the commissioners sent to Macedonia reported that they had found no Dacians there, but that the possibility could not be excluded that they might reappear once the bulk of the army had departed.[41] The Senate nonetheless gave command of these legions to Antony, while placing one of them under the authority of his brother and another under the authority of Dolabella in Syria. In the event, however, Antony was unable to exert control over the remaining Macedonian legions, the senatorial commission having emphasized the danger that might arise in the wake of their departure. Between Macedonia and Illyria, seven legions continued to be deployed in the Balkans.[42]

In Italy, the situation was becoming increasingly complicated. Cicero had begun to compose the *Philippics*. The second of these amounted to a manifesto against Antony, an unauthorized biography, in effect, if not also an incitement for his murder. Antony vigorously defended himself against Cicero's invectives, accusing him of being the principal instigator of Caesar's assassination. Before long, Antony's position had become more precarious, however, despite his having managed to obtain the proconsulship of Gaul while retaining command over the four legions garrisoned in Macedonia that he had recovered in Brundisium—where, accompanied still by Fulvia, he had to violently suppress a revolt of local soldiers and aristocrats.

The years following were marked by the vagaries of the relationship between Mark Antony and Octavian, two very different men. First of all, there was the significant difference in age between them (in the autumn of 44, Antony was almost forty years old, Octavian only nineteen). Both of them, each in his own way, claimed to be Caesar's heir, the one legitimate and the other spiritual. There was also the matter of personal temperament, amounting almost to a difference in religious allegiance: Caesar's former right-hand man obeyed the counsels of Dionysus, god of drunkenness and excess, the young Caesar those of the more rational Apollo. The two men were also distinguished by their manner of public speaking, Octavian preferring the gravitas of the "neo-Atticist" rhetorical style, which had recently become fashionable, and disparaging the turgidness and redundancies of the so-called Asiatic tradition in which Antony had been trained as a student in Greece.[43]

From autumn 44 onward, Octavian and Antony "in all their acts were opposing each other, but had not yet fallen out openly, and while in reality they had become enemies, they tried to disguise the fact so far as appearances went."[44] In this passage, modeled on Thucydides, Cassius Dio likened the two men to Athens and Sparta. The young Caesar, exploiting the common interest of military veterans and the plebian class, created his own political network and recruited legions in Samnium and Etruria. In Rome, he delivered an address to the Plebeian Assembly in which, to Cicero's great consternation, he restated his determination to assume his father's responsibilities.[45] Between October and December, the *Philippics* had begun to circulate among influential citizens.

Shortly afterward, Antony, who had suffered the defection of two legions, was obliged to leave Rome for the winter. In Cisalpine Gaul, the acropolis of Italy, as it was called, after replacing the proconsul Decimus Brutus, he went on to recruit troops and conduct military operations in the Alps, where his soldiers proclaimed him *imperator*. Brutus, for his part, sent a report to the Senate, hoping to obtain for himself the honor of a *supplicatio*, an official ceremony thanking the gods for victory. In a letter sent to Cicero in early autumn, he told of his exploits against an indigenous people, the Inalpini, who seem to have lived in what are now Piedmont and Savoy, and of his operations against "the most warlike people in the world," with the conquest of several fortresses and the devastation of a certain amount of territory. The chief aim of these operations, he says, was not personal glory; their purpose was mainly to train his soldiers and raise their spirits to "strengthen them in support of our cause," which is to say in anticipation of a civil war against Antony.[46] Cicero promised to do his utmost to support Brutus's "patriotic designs" and to assure him of the glory that was rightly his.[47]

At the same time he set about concluding an alliance, as surprising as it was necessary, with Caesar's adoptive son in the hope of bringing him under his control. On 20 December 44, he formally called upon the Senate to declare Antony a public enemy. The assembly, though it did not approve the request, annulled the consul's most important decisions and barred him from holding public office for the following year. This was the beginning of a new civil war, the first war between Dionysus and Apollo.

2

Western Warlords

THE CONSERVATIVES' attempts to reestablish the republican order had collateral effects. The amnesty granted to Brutus and Cassius allowed them, once the first weeks of confusion had passed, to occupy positions of power in the East. In the West, another figure profited from the political and military disorder: Sextus, Pompey's second son, who had survived Caesar's war in Spain, unlike his older brother, Gnaeus, whose severed head was exhibited before the people of Hispalis (modern Seville).[1] In theory, Caesar had pacified Spain, but Sextus managed to flee, apparently with the aid of local aristocrats and Roman colonists, ever faithful to the Pompeian cause.

In order to counter rearguard attacks, Caesar had been obliged to remain in Spain until September 45, Octavian having joined him there in the meantime. But once Caesar had returned to Italy, Sextus set about harassing his legates, carrying out raids throughout the Iberian Peninsula in the months leading up to the Ides of March. The governor of Hispania Ulterior in 44, based in Corduba (now Córdoba), was Gaius Asinius Pollio, a Caesarian loyalist and a veteran of Pharsalus and other battles of the civil wars, the last ones of which he recounted in his *Histories* in seventeen books. Pollio had directed the campaign against Sextus, but he seems not to have had any greater success than his predecessor, Gaius Carrinas. Appian relates a very unconvincing detail in this connection, saying that Sextus did not immediately reveal his identity to the men whom he had recruited for his acts of piracy; but that once it became known that he was Pompey's son, all the veterans who had fought with his father and his brother, now widely dispersed, hastened to join his camp.[2]

Syme described Pompey's younger son as an adventurer (a term he often applied to people he did not like). In fact, Sextus was a much more formidable adversary than Brutus or Cassius, for the renown of his father was not less than that of Caesar himself. The contest between Pompey the Great and Caesar continued long after they had died. The last phase of the civil wars, which determined the end of the Republic, should therefore be seen as a prolongation of their conflict, at least until Sextus's defeat in 36. Sextus had chosen "Pius" as a cognomen, to emphasize his filial piety and his desire to avenge the deaths of his father and brother. Although he influenced events in the Mediterranean from this time onward, Sextus is often considered to have been a figure of the second rank.

The propaganda of his enemies granted him no more than a minor role as a brigand, indeed a pirate, insinuating that whereas his father had made the Mediterranean "one safe and enclosed harbor in the control of the Roman people," his son undid this work.[3] Velleius Paterculus characterized Sextus as "a young man without education, barbarous in his speech, vigorous in initiative, energetic and prompt in action as he was swift in expedients, in loyalty a marked contrast to his father, the freedman of his own freedmen and slave of his own slaves, envying those in high places only to obey those in the lowest."[4] In the second century CE, Florus exclaimed, "But how great the difference between him and his father! The latter had exterminated the Cilician pirates, his son protected himself by piracy."[5] This was no longer a civil war: Sextus's operations amounted to banditry.[6]

The underestimation of Sextus Pompey's influence is due to the legend created by his principal adversary, Gaius Julius Caesar Octavianus. It is true that the prestige of his family name assured Sextus of the loyalty of his troops, but he was by no means an incapable commander; as the course of events was to show, his talent as a strategist was decidedly superior to that of Octavian. A young man who had rapidly become an adult, by 44, when he was twenty-two years old, he had assembled an army of legionaries and auxiliaries, the equivalent of seven legions, in the northwest of the Iberian Peninsula. Two days after the Ides of March, Decimus Brutus wrote to Brutus and Cassius, expressing the view that Sextus Pompey and Caecilius Bassus alone could guarantee their security—in other words, that the only possible refuges were territories controlled by Caesar's enemies, Spain and Syria.[7]

Just after the Ides, however, after negotiations with the consuls, Sextus finally "show[ed] the white feather."[8] Shortly afterward, Decimus Brutus managed to rejoin his legions in Cisalpine Gaul, where Cicero had also considered taking refuge, though he did not rule out the possibility of seeking the protection of Sextus Pompey.[9] On 10 July 44 Cicero learned that Sextus, having set out with a legion from Carthago Nova (New Carthage, present-day Cartagena), was laying siege to Baria (Vera, in Andalusia). It was while taking this stronghold that news reached him of Caesar's assassination, the cause of much rejoicing.[10]

The situation changed as the result of intervention by the governor, Marcus Aemilius Lepidus. Formerly commander of the cavalry under Caesar, Lepidus succeeded him as pontifex maximus, the highest official of the civic religion, thanks to Antony's influence. Lepidus had evidently learned from the experience of his father, who bore the same name and was the unhappy protagonist of yet another one of the many earlier episodes of civil war, just after the death of Sulla. Lepidus's father, consul in 78, had adopted a demagogic policy, working to demolish all the measures taken by Sulla; the following year, he organized a rebellion. His mistake was deciding to march on Rome instead of going back to his own province, Transalpine Gaul.

During the same period, another rebellious military commander, Quintus Sertorius, was defeated in Spain, where he had ruled as a warlord for six years before his death in 73. Pompey, who was then in the process of consolidating his own power, managed to quiet the grumbling of Romans who could no longer tolerate Sertorius's close relations with Hispanic aristocracies. Sertorius was finally murdered. His fate must have convinced Lepidus of the necessity of cooperating with other regional governors. He well understood that, in order to control the western part of the Mediterranean, it was necessary to control the whole of Romanized Western Europe.

Caesar had confided to Lepidus both Gallia Narbonensis and Hispania Citerior, that is, the coastal region extending from the Pyrenees to New Carthage. Lepidus remained in Spain, where he negotiated the cessation of hostilities with the Pompeians; in October 44 he removed himself to Gaul. Even if our sources are primarily interested in what was happening in Rome, it was in the West that Rome's destiny was to be settled. It was there that Lepidus was decisive, by devising a strategy for consolidating Rome's control over Gaul on either side of the Alps.

In his funeral oration for Caesar, Antony had made clear what Caesar had intended to do in entering upon the Gallic Wars. Caesar's purpose was not limited to combating the enemies of allied peoples. Caesar had conquered all the peoples of these formerly unknown regions, accelerating the process of combining Cisalpine Gaul with the rest of Italy.[11] As for Transalpine Gaul, the Caesarian conquest had created a new geopolitical landscape. Until the end of the civil wars, these territories had been untouched by significant events apart from a few sporadic revolts.

A part of the Gallic aristocracy had supported Caesar's cause, and when the fighting was over he rewarded a number of tribal chiefs and members of the aristocracy with magistracies in their cities, distributions of land, even grants of Roman citizenship. The city of Arelate (Arles) was made a Roman colony. The same policy of integration was followed in Transalpine Gaul by the governor there, Lucius Munatius Plancus, another faithful lieutenant of Caesar who had fought alongside him against the Gauls, and later against the Pompeians in the wars of Spain and Africa.

One must nonetheless keep in mind what was at stake in the struggle for control of the region. The war did not end in 52 at Alesia. The Gauls continued to do battle with the Roman armies, and at the time of the Ides of March, Caesar's generals were still conducting operations. Foreign clients with whom Caesar had negotiated alliances also included Germanic populations beyond the Rhine, who formed a protective glacis of federated tribes. The news of Caesar's death spread very rapidly among the Gallic peoples; in Rome, there was fear of revolt, particularly among the Germanic peoples of Belgic Gaul. Late March brought the reassuring news that the Germans had declared their obedience to Rome.[12]

The Senate authorized Munatius Plancus to found two new Roman colonies: Lugdunum (Lyon) and, to the northeast of the Helvetii, Raurica (Augst). In the meantime, there had developed among the Gallic populations the practice of building *oppida*, fortified settlements that archeologists regard as a form of proto-urbanization. Alongside these agglomerations, mostly defensive in character, market towns grew up. In the countryside, Caesar noted various types of habitats, among them, in addition to *oppida*, villages (*vici*) and isolated farms (*aedificia*). The flourishing agriculture of these lands, combined with extensive rearing of livestock and hunting in the forests, allowed Caesar's legions to feed themselves. While Romanization, understood as the formation of a Gallo-Roman civilization, began to take shape only around the middle of the first century BCE, archeological research has revealed evidence of Mediterranean acculturation from the second century, for example, the earliest appearance of animal breeds imported from Italy (initially in sites of aristocratic occupation). Lepidus, for his part, was in charge of the territory of the old province, created around 100, which encompassed more or less Provence, southwestern France, and the Rhône Valley. Its boundaries were the Caesarian colony of Vienne and Lake Geneva to the northeast, the Pyrenees to the southwest, the Alps to the east, and the Massif Central to the north.

The Greek city of Massalia (Marseille), situated on the "Way of Hercules" (the route Hannibal had taken to reach Italy) and long a Roman ally, controlled a good part of the Mediterranean coast. Its prestige had been undermined by its attitude toward Caesar, who besieged the city in September 49. Massalia capitulated, and, though it did not lose its autonomy, it was forced to cede a fair amount of territory; its port nonetheless remained active. Furthermore, Massalia preserved its role as a cultural center, attracting young Gauls who could not afford to study in Rhodes or Athens. Strabo, scarcely concealing his disdain, spoke of it as a "training school for the barbarians."[13] Valerius Maximus, writing at about the same time, praised the conservative spirit of the Massaliotes and their determination to retain traditions that went back to the Greek colonists who had founded the city. Its citizens were very strict with regard to the freeing of slaves, immoral entertainments, overly elaborate funeral ceremonies, and cults considered to be inimical to the well-being of the community. "From the foundation of the city," Valerius notes, "there is a sword therein to kill the guilty. It is eroded by rust and scarcely adequate to its function, but a sign that even in the smallest details the monuments of ancient customs are to be preserved."[14]

The barbarians of this region were "friendly" Celts, such as the family of the Pompeii Trogi, belonging to the community of the Vocontii in Narbonnaise Gaul, the most famous *oppidum* of which was Vasio (present-day Vaison-la-Romaine). The family owed its name and its Roman citizenship to Pompey, who at the time of his campaigns against Sertorius in 76–72 had thus rewarded the grandfather of the historian Pompeius Trogus for his services as an officer in the auxiliary cavalry. Trogus's father had served in the Gallic Wars as Caesar's secretary; Caesar also assigned him certain diplomatic tasks, even entrusting him with his seal. He is probably the same Gnaeus Pompeius mentioned by Caesar as his interpreter, who in November 54 was sent as an ambassador to Ambiorix, a leader of the people of the Eburones in Belgic Gaul.[15] The son of this faithful servant, Pompeius Trogus, author of a universal history published during the Principate of Augustus, may have studied Greek at Massalia.

It was to Massalia, as well, that Lepidus had urgently summoned Sextus Pompey. In choosing as their meeting place this ancient Pompeian stronghold, which had been hard hit during the civil war, Lepidus had probably wished to show his good will, and all the more as Sextus had delivered a part of his legionary forces to him; but it also provided Lepidus with a pretext for keeping his distance from Brutus and Cassius, who had called upon him to return to Rome just after the Ides of March.[16] Sextus, on the other hand, had retained command of his fleet, which for the moment was stationed at Massalia and henceforth was to constitute the main part of his forces. Lepidus's diplomacy, in avoiding a further episode of civil war, enabled Sextus to recover his family's properties in Spain. In the meantime, the Senate appointed him to the

FIGURE 2.1. *Aureus* of Sextus Pompey

proconsular office of prefect of the fleet and the Mediterranean littoral (*praefectus classis et orae maritimae*) (fig. 2.1)[17].

The confused situation among the Gauls following their conquest by Rome nonetheless made it necessary to constantly negotiate with local aristocracies. It was for this reason that Lepidus, together with Plancus, became involved in the founding of Lugdunum.[18] Doubt has been cast on the account given by Cassius Dio, but it is clear that Lepidus, even if his role in establishing the colony was not officially sanctioned, had become the dominant figure in the western theater of operations. He alone had the prestige and the diplomatic skill needed to preserve a precarious geopolitical balance, apparently in agreement with Plancus and the other governor, Asinius Pollio.

In Africa, profiting from the disarray that followed upon the Ides of March there, the Numidian prince Arabio regained control over part of the territory he had had to abandon in 46 after Caesar's victory and the Roman occupation of the kingdom of Arabio's father, Massinissa II.

Since Sextus Pompey controlled the Strait of Gibraltar, Arabio was able to contribute to the provisioning of the troops he had loaned to Sextus in the expectation that they would come back to him very well trained.[19] On returning to Africa, he quickly recovered some of his domains, at the expense of the king, Bocchus II, who was obliged to retreat to the west. Arabio also killed Publius Sittius. Born in Nuceria, in Campania, between 95 and 90, Sittius was the son of a wealthy knight with extensive commercial interests. He grew up in Campania and Rome and, as a young man, experienced firsthand the violence of the revolt led by Spartacus, who sacked Nuceria during the winter of 73–72. Once the revolt had been suppressed, Sittius looked after the affairs of his father (first in Rome, where he was acquainted with Cicero and other important figures, and then in Spain, where as part of Crassus's entourage he probably met Caesar, who was quaestor there in 68).

Around the middle of 64, Sittius left Spain and settled in Africa with a group of companions who have been described as adventurers. In fact, he had to flee prosecution for unpaid debts, and he was very probably involved, at least to a certain degree, in the conspiracy directed by Catiline. He had assembled a small army and sought refuge with Sosus, the king of Mauretania, who named Sittius general. Between 64 and 47, he based his operations there, commanding an army of mercenaries and in due course a fleet. As an ally of Sosus's successor, Bocchus II, he supported Caesar in the civil war against the Pompeians and Juba I of Numidia. With the possible aid of a "fifth column" constituted by the Roman merchants of Cirta, one of the capitals of Numidia, Sittius laid siege to the city and took it; Bocchus occupied the region as far as the Ampsaga river. After Caesar's final victory in the African War, he rewarded Sittius with lands near Cirta as part of the political reorganization of northern Africa, with Bocchus being appointed king of western Mauretania, and Bogud king of the eastern part of the country. Numidia was annexed to Rome under the name of Africa Nova, to distinguish it from the "old" province of Africa.

Nevertheless a large part of the kingdom—the territory surrounding Cirta (present-day Qusanṭīna in northeastern Algeria) as well as the rest of Numidia to the east of the Ampsaga—even though nominally subject to the authority of the governor of Africa, was directly administered by Sittius and his associates. Bocchus and Sittius, acting in concert, succeeded in occupying Arabio's domains; Sittius himself effectively presided as a warlord over a region that included the cities of Cirta and Milev (present-day Mila) and, on the coast, Rusicada and Chullu (present-day Skikda and Collo). Cirta he made an independent enclave unencumbered by the usual apparatus of Roman provincial administration—a model going back to Gaius Marius that attracted Italian, African, and Spanish settlers. No one disputed Sittius's power, which, by virtue of this autonomous principality, formally recognized by Caesar, was sui generis.

A new Roman Africa was beginning to take shape. Among other things, Caesar contemplated refounding, only now as Roman colonies, two great commercial centers that the Romans had destroyed in 146: Corinth in Greece and Carthage in Africa. Carthage became a Roman colony in 123 at the urging of Gaius Gracchus, but its reorganization was carried out by Octavian on the basis of Caesar's plans. Three thousand colonists are said to have been sent under the consulship of Antony and Dolabella, which is to say in the months following the Ides of March. This dating is implausible, however; in all probability, the colony was created a little later. Be that as it may, Caesar's designs were destined to upset the world's political and economic equilibrium.[20]

The juridical precedent set by Sittius, a Roman citizen who almost single-handedly created an autonomous province, heralded the emergence of new ways of thinking about the international balance of power in the face of changing circumstances. The notion of *provincia* in our sources from this period is rather vague. Peoples outside Rome and Italy were referred to as *exterae nationes* or *exterae gentes*, without any further indication as to whether they were located within or without Roman provinces. At a time when the world was conceived as a chessboard where non-Romans were insignificant pawns, easily sacrificed, it is not surprising that Roman sources should have been chiefly concerned with Romans.

Antony, for his part, sought to evict Decimus Brutus from Cisalpine Gaul, considering it to be his own province. Two of his legions having defected, Antony's army now comprised five units: In addition to two legions in Macedonia, there were two legions of veterans recruited in Campania by Caesar's former lieutenant Publius Ventidius Bassus; a fifth legion, called Alaudae, consisted of soldiers from Transalpine Gaul enlisted by Caesar himself.[21] This last unit probably also included veterans of Caesar's campaigns, and perhaps other foreigners as well (as a funerary inscription of the soldier Gaius Valerius Arsaces, found in the territory of the Ligures Baebiani, in the present-day province of Benevento, seems to attest).[22]

Harried by Antony's troops, Decimus Brutus was obliged to retreat to the colony of Mutina (now Modena). At this same moment the Senate co-opted Octavian, granting him extraordinary powers that raised him to a rank equivalent to that of a propraetor, in January 43. Octavian's army was financed with public funds, which he used in turn to co-opt Antony's auxiliaries, horsemen (some of them Gauls), archers, and even elephants, possibly transported from Africa.[23] If their tactical usefulness remains unclear to us, they nonetheless enjoyed a certain symbolic significance; already in 46, they had appeared on Caesar's monetary coinages.

The Senate decreed a state of emergency and authorized armed intervention with Octavian's assistance. Antony, driven out of the cities of Cisalpine Gaul and lacking auxiliary forces, was forced to enlist gladiators as well as inexperienced soldiers, feeding them by resort to pillage and requisition. The colony of Parma, conquered by Antony's younger brother, Lucius Antonius, became a theater of massacres. The arrival of the consular armies culminated in a major setback for Antony's forces, Cicero having in the meantime rallied to the conservatives' cause both consuls for the year 43, Aulus Hirtius and Gaius Vibius Pansa, former loyal lieutenants of Caesar who were troubled by Antony's intemperate behavior. Ventidius Bassus was obliged to retreat to the region of Picenum, where he recruited a new legion.

Cicero already saw himself as the victor. Owing to his influence behind the scenes, a coalition against Antony had been approved by the Senate consisting of the two consuls, the propraetor Decimus Brutus, and the young Caesar, whose praetorian *imperium* sanctioned hitherto illegal actions. On the pretext of punishing Decimus for his role in assassinating Caesar, Antony besieged him at Mutina; Hirtius and Pansa, supported by Octavian, went to his aid at once. On 14 April 43, a first battle took place near Forum Gallorum (Castelfranco Emilia). Pansa, captured during an ambush set by Antony in the forest (employing a technique of guerilla warfare very probably learned in Gaul), was seriously wounded and died ten days later; Antony, on the other hand, succeeded in taking revenge on the men of the Martia legion who had abandoned him six months earlier. The decisive encounter took place near Mutina on 21 April, with the result that Decimus was delivered from the siege. But the triumph of the conservatives was qualified by the death of both consuls. Pansa's death came two days after that of Hirtius at Mutina. The poet Ovid later recalled his own birth in that terrible year "when both consuls died at Mutina."[24] Cicero, in his overconfidence, had underestimated either Antony's ability to regroup or the character of Octavian, whom he still thought he could manipulate. Antony's army, having been put to flight, left behind on the battlefield a great many standards and cadavers. Antony nonetheless managed to reorganize his troops during the course of their retreat, rearming them with whatever was at hand (shields made from the bark of trees, for example), and encouraging them by his own personal example.[25]

The cycle of *Philippics* was now complete. Four days after his defeat, Antony was declared a public enemy, along with all his supporters. The Senate, who refused his proposal to negotiate, sent away Antony's ambassador, Lucius Varius Cotyla. But if Cicero thought that he had won, others among Antony's enemies considered the battle of Mutina to have been a Pyrrhic victory. Cicero wrote to Cassius and Gaius Trebonius, another member of the conspiracy against Caesar, that had he been invited to "that splendid feast on the Ides of March, we should then have had no leftovers."[26] The death of the consuls had weakened the faction opposed to Antony, who likewise could muster three legions, stationed in Picenum under the command of the able and energetic Ventidius. Even if Antony did not always manage to carry the day, his political experience and the loyalty he inspired among his soldiers permitted him to reconstitute alliances and restore the fortunes of his house.

Thanks to the example set by its leader, the army's morale was strong once more, and after crossing the Apennines, Antony's men took the road along the Ligurian coast. On arriving in Gaul, they were welcomed by Lepidus, who had renounced his neutrality and gone over to Antony's side, as a consequence of which he too was declared a public enemy. Octavian, having grasped the situation at once after conferring with Ventidius, decided to remain on the other side of the Apennines rather than come to the assistance of Decimus Brutus and pursue Antony.[27] Decimus Brutus complained about Octavian to Cicero, warning him that the young man could no longer be controlled.

It was at this moment, the most critical for Antony, that the tide turned in his favor, now that Octavian, in the aftermath of Mutina, had divined the intentions of Cicero and Decimus Brutus. Octavian justified his volte-face later on the grounds that certain senior senators, who ridiculed him on account of his youth, were resolved to marginalize him. They called him *puer*, a word that means not only "little boy" but also "slave."[28] It mattered little to him that Cicero, in the fourth *Philippic*, praised his courage and merit, by virtue of which he ought to be regarded as an adult deserving of the acclamation of victorious general (*imperator*).[29] The senators' condescension revealed their suspicions regarding Caesar's heir; Decimus Brutus was therefore awarded the triumph rather than the young Caesar. They had not taken into consideration the army's loyalty to Caesar and his descendants.

According to the Augustan version of these events, reported by Nicolaus of Damascus, Octavian had no choice but to measure himself against seasoned generals whose power was proportional to the number of soldiers they commanded.[30] These men were not only Romans, of course. Even Cicero, who not long before had criticized the use of barbarian auxiliaries, wrote to Brutus to tell him of the hopes he placed in the armies of Decimus Brutus and Plancus, whose legionaries, some of them rather inexperienced, were supported by "large, very loyal contingents of Gaulish auxiliaries."[31]

Decimus Brutus, pursued by Antony, had taken flight after Mutina with four legions of veterans and six formed by untrained recruits who deserted him in the days that followed. Abandoning the idea of doing battle, he elected to take refuge with Brutus in Macedonia, taking the road along the Adriatic that passed through Ravenna. From there he headed northward, accompanied by a personal bodyguard of loyal Gallic horsemen, most of whom he subsequently dismissed. He reached the Rhine with three hundred mounted troops; the crossing was difficult, and only a dozen or so joined him on the other side. Then, dressed as a Gaul (Decimus Brutus also spoke the language), he continued onward to Aquileia, but en route he was captured by bandits in the service of a chieftain named Camilus, for whom Decimus Brutus had done many favors in the past.[32] Having asked his captors to bring him to Camilus, he was welcomed with all honors; but Camilus had taken care to notify Antony, who ordered him to kill his prisoner and send his head to him.[33]

That Decimus Brutus should have mastered a Celtic dialect is by no means implausible, though at the time fluency in a barbarian tongue was not something one boasted about. Veterans of the Gallic Wars had long experience of the country and its inhabitants; Antony himself, who was so fond of strutting about in exotic costume, surrounded by barbarian bodyguards (and who had tried to bring elephants to Mutina), must have had a certain familiarity with the Gauls, possibly enough to allow him to intervene with them directly. Asinius Pollio, in a letter sent to Cicero from Corduba in June 43, confided to him his fear that Antony might stir up slaves and the native ethnic groups (*nationes*) to revolt—perhaps an allusion to his facility in communicating with barbarians, as in the case of Decimus Brutus, who had been forsaken by the Romans more quickly than by the Gauls.[34] In Rome, the decisive event was the coup d'état staged by Octavian. Profiting from the death of the consuls and protected by his soldiers, Octavian marched on Rome and in August 43 acceded to the consulship together with Quintus Pedius, Caesar's nephew and a veteran of his campaign. Then, relying on Fulvia's diplomacy, which was to be of fundamental importance in what followed, he sought the support of Antony and Lepidus. Plancus and Pollio soon followed Lepidus's example. Antony and Pollio came back from Gaul at the head of an enormous army, augmented by Ventidius's legions. Antony, Lepidus, and Octavian met in Bononia (Bologna), where they negotiated an accord that was to last for five years, with the possibility of renewal. This was not a private agreement like the ones concluded by Caesar, Pompey, and Crassus in 60 and 56, incorrectly called the "first triumvirate." The so-called second triumvirate was the first official triumvirate: an extraordinary magistracy officially instituted on 27 November 43, when the three men were appointed members of a commission created for the purpose of setting the Roman state in order (*triumviri rei publicae constituendae*), pursuant to a resolution proposed by the tribune of the plebs, Publius Titius.

Even if the Senate remained the paramount organ of government, the triumvirs were equipped with unprecedented powers. Unlike traditional magistrates, they were accountable neither to the Senate nor the people. Their word was law. They had the authority to appoint magistrates and provincial governors, even before the end of an incumbent's term, if necessary; they directly controlled the legions; what is more, they enjoyed *imperium maius*, which allowed them to move about without having to respect fixed territorial boundaries. The political union of the triumvirate was also sealed by matrimony: Octavian wed Antony's stepdaughter Claudia, the daughter of Clodius and Fulvia, a brief and unhappy marriage.

The triumvirs drew up a list of senators and knights considered to be major figures in the Ides of March plot against Caesar, who were then sentenced to death or exiled, and their assets expropriated. Pride of place on this list went to Cicero. Captured by hired assassins even before Antony, Lepidus, and Octavian had entered Rome, he was beheaded. Appian tells us that Cicero's head, after having been exhibited on the rostra—the platform for speakers in the Forum—was displayed for some time on a table in Antony's home. The exhibition of Cicero's remains had a comparable symbolic significance, which was in no way incompatible with the behavior of the leading figures of the late Republic. Careful not to neglect the people's attachment to tradition, they practiced a kind of politics-as-spectacle that permitted them to undermine it at every turn while at the same time taking cover under the *mos maiorum*—the morals of the ancients, to which conservatives piously appealed when it suited them.

Unlike the other proscripts, Cicero's corpse was desecrated in an altogether singular manner, the head being placed on the rostra together with his right hand. In literary tradition, this last detail signified a desire to punish the hand that had written the *Philippics*. Cassius Dio gives another explanation, that the hand symbolized the oratorical gestures that accompanied Cicero's speeches against Antony.[35] Rationalizations of this sort do not account for the brutality of such an act of mutilation, however. The efforts of ancient authors to discover a motive show how foreign it was to the Roman code of conduct, unless it is to be considered simply as an expression of ungovernable rage against Cicero's mortal remains. The solution is to be found elsewhere: Scarcely ten years earlier, the Parthians had treated Crassus's cadaver in the same fashion, cutting off his head and his right hand.[36] Once again, Antony's "orientalist" side influenced his political language.

Cutting off the head and the hand was not an invention of the Parthians; this custom went back to Egypt during the second millennium BCE. The right hand represented power, for the integrity of the body was a necessary condition for a king, whose authority was legitimated by the right hand. Unsurprisingly, the same indignity was inflicted upon Cyrus the Younger after his death at Cunaxa in 401 BCE, as reported by Xenophon, an author much appreciated by Cicero himself.[37] Finally, the non-Roman practice of regarding the head and hand as possessing particular symbolic significance was part of the inventory of exotica that colored Antony's approach to governance, well before his long stay in the East. The fate of Cicero's corpse is revelatory in this regard. During the heroic era when Rome began to assert its power in the Mediterranean, few Roman politicians could be described as experts on international affairs; many of them, in fact, perhaps for reasons of ideological prejudice, were pleased to go on ignoring even Greek culture. However much Antony's taste for the exotic may have dismayed conservatives, it was not difficult to decode its macabre message: The head of Cicero, nailed to the rostra, was a trophy of war (and, more generally, of hunting), and the hand the symbol of power usurped.

3

The Wars of the Tyrannicides

CAESAR'S ASSASSINS had gone away from Italy for good. Brutus, when he was still urban praetor, realized that he could no longer stay in Rome. Once the identity of the two chief assassins became known, leaving was their only practical option.[1] Both Florus and Appian maintain that Caesar had meant to assign the provinces of Macedonia and Syria to Brutus and Cassius, respectively, but this is very doubtful.[2] By contrast, other figures involved in the plot had already been appointed proconsuls. While Decimus Brutus was unsuccessful in preventing Antony from gaining control of Cisalpine Gaul, two members of the conspiracy governed key provinces of Anatolia, Gaius Trebonius in Asia and Lucius Tillius Cimber in Bithynia. Brutus and Cassius, having no other choice, set off for the East as well. For want of any juridical justification, they sought to justify their murderous act by appeal to philosophical principles. Brutus was a Platonist; Cassius had for some years aligned himself with the Epicurean school. Platonism approved tyrannicide; Epicureanism, for its part, licensed a certain political and ethical flexibility, particularly in relation to what later came to be called the concept of utility, that a number of eminent Romans (Caesar among them) found convenient, not least as a supplementary proof of their Hellenic learning.

The Senate had granted two small provinces to the chiefs of the conspiracy, Cyrenaica to Cassius, Crete to Brutus. Brutus ended up seizing Macedonia, which was governed by Gaius Antonius, and Cassius went to Syria, which Caesar had entrusted to Dolabella in preparing for the campaign against the Parthians.[3] The peoples of the Roman East were bound to take sides, and the support of the Greek cities was essential, all the more as the process of integrating Greeks into the empire after the civil war between Caesar and Pompey had greatly accelerated. The province of Syria was a particularly delicate matter, for the Parthians had every interest in sustaining and, if possible, deepening the discontent of local communities. It was therefore necessary to revive the policy pursued by both Pompey and Caesar, courting the favor of various kings and petty rulers in addition to that of the Greek cities. For this reason, in the autumn of 44, Brutus and Cassius made a first symbolic visit to Athens, a city that more than forty years earlier had paid for its decision to back Mithradates when Sulla sacked it after a long siege, in 86. Much blood was shed, but the proconsul ordered that the city was not to be burned. Athens kept its liberty, was restored to something like its former condition, and, as we noted, warmly received the young Romans who, like Brutus himself, came to study there. On their arrival, Caesar's murderers were welcomed as liberators, and bronze statues were erected in their honor alongside those of Harmodius and Aristogeiton.

The comparison with the Tyrannicides, symbolic founders of Athenian democracy, is instructive. Aristogeiton and the young Harmodius, who plotted unsuccessfully against the tyrant Hippias, were put to death for the murder of Hippias's brother Hipparchus in 514; the tyrant was deposed four years later. Not long afterward, bronze statues cast by the sculptor Antenor were raised in their memory in the Agora, but in 480, at least according to tradition, they were taken by the Persians as spoils of war and later replaced by another group made by Kritios and Nesiotes. Antenor's group was returned to the city by Alexander the Great, or possibly Seleucus I, and reinstalled in the same place. The ship that transported the original statues stopped at Rhodes on the way, where they were honored with great ceremony, for the symbolic value of the effigies of the Tyrannicides, the first ones representing mortal men to have been erected in Athens, was recognized in cities throughout Greece, and still more after the arrival of the Romans.[4] A friend of Brutus by the name of Empylus dedicated a work on the death of Caesar to him; very probably this was the rhetorician Empylus, a native of Rhodes, whom Cicero praised for his memory.[5]

By means of these statues the Athenians offered thanks to Brutus and Cassius for having eliminated Caesar, who had humiliated them after Pharsalus, Athens having taken Pompey's side. Immediately after the battle, it had to bow down once more before a Roman, hastening to send an embassy to Caesar to plead for forgiveness. Caesar showed clemency, while issuing a warning that no doubt was meant to recall the magnanimity displayed earlier by Sulla: "How often will the glory of your ancestors save you from self-destruction?"[6] Nevertheless the principal reason for the Athenian animosity toward Caesar was economic in nature. Among his future projects was a plan, initially put into effect at the beginning of 44, for refounding Corinth as Colonia Laus Iulia Corinthiensis, this for the purpose not only of reviving commerce and establishing the city as a counterweight to Athens but also of romanizing depopulated regions in the East while at the same time emptying Rome of disfavored citizens and unwanted foreigners. Even so, though he granted citizenship to many Greeks on an individual basis, he rewarded no oriental city with corporate Roman citizenship or Latin status, perhaps realizing that the Greek world could not be wholly Romanized.

A bit earlier, attempting to resettle some of his veterans in the southern part of Epirus, around Buthrotum (present-day Butrint, in Albania), with a view to strengthening the strategic position of this area on the northeastern coast of the Ionian Sea, Caesar had threatened to interfere with the interests of a wealthy landowner who was well connected with the Roman aristocracy, Titus Pomponius Atticus, Cicero's great friend. One of Atticus's favorite properties was called Amaltheum—an allusion to Zeus's goat nurse, Amalthaea, and probably, by extension, to the rearing of animals.

Caesar was to have greater success with Corinth. The renaissance of the ancient port city, newly settled by Roman colonists and soon the residence of the proconsul of Achaia, was part of a larger program aimed at arresting the depopulation of Greece as the result of wars and the enslavement that followed from them, on a scale that substantially increased the presence of oriental immigrants in Rome. But this refounding could not help but arouse apprehension among the Athenians, who feared a reduction in the volume of traffic passing through Piraeus, and all the more as

FIGURE 3.1. Fragment of the base of the statue of Brutus

the Mithridatic wars had all but shut down shipping through the island of Delos; onomastic analysis shows that the colonists of the new Corinth, in addition to military veterans and freedmen, included a colony of merchants from Italy who had settled in Argos, a land famous for horse breeding, hoping to profit from the business of ensuring that Roman soldiers had the foodstuffs they needed for overseas operations. One of them was almost certainly a certain Gnaeus Seius, who went down in history for purchasing a wonderful purebred horse that, as we shall also see later, had the power to bring misfortune to its owners—beginning with Seius himself, sentenced to death by Antony around 44.[7]

The Athenians were quite pleased to erect statues in honor of new tyrannicides. Excavations at the Agora have uncovered the base of the statue of Brutus (fig. 3.1), from which it is possible to reconstruct his official name, Quintus Servilius Caepio Brutus.[8] He had long claimed kinship with Lucius Iunius Brutus, the semilegendary founder of the Republic and a tyrannicide himself. The Athenians erected another statue of Brutus at Delos, in gratitude for his "services" to the city. A third was also raised by the Athenian deme of Oropus in the sanctuary of Amphiaraus.[9]

The Athenian network of influence cultivated by Cicero and his friends seemingly favored this consensus; Cicero's son, ardently opposed to tyranny, was one of the most devoted supporters of Brutus, who attended the lectures of philosophers in Athens and engaged Roman students there in debate.[10] Taking Cicero as his model, Brutus also wrote a treatise titled *Concerning Duty*, now lost.[11] This show of intellectual activity concealed from everyone's view the fact that he was preparing for war. He had salvaged ships and sent to Macedonia a Greek envoy, a certain Herostratus; in the meantime Gaius Antistius Vetus, the outgoing governor of Syria who had replaced Sextus Caesar, had been induced to hand over a part of his province's revenues. In Thessaly, Brutus had marshaled arms and troops, including a unit of cavalry assigned to Dolabella for the war against the Parthians, and a good number of Pompey's soldiers who were said to have stayed on in the region after Caesar's victory at Pharsalus, to the south of Larissa, the principal center, which some authors associate with the kingdom of Achilles.[12]

If this information is trustworthy, it would appear that these veterans survived for more than four years as roving brigands—unsurprisingly, perhaps, since Thessaly, which had always occupied a special place in the Greek imagination, was known as a land of sorcery and magic. It seems more probable, however, that they were natives of Thessaly who had been incorporated in Pompey's legions together with Boeotians, Achaeans, and Epirotes.[13] Caesar had, of course, after Pharsalus, granted liberty to Thessalians who had fought in his ranks.[14] Later, at Philippi, Thessalians served in the army commanded by Brutus.[15] At all events, it was with these troops that Brutus, armed with the authority of a *senatus consultum* that gave him plenary powers over the Western Balkans and Greece, occupied Macedonia, Epirus, and Illyria, profiting from Vatinius's difficulties in responding effectively to the attacks mounted by the Dalmatians.[16]

Furthermore, Brutus regained control of the legion led by Gaius Antonius, who had been wounded and taken hostage, with the support of the governor, Hortensius, Brutus's uncle. Brutus had a total of eight legions at his disposal, partly comprised of veterans, with a good many horsemen, light infantry, and archers; he "had a high opinion of the Macedonians, enlist[ing] two legions from them, [which] he trained in the Italian way."[17]

Cassius, for his part, headed eastward as well, occupying Syria, where he had distinguished himself a few years earlier. A succession of Roman governors there had attempted to put down the insurgency of Caecilius Bassus and his local and Parthian supporters. Sextus Caesar had been replaced by Antistius Vetus, who, as we have noted, gave Brutus a share of the revenue collected in Syria. Antistius had taken up the fight against Bassus with the support of Antipater, a close adviser to the high priest Hyrcanus II of Judaea, husband of the Nabataean princess Kypros, and father of Herod the Great. Antipater, whose position had been strengthened by Pompey's reorganization of the province, was a faithful ally of the Romans, who had come to his aid in the struggle against the Hasmonean king Aristobulus II and his sons; thanks to his wealth and his diplomatic skills, Antipater managed to avoid becoming a collateral victim of the Roman civil wars.

The Jews were hostile to Pompey for having committed the sacrilege of forcefully entering, and possibly looting, the Temple of Jerusalem in 63. They pledged their allegiance to Caesar, whose life Antipater had saved some fifteen years later, in 47, during the Alexandrian War.[18] Caesar entrusted the administration of Judaea to Antipater and bestowed upon Hyrcanus and his descendants the title of Prince and High Priest of the Jews, together with other privileges and exemptions. Moreover, he authorized the reconstruction of the ramparts of Jerusalem, which Pompey had destroyed, and granted Alexandrian citizenship to the Jewish community of that city.[19]

Mark Antony, for his part, had gotten to know Antipater's family in 57–56, when he was a promising young officer taking part in the campaigns conducted by Gabinius, then the governor of Syria.[20] On the order of Gabinius, who had also authorized him to intervene in the affairs of neighboring kingdoms, Antony went to the aid of Hyrcanus in Judaea and, in the company of other officers, formed an army consisting of Roman legionaries and Jewish auxiliaries to take up arms against the enemies of the high priest.

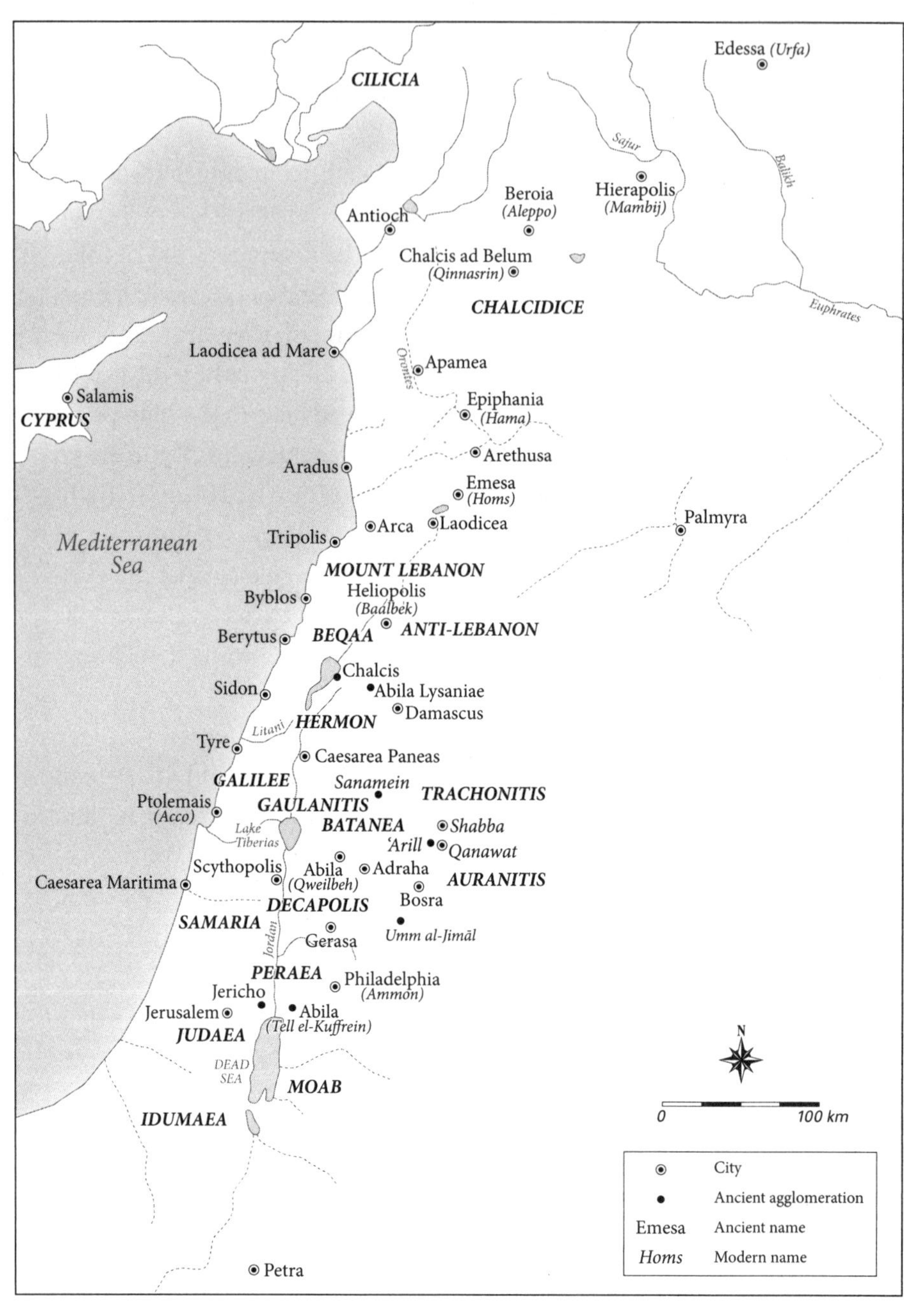

MAP 2. Roman Syria

As for Bassus, he was supported by Alchaidamus (or Alchaudonius; from the Arabic *al-ḫiḍamm*, magnificent lord), chief of an Arab tribe, the Rhambaeans, rivals of the Osrhoenians of Edessa whose loyalty wavered between Rome and Parthia. In 69 Alchaidamus (or, more probably, his father) had backed Lucullus during the war against Mithradates and Tigran of Armenia; subsequently he took the side of the Parthians against Crassus.[21] Bassus also enjoyed the support of Sampsiceramus of Emesa (modern-day Ḥomṣ) and his son Iamblicus (who was stationed at Arethusa, a strategic town on the Orontes River). The list of minor regional powers also included two anonymous chieftains, one from Lysias, a city to the north of Apamea, and the other from Heliopolis (Baalbek). Another person of whom one would like to know more is the Ituraean Ptolemy, who ruled the Syrian frontier of the Seleucid Empire, a region the Greeks and the Romans called Coele-Syria. Its principal center was Chalcis in eastern Lebanon, in the Beqaa Valley.[22]

Pompey's Syrian campaign in 64 had discouraged the expansionist ambitions harbored by Ptolemy, who until then had profited from the disintegration of the Seleucid Empire; he subsequently furnished Caesar with auxiliaries who fought at Pharsalus and then followed him to Africa and, as we saw earlier, to Rome, where they formed Antony's bodyguard during the time of his consulship.[23] The Ituraean leader, together with other phylarchs of the region, also supplied soldiers to Bassus, who, in command of two legions, had established his headquarters at Apamea, a fortified city surrounded by very fertile lands.[24] Bassus and Antistius Vetus eventually concluded a truce.[25] The new governor of Syria, Lucius Staius Murcus, was also a supporter of the plot against Caesar, but the Parthian menace made it necessary to suspend fighting among the Roman forces. Murcus had three legions at his disposal, reinforced by three others sent by Quintus Marcius Crispus, proconsul of Bithynia and Pontus.[26]

The arrival of Cassius, whose prestige and experience against the Parthians could only inspire confidence, was enough to sort things out. On 7 March 43 he wrote to Cicero, from his camp at Tarichea in Judaea, that Murcus and Crispus had given him their soldiers and that he had also gained control of Bassus's legions, while Dolabella's legate Aulus Allienus (earlier a proconsul in Sicily) delivered four legions from Egypt with Cleopatra's blessing.[27] In another letter, he noted that he had retained Staius Murcus as legate and confirmed Crispus in his military office; two months later, on 7 May, he cursed Bassus for stupidly having closed the gates of Apamea, refusing to hand over his soldiers to him, until finally they disobeyed his orders and negotiated their own settlement with Cassius.[28] According to Cassius Dio, Cassius had entrusted command of the fleet to Murcus while letting Crispus and Bassus go, unharmed, whereas according to Josephus (who reported the events from a Jewish perspective), Bassus had collaborated with Cassius and Murcus in requisitioning arms and men and levying tribute in the cities.[29] However this may be, both men soon disappeared from history.

Cassius acted severely toward the Jews, who felt no regret for their loyalty to Caesar (Antipater was also a friend of Octavian) and had supported the operations against Caecilius Bassus. The new Roman master demanded a colossal tribute and reproached Antipater's lieutenant, a certain Malichus (very probably a Nabataean; the name means "king") for having shown insufficient zeal in reducing the cities of Judaea to servitude. Malichus was bent on stirring up revolt against Antipater, all the more as Cassius and Murcus had confided the government of Coele-Syria to Herod, promising him the throne of Judaea.[30] The Parthians did not seem to pose a threat: Cassius had probably sought to convince them to join forces with him against Dolabella, who had been given responsibility for carrying out the campaign envisaged by Caesar.

By the autumn of 44, Dolabella had moved on to Greece, where, learning of the splendid horse of Seius, he made a detour and went to Argos to seize it.[31] Shortly thereafter, in January 43, Dolabella had the governor of Asia, Gaius Trebonius, put to death; Tribonius, a member of the conspiracy against Caesar, had detained Antony in conversation outside the Curia of Pompey on the Ides of March, delaying his entry to the meeting of the Senate. On the pretense of wishing to negotiate with the proconsul, Dolabella took the city of Smyrna and captured Trebonius. When the news reached Italy, Antony was laying siege to Decimus Brutus at Mutina. Cicero exploited the event in order to foment war, recounting the manner of Trebonius's gruesome death in *Philippic* 11, omitting no detail.

Trebonius was the first one of Caesar's murderers to fall. Cicero revealed the existence of a plot against the Republic by Antony and Dolabella, who had respectively usurped the provinces of Cisalpine Gaul and Asia, and castigated Dolabella for proceeding to Syria, where one of his legates, Octavius Marsus, had plundered the cities and the countryside—part of a broader strategy, Cicero insisted, for regaining control in both the East and the West.[32] But Dolabella, a less experienced commander, had less luck than Antony. From the reconstruction of events by Appian and Cassius Dio, though it is not always straightforward, it appears that, by eliminating Trebonius, Dolabella had gotten back his money, which allowed him to form a second legion and a fleet manned by mercenaries who had been recruited along the whole of the southern coast of Asia Minor, in Rhodes and Lycia, and from Pamphylia eastward as far as Cilicia.[33] In the meantime, Dolabella had been declared a public enemy and the Senate instructed Cassius to wage war against him.

Two letters from Publius Lentulus Spinther, one to the Senate and the other to Cicero, inform us about Dolabella's movements. Lentulus, son of one of Pompey's most trusted allies, executed by Caesar, had served as a young man under Trebonius as quaestor and now found himself in Perge, the capital of Pamphylia, a few days before Dolabella's defeat in Syria. In the event of disappointment, Lentulus believed, Dolabella would return to Italy to aid Antony. Because of Rhodes's support for Dolabella, Lentulus had not succeeded in thwarting the advance of his fleet, but he did manage to disperse it, partially neutralizing its capabilities.[34] Lentulus made a point of denouncing the attitude of the Rhodians, who in the past had closed their gates and harbor to the Pompeians, his father among them, when they were being hunted down after their defeat at Pharsalus.[35] On a personal note, he asked Cicero to stand surety for his debts and begged him to ensure that he would be treated on the same level as Cassius and Brutus. His attitude, in other words, was that of an aspiring warlord.

The situation in Cilicia was delicate. The conflict between the two Roman armies had had repercussions throughout the land, notably in the prosperous city of Tarsus, which in 47 had taken the name of Iuliopolis in honor of Caesar. Here the far-flung Roman civil war came to be reproduced in miniature. The local authorities offered the crown initially to Cassius, the first to arrive, then later to Dolabella. Both men assumed the office of *stephanophoros*, the eponymous magistracy of the city; both men disparaged Tarsus as a city of "changeable loyalties" (*eumetabolos*).[36]

Cassius, however, could count on the support of the dynast Tarcondimotus,[37] an old ally of Pompey whom Cicero, at the time of proconsulship in 51, had called "the most faithful ally and the most devoted friend of the Roman people beyond Mount Taurus."[38] After Pharsalus he had abandoned the Pompeians, and Cato the Younger accused him of having reverted to robbery on the seas; this detail, attested by Lucan, and so perhaps not a piece of poetic license, suggests that Tarcondimotus had been a piratical chieftain in his earlier career.[39] Since his descendants took the name Iulius, it seems reasonable to suppose that Caesar had granted him Roman citizenship, possibly on passing through Tarsus in 47, when he had "settled all the affairs of the province and its neighboring states."[40] Caesar surely had no difficulty judging the qualities of a man whom Strabo described as an able politician, endowed with "manly virtues" (*andragathia*), who had managed to become the sole lord of the Amanus mountains, which until then had always dominated by "several powerful tyrants"; a man whom the Romans at one point had favored with a royal title.[41]

Tarcondimotus controlled a part of the surrounding region, whose most important center was the Hellenized city of Kastabala/Hierapolis, on the edge of the forests of the Amanus range (Nur Dağları). His territory overlooked the Plain of Issus, where Alexander the Great had won a pitched battle against the Persians in 333. The Tarsians tried to prevent Tillius Cimber from meeting up with Cassius, by closing their gates. Cimber continued on his way, probably passing through Aigai, a port situated near the present-day city of Adana, which, in the Middle Ages, under the name of Ayas (or Laiazzo), was an important trading post. Cassius had installed a garrison there that later was defeated by Dolabella, with the help of the Tarsians.[42]

Dolabella was later turned back at Antioch, former capital of the Seleucids, where Caesar was fondly remembered: The city having sided with him against Pompey, its administrative freedom, granted in the first place by Pompey, was then reconfirmed.[43] The Caesarian era inaugurated on 1 September 47 was marked by the construction of a new basilica, the Kaisareion (named after the one in Alexandria), as well as other public works, testifying both to the importance that Caesar attached to Syria and to the prestige that still accrued to the former royal capital, one of the great Mediterranean cities of its time.

Cassius, for his part, having occupied Antioch, knew the city and its inhabitants very well, going back to the period when it had resisted the Parthians, in 53–51. He did not enjoy the same popularity as Caesar, but he was nonetheless feared. Lentulus, in his report sent to the Senate on 2 June 43, made a point of mentioning a small group of soldiers whom Dolabella had enlisted in Asia and brought down to Syria. These men subsequently deserted and reported from Pamphylia that Antioch had repelled Dolabella's attacks. Dolabella, having been obliged to leave his wounded behind, pulled back as far as Laodicea (al-Lādhiqiyya), a maritime city loyal to Caesar, where he set up his headquarters. Taking advantage of this nocturnal retreat, almost all the soldiers he had recruited in Asia abandoned him. Eight hundred of them returned to Antioch, submitting to the authority of Cassius's legate, while the others crossed the Amanus mountains. Cassius himself, a march of four days away, was closing in on Dolabella and what was left of his army. Lentulus, writing to Cicero, expressed the opinion that Dolabella would soon be punished for his crimes—indeed, he suspected that Dolabella had already been crushed.[44]

Lentulus's wishes were fulfilled, but not right away. In spite of everything, Dolabella still had a fair number of ships at his disposal, with which he tried, unsuccessfully, to take the ancient city of Aradus (present-day Arwad), a major port on an island off the Syrian coast. Cassius had already assured himself of Aradus's support, as well as that of Tyre, the other major Phoenician commercial center. Cleopatra, on the other hand, who controlled Cyprus in the person of her governor, Serapio, continued to support Dolabella; the Rhodians and the Lycians (the latter having concluded a treaty with Rome in 46) remained neutral.[45] Having had to regroup on the Syrian coast, Dolabella found himself confronted there with Cassius's troops, reinforced by auxiliaries that included mounted archers—a sign that Cassius had reached an agreement with the Parthians.[46] Dolabella was therefore forced to barricade himself at Laodicea.

Cassius, protected by a guard of centurions, entered the city. The confrontation ended with Dolabella's suicide and that of his legate Octavius Marsus, who earlier had refused Cassius's offer of a pardon.[47] Cassius then seized Dolabella's possessions, beginning with Seius's horse.[48] All this took place in the month of July. Laodicea was severely punished by heavy exactions; the same treatment was reserved for Tarsus, some of whose citizens were reduced to slavery.[49] In the meantime Brutus and Cassius had realized that the situation in Italy would soon change and that the only way to maintain their position in the East was to institute a policy of terror. This led to the enslavement of the Jews of Aradus, Tyre, Sidon, and Antioch, under Cassius's direction.[50]

Appian, in *The Civil Wars*, tried to impose some order on a most unruly narrative. After describing the creation of the triumvirate and the proscription lists at once drawn up by its members, he recalls prior events (the troubles in Africa, the conflict between Cassius and Dolabella in Syria, and the operations conducted by Sextus Pompey in Sicily), not omitting to mention the calamities that fell upon cities of the Levant: Rhodes, Patara, and Xanthus in addition to Laodicea and Tarsus.[51] We have already reviewed a few of these episodes; the rest we will consider in due course. The crisis of the African provinces and the operations of Sextus Pompey there, which we will go on to examine in what follows, were by no means insignificant in this regard.

In May 43, after having received news of the battle of Mutina, Brutus quit the Adriatic and traversed Macedonia along the Via Egnatia. He left his legates to look after matters in Macedonia, among them Cicero's son, who was delighted to abandon his studies and devote himself at last to war. Cicero himself, acutely aware of the impending danger, urged Brutus to return to Italy, but Brutus preferred to prepare the way for a future campaign in the western part of Asia Minor, where he succeeded in obtaining the support of the aged Deiotarus.[52] Control of this area also depended on suppressing resistance in Thrace, where local dynasties, which seem to have confidently anticipated the success of Caesar's expedition against the Dacians, now found themselves in a bind.

We know nothing of the attitude of Sadalas II, king of the Astaean Thracians, successor to Cotys VI and formerly an auxiliary commander at Pharsalus, but it is reasonable to suppose that he was inclined to side with the Romans and take advantage of their need to vanquish the formidable Bessi, and all the more since they might be expected also to launch the campaign against the Dacians that had been delayed by Caesar's death. However this may be, Sadalas was struck down in a battle against unidentified enemies, and his widow Polemocratia (a telling name, in the event) handed over the gold and silver in his treasury to Brutus, who placed her son Cotys in the care of the citizens of Cyzicus, a Greek city on the Sea of Marmara. The precious metals were minted, and the currency created in this way was used to wage war.[53]

Brutus already knew this part of the world. If Caesar had pardoned him after Pharsalus, it was because he counted on being able to profit from Brutus's prior experience in the East. In the 50s, having already earned a reputation as an author of philosophical treatises, Brutus set out for Cilicia in the company of his father-in-law, Appius Claudius, to enrich himself as a banker and to create a network of clients, loaning large sums not only to the town of Salamis in Cyprus but also to Ariobarzanes III, king of Cappadocia and Lesser Armenia, recommended by his friendship to the Roman people. Several years passed, and sometime around the beginning of 50 Brutus vehemently insisted that Ariobarzanes repay his debt, notwithstanding the king's straitened financial circumstances.[54] The anonymous rhetorician who compiled the apocryphal collection of Brutus's letters gives us some idea of his peremptory attitude and the difficulties of the Greek cities. In a short note addressed to the citizens of Samos, Brutus reproached them for not promptly providing him with the information he had asked for, menacingly enjoining them to consider the consequences of their recalcitrance. The Samians limited themselves to replying with a comparably short note begging his pardon.

The eastern provinces were accustomed to furnishing Rome with substantial fiscal resources in the form of exactions, land taxes, and custom duties. But cities and kings were now beginning to balk—Ariobarzanes III, for example, surnamed Eusebes Philoromaios (Pious Friend of the Romans), had no desire to help someone like Brutus.[55] When Ariobarzanes refused to accede to the demand of the Caesaricides that he supply them with troops, Cassius had him killed after first harshly repressing the cities of southern Asia Minor.[56] There were several reasons for the king's disinclination to cooperate. Apart from loyalty to the memory of his benefactor, Caesar, Ariobarzanes possibly feared the prospect of an agreement between Brutus and Cassius and the Parthians, from which the king of Commagene Antiochus I, who controlled the "junction" (*zeugma*) of the Euphrates, a strategic passage permitting access to Mesopotamia, could not help but profit.

The preface to the apocryphal Greek letters ascribed to Brutus, which were already circulating in the first centuries of our era, notes in connection with his activity in the East that "as a man making war against many regions, [Brutus] conducted diplomacy through countless letters." Composition of this collection (which also includes a few authentic letters) is conventionally attributed to a certain Mithridates, nephew of an oriental king of the same name—perhaps Mithradates II of Commagene, son of Antiochus, who reigned between 36 and 20—which would explain why a teacher of rhetoric should have been so well acquainted with the geopolitical situation.

By the end of 43, reports of the situation in Rome had undermined the credibility of the Caesaricides. The creation of the triumvirate and the execution of political adversaries, most notably Cicero, heightened tensions, with the result that Brutus ordered Antony's brother Gaius Antonius to be killed.[57] Antony, it was said, had sought a compromise with Brutus, but negotiations broke down with the murder of his brother, accused of having tried to persuade Brutus's troops to mutiny. Lepidus depended on legates to look after the affairs of western Europe, having been elected consul, together with Munatius Plancus, for the year 42. Antony and Octavian, having appropriated the wealth of their enemies once they had been eliminated, now set about recruiting troops. The triumvirs, Appian observed, "needed a great deal of money to carry on the war, for the taxes from Asia had been paid to

Brutus and Cassius, and were still accruing to them, and kings and satraps were also contributing, while they themselves were short of money in a Europe, particularly Italy, worn out by wars and imposts."[58] Cassius even thought of plundering the wealth of Egypt, which was ravaged by famine just then, on learning that Cleopatra had equipped a large fleet with the purpose of coming to the aid of Antony and Octavian.[59] Since these two men were already crossing the Ionian Sea, Caesar's murderers had to react at once. The fate of the East was still far from having been decided.

4

Avenging Caesar

AFTER HIS apotheosis, Caesar was called *Divus Iulius,* the divine Julius. To encourage popular acceptance of Caesar's divinization, the triumvirs relied on the prestige of his territorial conquests, including that of Britain (notwithstanding that it was, in reality, a failed attempt at conquest). Caesar was to go down in history for his discovery of unknown lands. The temple of Venus Genetrix, in the Forum of Caesar, conserved as part of the dictator's donation following his triumphs of 46 a pearl cuirass, as though to memorialize the extension of Roman *imperium* as far as the Ocean.[1]

A denarius struck in 42 by the monetary magistrate Lucius Mussidius Longus (fig. 4.1) displays the insignia of world domination, over land and sea: globe (symbol of *orbis terrarum*), scepter, and oar. A similar iconography had figured on a coin more than thirty years earlier, in 74, associated with the extraordinary powers conferred on Marcus Antonius Creticus, Antony's father, in his campaign against piracy.

Control over the world depended in the first place on controlling the Mediterranean, but this body of water was once again practically held hostage by pirates. We saw earlier that the Senate had named Sextus prefect of the fleet and the seacoast in early 43. Given that he was a direct descendant of Pompey the Great, however, there was a risk that he might overshadow Caesar the Younger; Sextus therefore had to be sidelined, if not actually eliminated. Accused of having taken part in the conspiracy of the Ides of March, he found his name entered on the proscription

FIGURE 4.1. Denarius struck in honor of I. Mussidius Longus

list later that same year.[2] The civil war between Pompey and Caesar had not yet really ended.

While the triumvirs were busy preparing for war against Caesar's murderers, Sextus moved at once to assert his mastery of the seas. Whereas the triumvirs had put a price on the heads of the partisans of Brutus and Cassius, Sextus offered double the amount to anyone who saved their lives.[3] The son of Neptune, as he liked to call himself, had lieutenants of exceptional ability. In addition to Roman admirals, he also had in his service four very experienced commanders of more doubtful reputation, all of Greek (or at least oriental) ancestry: Apollophanes, Demochares, Menecrates, Papias, and Menodoros (also known as Menas). The historiographical tradition, hostile to Sextus Pompey, considers these figures to have been pirates; and with good reason, it would appear, since when Pompey the Great succeeded in temporarily eradicating piracy in 67, he was not content simply to seize the boats that he had not sunk—he also imprisoned their most capable commanders, reducing them to slavery before finally freeing them.[4] Apparently, after the death of their patron these robbers transferred their allegiance to his son, and in the years that followed accounted for a large part of his naval successes.

Sextus's first military exploit was the siege of Messana (present-day Messina). After an initial uprising the governor, Aulus Pompeius Bithynicus, authorized him to come to Sicily in late 43 or early 42, on the condition that they shared power (Sextus later had him put to death). Sicily, the largest island in the Mediterranean and the first province acquired by Rome, occupied a position of the highest strategic importance. The Romans had controlled Sicily since the end of the First Punic War in 241, but its cities had been allowed to retain their institutions. Greek and Punic were spoken there, and local cultural and religious traditions reflected centuries of Hellenic influence.

The Roman order, by contrast, came to be established only with difficulty, particularly during the slave wars of the second half of the second century. Around the middle of the first century, the major urban centers were allied with Pompey; after Caesar's crossing of the Rubicon, however, the island came under his authority. In 46, following the defeat of Pompey's partisans in Africa, Caesar granted Sicilian cities the Latin right (*ius Latii*), which guaranteed local autonomy while awarding Roman citizenship to outgoing municipal magistrates and their near relations.

The importance of Sicily was not only strategic, however. Its cereals had long been essential for provisioning Rome and Italy as a whole. From the military point of view, control of the island facilitated operations in the Western Mediterranean, and particularly Africa, a new source of grain supplies for the capital. Sextus, by virtue of his ability to block commercial shipping, represented a serious threat to the triumvirs' plans; the Sicilian cities, for their part, now freed from the obligation of acting as an economic intermediary, had no reason not to support him. Moreover, fear of Sextus's fleet discouraged eastern merchants from sailing to Italy.[5] Sextus also welcomed fugitive slaves. During the seven years that he occupied Sicily, from 42 to 36, he was the undisputed master not only of the island but also of a large and crucial part of the Mediterranean, with the result that he "reduced Rome to famine."[6]

The Young Pompey offered a safe asylum to many Romans as well, among them some twenty senators seeking to escape proscription and a number of military deserters. Cassius himself, before departing for the East, visited Sicily. Sextus not only welcomed outlaws, he encouraged them to flee, promising handsome rewards to anyone who saved them. His fleet was mobilized to assist their passage, and he himself came to meet them. The most distinguished proscripts were granted commands in his armies and naval forces.[7] Others, in the territory of the Bruttii (now Calabria), mounted resistance under the command of a certain Vetulinus, who had assembled a force made up of proscribed dignitaries and civilian volunteers from eighteen towns at the mercy of the triumviral armies. Hopelessly outnumbered, he sent his son and the others to Sicily and then threw himself against the enemy in a suicidal attack.[8]

Sextus's control of Sicily also complicated the situation in Africa, which in 44 was governed by the praetor Cornificius, formerly a legate of Caesar who the year before had fought in Syria against Caecilius Bassus. Loyal to the Senate, Cornificius withheld his support from the triumvirs and likewise gave proscribed refugees a warm reception. For this reason he came into conflict with Titus Sextius, the governor of Africa Nova, who had succeeded in winning over the Numidian king Arabio to his cause. Arabio, as we saw earlier, was responsible for the death of Sittius; ironically, in a letter to Atticus, dated 14 June 44, Cicero (who two years earlier had said that Africa was born to wage war against Rome) expressed his satisfaction on hearing this news.[9]

Arabio, setting aside his fidelity to the Pompeian cause, put his horsemen at Sextius's disposal; with an elite corps of troops, he breached the ramparts of the enemy camp, while his cavalry attacked Cornificius's troops, killing their commander. Cornificius's legate Decimus Laelius Balbus, who had laid siege to Cirta, was killed as well. The death of these republican military leaders threw their soldiers into disarray and put the proscripts to flight, some of them heading to Sicily. The African cities came over to the side of the triumvirs, and the provinces of Africa Vetus and Africa Nova were consolidated.[10] Appian, who relates these events, likens the conflict between Cornificius and Sextius to the one between Cassius and Dolabella in Syria, laying emphasis on the rapidity with which operations in Africa were conducted—a sort of Blitzkrieg.[11]

In the meantime, Lepidus had ensured the cohesiveness of the western provinces by means of a policy of municipal expansion in Spain and Transalpine Gaul; in Spain, he founded Colonia Iulia Victrix Lepida near the site of the city of Celsa, on the Ebro, near present-day Velilla de Ebro in Aragon. Other colonies were established, among which the most important around 42 were Carthago Nova (New Carthage), on the southeastern coast of the Iberian Peninsula, and Nemausus (Nîmes), in southern Gaul. Additionally, he was generous in granting Roman citizenship, which enabled him to increase his prestige while at the same time recruiting new legionaries.

In early 42 Lepidus assumed his second consulship and concerned himself with the administration of Rome and Italy, while the other two triumvirs prepared for the war against Brutus and Cassius, awaiting the arrival of fair weather to embark. Antony had lost his brother Gaius, but he could still rely on the support of his friends and, above all, members of his family. His elderly uncle, Gaius Antonius Hybrida, who had been consul with Cicero in 63 and whom Caesar had recalled to Rome from a gilded exile in the Ionian island of Cephalonia, was given the office of censor. The prerogatives of this important magistracy, which had a term of five years, included control over the composition of the Senate through the appointment of favorably disposed members and, if necessary, the expulsion of undesirables. Until then the Senate had taken such decisions itself, but now a large part of its traditional authority had been appropriated by the triumvirs, whose exceptional powers allowed them to adopt resolutions without having to consult the popular will.

With the elimination of their principal enemies, the triumvirs dominated the executive organs of the Republic; the cooperation of a largely remodeled Senate forestalled any serious opposition. Lucius, the youngest of Antony's brothers, had stayed on in Gaul to fight the Alpine chiefdoms, over whom, as we shall see, he was to celebrate a triumph in 41.[12] The tyrannicides, for their part, continued to exact tribute and requisition troops in Asia Minor, not hesitating to use force and terror while occasionally punishing kings, chieftains, and cities that had not supported them, or not enthusiastically enough. They too welcomed proscripts, notably Lucius Aemilius Paullus, Lepidus's elder brother, whom the triumvirs had allowed to escape to the East.

Our sources contain fairly detailed accounts of the exactions of Brutus and Cassius, who on the whole were more interested in extracting wealth than in settling scores with adversaries. Cassius, for example, did not destroy Rhodes as punishment for its resistance. It needs to be kept in mind that in his youth he had gone there to study and that the Rhodians later sent to him as an ambassador his old teacher Archelaus, who stressed the essential point, namely, that a philhellene who cherished liberty could not lay waste to a Greek city. To this, Cassius replied that a *senatus consultum* had enjoined all the peoples of the East to defend Brutus and himself; moreover, the inhabitants of the Ionian Sea ought to obey not only Brutus but also Sextus Pompey, whose fleet ruled the waters off the coast of Sicily.

Octavian's admiral, Salvidienus Rufus, though he was unsuccessful in his bid to nullify Sextus's maritime supremacy, did nonetheless manage to prevent him from invading Italy.[13] Lead sling bullets bearing the Caesarian symbol of a thunderbolt and the inscription *Q*[*uintus*] *Sal*[*vidienus*] *im*[*perator*] have been recovered near Leucopetra, on the Calabrian side of the Strait of Messina.[14] Octavian later visited the Strait but had to leave to meet up with Antony at Brundisium.[15]

Proscribed senators in search of refuge had to be protected as well.[16] Confident of their superiority, the Rhodian admirals Alexander and Mnaseas initially attacked Cassius's fleet off the coast of Myndus (present-day Gümüşlük) in Asia Minor, and, in a second engagement, launched an assault against Staius Murcus; in both cases the Romans prevailed. In the meantime, Cassius dispatched infantry under the command of his two legates, Lentulus (who, it will be recalled, wished to be seen as an equal of Caesar's assassins) and Fannius. Cassius's troops entered Rhodes with the aid of its citizens and the siege of the city culminated in a riot of plunder and pillage. Nevertheless Cassius decided not to seize the "Chariot of the Sun," probably a statuary group dedicated to the island's most important divinity.[17]

Brutus's operations in Lycia gave rise to other horrific scenes, particularly the siege of Xanthus, where he was aided by the neighboring cities of Oinoanda and Patara. The resistance of Xanthus, fomented by the popular leader Naucrates, ended in mass suicide; many of its inhabitants immolated themselves after having killed their own families. Ultimately the Lycian league accepted Brutus's conditions, probably agreeing to revise the treaty concluded with Caesar in 46.[18] Furthermore, and again in contrast with Shakespeare's "gentle" Brutus, the man himself commanded the death of Theodotus of Chios, a rhetorician and tutor to Ptolemy XIII, who was among the royal advisers responsible for assassinating Pompey on his disembarkation in Egypt. This decree is attested by Plutarch, though Appian disagrees, saying that Cassius had ordered his crucifixion (according to Appian, Theodotos was from Samos).[19] Be that as it may, the execution was inevitable, for Sextus was not simply an ally of the Caesaricides; the accord between the three military leaders was a sort of republican alternative to the triumvirate.

The scale of Brutus's and Cassius's exactions was very considerable: at least twenty-five to thirty thousand talents in Asia and Lycia (a talent was then worth six thousand drachmas), plus the fortune of Ariobarzanes III. The army of Octavian and Antony, by contrast, was having trouble obtaining the supplies it needed owing to a naval blockade in the Mediterranean: A part of Cleopatra's fleet had been sunk and grain from Hispania and Africa had been intercepted by Sextus Pompey; the Adriatic and Ionian Seas, for their part, were controlled by Staius Murcus and Gn. Domitius Ahenobarbus (grandfather of the emperor Nero), member of a prominent aristocratic family and son of Lucius, a great enemy of Caesar, who, at least according to Cicero, had succumbed to the blows of Antony shortly after the battle of Pharsalus.[20]

Antony and Octavian attacked the Balkans in the fall, a massive demonstration of force that the Caesaricides' fleet was incapable of withstanding. Brutus and Cassius, having finally joined forces, set out at the head of twenty legions to do battle with Antony and Octavian, who now occupied Macedonia. The two battles of Philippi showed that Antony, at least on the tactical level, was a worthy successor to Caesar. Philippi was situated on a hillside overlooking the Via Egnatia. Founded in 355 by Philip II, the city was part of Macedonia, but it was not far from Thrace, where, as we have seen, Brutus had seized Sadalas's treasures.

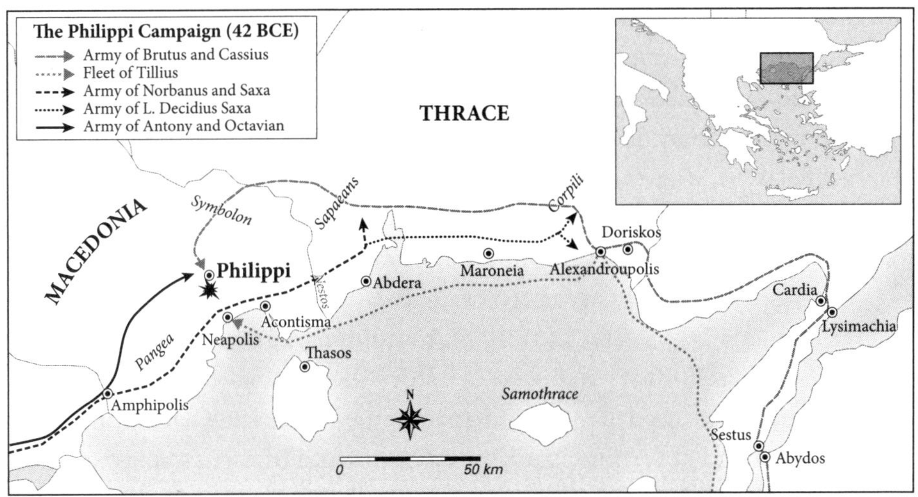

MAP 3. The Philippi campaign

There was another Thracian dynasty of consequence, however, the Sapaeans, whom we encountered earlier; at that time power was shared between the two sons of Cotys VI, Rhascupolis and Rhascus. Now, while the fleet commanded by Tillius Cimber patrolled the seas on behalf of Brutus and Cassius, Octavian and Antony had sent eight legions to Macedonia under the direction of Gaius Norbanus Flaccus and a veteran of Caesar's civil wars, Lucius Decidius Saxa. Saxa was a native of Spain; in the *Philippics*, Cicero described him as a military surveyor "from the farthest parts of Celtiberia." There is no evidence that Saxa was a *Hispanus*, that is, someone of Spanish blood to whom Caesar had granted Roman citizenship, let alone a native of a region that was still rebellious; he might well have been a *Hispaniensis*, which is to say a Roman citizen born on provincial soil.[21]

Norbanus and Saxa had crossed the plain of Philippi, in western Thrace, taking up a favorable position in the mountainous territory of the Sapaeans and the Corpili (a less well-known Thracian chiefdom that had been subjugated by its more powerful neighbor). At Pharsalus, it will be recalled, the Astaeans and the Sapaeans each failed in their attempts to put themselves on the winning side, for they had sent auxiliary troops to Pompey chosen by the crown princes, Sadalas and

Rhascupolis, respectively. The death of Sadalas having put the Astaeans out of play, the Sapaeans prudently decided this time to hedge their bets by sending reinforcements to both camps of the Roman armies, Rhascupolis in support of Caesar's assassins, with three thousand horsemen, and Rhascus, with the same number, in support of his avengers.[22] The two brothers' reported disagreement was no doubt a pretense; they must have felt sure that they would be granted clemency by the victors, who in any case would have need of Thracian allies to assert control over strategically important, but difficult and dangerous, terrain. In the course of preliminary maneuvers before the first battle of Philippi, Rhascupolis succeeded in placing a part of the Caesaricides' army under the command of Lucius Calpurnius Bibulus, and Rhascus managed to avoid being ambushed by Norbanus. "Both the Thracians," Appian tells us, "were the talk of their armies."[23]

But the outcome of the two battles that took place on the plain of Philippi on 3 October and 23 October 42, which ended with the suicides of Cassius and Brutus, did not concern only the peoples of this immediate vicinity. They were events of major importance for the Mediterranean as a whole and the Middle East. Brutus and Cassius, just as Pompey had done six years earlier in advance of Pharsalus, sought the support of the Parthians. The triumvirs were already aware of this: The edict of proscription mentioned Brutus's and Cassius's traitorous attempt to raise an army "from barbarians ever hostile to our empire."[24] Antony, unsurprisingly, took possession of Seius's horse, which Cassius had made his emblematic mount. Antony, its fourth owner, met with a wretched end as well—hence the proverbial expression *equus Seianus*, already current, applied to unfortunate men.[25]

The Parthians were nonetheless content to wait and see how matters played out. In the event, Brutus and Cassius's request for additional reinforcements, communicated through their ambassador Quintus Labienus, came to nothing. Labienus was the son of Titus, Caesar's former lieutenant who went over to Pompey's side and carried on the war after the defeat at Pharsalus, finally falling in 45 at the battle of Munda. We do not know whether his son had followed him, or what he was doing during Caesar's dictatorship; the young Labienus enters history at just this moment, before the Philippi campaign, when Cassius sent him to negotiate with the Parthians. After Philippi, fearing the vengeance of the triumvirs, Labienus chose to remain at Orodes's court.[26] In due course we will see what became of him.

Cassius nonetheless had at his disposal a sizable number of Parthian troops, who may have joined up with him in the wake of the operations against Dolabella in Syria. They included some four thousand mounted archers accompanied by Parthian, Median, and Arab horsemen, these in addition to auxiliary forces furnished by the Galatian tetrarchs and other kings, and a cavalry corps consisting of Iberian and Gallic veterans. Brutus's cavalry depended less heavily on recruits from the East, being comprised of Gauls, Lusitanians, Thracians, Illyrians, and Thessalians.[27] A horseman bearing the Celtic name of Camulatus defected to the enemy shortly before the second battle.[28] The Lycians, who had promised military assistance to Brutus as a sign of submission, may have contributed a fleet.[29] These troops, in combination with the legions of the Caesaricides, amounted to an army of eighty thousand men; the origin of the Gaulish troops is unknown to us, but the Lusitanians may have had some connection with Sextus Pompey.

As in the case of Pharsalus, the foreign component was substantial. Moreover, not all the legionaries came from Roman families; there were also foreign-born recruits trained in the Roman manner. In the speech Appian reports Cassius making to his troops, republican in tone, he once more remarks that the army benefited from alliance with many different peoples and kings, in the provinces and beyond.[30] Black soldiers were not unknown. As they were leaving camp, Brutus's men encountered an "Ethiopian," which was taken as a bad omen (in classical literature, Blacks were associated with the underworld); yet this man might well have been part of an auxiliary sent from Egypt or North Africa. Nor was the avengers' army unmixed.[31] The triumvirs surely could have counted on Rhascus's horsemen and other supporting troops: The Spartans had given Octavian two thousand soldiers who subsequently died in combat; Thessalonica had also furnished aid, and Brutus, to motivate his legionaries, promised them the right of pillaging the city following their victory (something that was never to be spoken of in advance of its actually coming to pass).[32] This arrogance, as well the policy of terror practiced by the tyrannicides in the eastern Mediterranean, almost certainly affected the conduct of the war and, especially, its aftermath.

At the end of the first battle of Philippi, Cassius committed suicide upon witnessing the retreat of a part of his army. Brutus took his own life following the second battle. In the self-interested telling of the *Res Gestae,* Augustus refers to the two battles as a personal success, in order to discredit Antony's military prowess, and goes on to try to show that the first battle had its ups and downs and that the outcome was due to the death of Cassius.[33] But, in fact, victory at Philippi belonged to Antony; Octavian's performance there hardly rose to the level of his adoptive father. He did, however, manage to take vengeance, massacring captives and sending Brutus's head to Rome, where it was to be placed at the foot of Caesar's statue.[34]

Once again Octavian demonstrated the *crudelitas* of which he had given proof earlier during the time of the proscriptions, when the praetor Quintus Gallius had made an attempt on his life. The young Caesar ordered a band of centurions and soldiers to remove Gallius from the tribunal where he was being tried, then tortured him as if he were a slave, and finally ripped out Gallius's eyes with his own hand—a scene straight out of the HBO series *Rome.* In his autobiography, however, Augustus says that Gallius was banished and "either lost his life by shipwreck or was waylaid by brigands."[35] However this may be, the case of Brutus was charged with political significance, for the dispatch of his head (Antony saw to it that the rest of the body was honorably cremated) agreed both with the edict of proscription and the principle of *pietas* in respect of the divine Caesar, Augustus's father.

The surviving legionaries took refuge on the nearby island of Thasos, where Brutus had arranged for Cassius's remains to be sent. They surrendered shortly afterward, handing over their arms and money in exchange for their own safety. Among their officers were Lucius Valerius Messalla Corvinus, whose name had figured on the list of the proscribed, and Calpurnius Bibulus, son of a formidable enemy of Caesar; both men in their youth had studied in Athens, along with Horace and the younger Cicero; both pledged allegiance to Antony after negotiating the surrender of their troops, their equipment, and everything that was precious to them.[36] The remnants of the tyrannicides' armies were absorbed into Sextus Pompey's forces in Sicily.

The Roman Republic was said to have died at Philippi.[37] Whether it had or not, Caesar had been avenged. The foreign allies of Brutus and Cassius hastened to reach a new understanding with the triumvirs, beginning with the Thracians. Rhascus handed over some number of prisoners in exchange for the safety of his brother Rhascupolis. "This showed clearly," Appian says, "that even right from the start these Thracians were not at odds with each other, but with two mighty and evenly matched armies fighting it out in their country, they divided up the risk posed by the uncertainty of fate, so that the victor might save the vanquished."[38]

PART II

Joys and Sorrows of the Triumvirs

5

Between Concord and Discord

CAESAR HAVING been avenged, the triumvirs could devote themselves at home to restoring the *res publica* and remunerating discharged soldiers. Their approaches differed, but they had a common—and complicated—mission, namely, to see to it that the task of reconstituting the republican order and establishing new colonies for veterans would be accomplished without arousing an unmanageable degree of protest. Abroad, Brutus and Cassius had bled the cities of the eastern Mediterranean white to finance so much violent conflict, and, in view of the formidable challenges facing the triumvirs, additional exactions were unavoidable; even so, there was scarcely any consensus among them as to how these challenges should be met. "For it is a difficult matter," Cassius Dio observed, "for three men, or even two, who are equal in rank and as a result of war have gained control over such vast interests, to be of one accord."[1]

The authority of the triumvirs was equal to that of consuls, but unlike the extraordinary powers enjoyed by Pompey and Caesar, it was not a matter in this case solely of pursuing military objectives; they had to find a way to put an end to political discontent as well. In theory, their appointment did not supersede republican institutions, but they had important prerogatives that recalled those of Caesar's dictatorship, notably including the right to convene the Senate.[2] On 11 November 43, during their meeting in Bononia prior to officially taking power, they had reached an agreement that also provided for the sharing of the Roman territories they controlled by means of virtually all the legions in the West: Octavian was placed in charge of Africa and the islands of the Tyrrhenian Sea (where Caesar's son could test his strength against Pompey's son), Lepidus of Spain and Gallia Narbonensis, and Antony of both Transalpine and Cisalpine Gaul, the latter having now been definitively made part of Italy.[3]

The need to settle soldiers who had served in Caesar's armies led to the founding of new towns and cities in Cisalpine Gaul, in addition to the ones already created by Caesar himself, such as Tergeste (Trieste) and Pola (Pula) in Istria, which were guarded by a network of fortresses. A commission created by the triumvirs established the colony of Iulia Concordia in a strategically important area, populated since prehistoric times, where two major roads crossed, the Via Postumia and the Via Annia. The name of the new colony, given to other such settlements as well, alluded to the public purposes the triumvirate sought to promote (the convergence of roads from surrounding lands was thought to be conducive to municipal harmony), while at the same time marking the high point of the Romanization of the Venetia, which carried with it a romanticized conception of physical space and the countryside that was closely linked to Roman values. The plains of the Po Valley, divided up in accordance with surveyors' measurements and memorialized by Virgil's *Georgics*, embodied the ideal of a well-ordered and cultivated landscape, by contrast with the barbarian wilderness. But the process of Romanization was by no means peaceable or without lasting consequence. The recent past, with its wars of conquest and its revolts, could not help but continue to weigh upon relations between Romans and local peoples, even in territories that were relatively close to the heart of the empire.

It is against this background that the importance of Lucius Antonius's activity may be better appreciated. On 1 January 41 Lucius assumed the office of consul and, at the same moment, celebrated his triumph *ex Alpibus*, the last in a long series of victories over Transpadane peoples and Ligurians that had punctuated the conquest of Cisalpine Gaul. Augustan propaganda saw in this latest celebration evidence of designs by Fulvia, Antony's wife, to draw glory from the defeat of "certain peoples dwelling in the Alps" and to rebuke Lucius for considering himself on this account superior even to Gaius Marius.[4] Nevertheless, one must not underestimate the ideological importance of a triumph over such peoples. In the Roman imagination, the Alps inspired terror; they were controlled by tribal chieftains and petty kings who ruthlessly regulated the transit of merchants and armies (Camilus, who killed Decimus Brutus on the orders of Mark Antony, was one such chieftain). Just the same, the wars waged by Caesar between 58 and 50, and the progressive Italianization of Cisalpine Gaul that accompanied them, had accelerated the process of Alpine integration. And even if Fulvia was certainly not a housewife (there can be no doubt that she played an important social and political role), her influence must not be exaggerated, following the propagandistic derogation of Antony (and his brother) as a puppet of women.

The rivalry between Antony and Octavian grew stronger with time, not least because the prestige attaching to victory at Philippi belonged entirely to Antony; Octavian, already ill during the battle, had had to undergo a long convalescence. Octavian nonetheless he had the advantage of Caesarian descent; sometime in 41 he assumed the patronym *divi filius* (son of the deified one), which elevated him above the two other triumvirs as well as the other members of the aristocracy. His most important allies included influential political figures and senior military officers; senators were enlisted to manage Antony and Lepidus. Even during this phase of equilibrium, however, most citizens tended to prefer Antony, for they found it easier to look up to a man from the Roman *nobilitas* than a Caesar from the equestrian branch of a plebeian *gens*. Antony did everything he could to draw attention to his patrician origins and to his privileged association with the dictator. It was for this reason that he gave the ancient cognomen Iullus as a praenomen to his second son with Fulvia. This name was charged with symbolic significance: Tradition located an early instance of it in the principal branch of the *gens Iulia* in the fifth century BCE, and scholars traced it back as far as the mythical son of Aeneas, Iulus (alternatively, Ascanius), founder of the line; the archaic variant Iullus gave Antony's line of descent additional luster.

Restoring order on Rome's terms over the entire Mediterranean made it necessary from time to time to resort to realpolitik. Antony and Octavian had no choice but to join forces against Lepidus, who now found himself disadvantaged by a new distribution of provincial authority. After Philippi it was agreed that Lepidus was to have Africa Vetus, originally meant for Antony; later he was given both African provinces. Spain (which seems to have been treated as a single province) was now assigned to Octavian, and Gaul to Antony.[5] But with his victory over Cornificius in 42, Titus Sextius now effectively governed both African provinces. Octavian nonetheless gave Africa Nova to another veteran of Caesar's armies, Gaius Fuficius Fango. To be sure, this new power-sharing arrangement involved only those provinces that were fully under the triumvirs' control; up until Philippi, the Adriatic was still subject to the authority of Staius Murcus and Domitius Ahenobarbus, who operated outside their command.[6]

From this time onward, our sources concern themselves for the most part with Antony and Octavian, making little mention of Lepidus. Lepidus was not completely powerless, of course, for he had at his disposal three legions and still enjoyed a certain respectability; after all, he was pontifex maximus and therefore untouchable. In short, Philippi had brought about important changes within the triumvirate: Lepidus, though he had been given a wealthy province, was nonetheless marginalized, whereas Antony, the true victor, had drawn political advantage from it. Lepidus stayed on in Rome until 40, however, which allowed him not only to stay in touch with local allies but also to deal with the crisis that emerged in Italy in the meantime, during the second half of 41.

Plutarch, in a passage of his *Life of Pompey*, before turning to the battle of Pharsalus, deplored the "contentiousness and greed" of the Romans, observing that Caesar and Pompey would have done better to join forces against the barbarians:

> For with kindred arms, fraternal ranks, and common standards, the strong manhood and might of a single city in such numbers was turning its own hand against itself, showing how blind and frenzied a thing human nature is when passion reigns. For had they now been willing quietly to govern and enjoy what they had conquered, the greatest and best part of earth and sea was subject to them, and if they still desired to gratify their thirst for trophies and triumphs, they

> might have had their fill of wars with Parthians or Germans. Besides, a great task still remained in the subjugation of Scythia and India, and here their greed would have had no inglorious excuse in the civilization of barbarous peoples. And what Scythian horse or Parthian archery or Indian wealth could have checked seventy thousand Romans coming up in arms under the leadership of Pompey and Caesar, whose names those nations had heard of long before that of Rome, so remote and various and savage were the peoples which they had attacked and conquered?[7]

Here Plutarch is engaging in an exercise of counterfactual history, no doubt inspired by techniques that were taught in schools of oratory, but his assessment of the ambition of Roman leaders of the late Republic, and the predicament in which they found themselves, is no less instructive for that. The alternative facing Antony and Octavian was no different than the one that faced Caesar and Pompey.

After Philippi it was necessary to impose order on the Balkans and the eastern lands inherited from Brutus and Cassius, namely, Asia Minor and Syria, which had been constantly threatened by the Parthians since Carrhae. Caesar's plan of subjugating the East had not been set aside, but Sextus Pompey's maneuvering and the complicated relations among the triumvirs combined to delay its being put into effect. Sextus rapidly took advantage of the situation to make himself master of the seas. And although the avengers' admirals had prevented him from assisting the military efforts of the Caesaricides, that permitted him to become the new champion of the republican cause: Whereas the triumvirs had put a price on the heads of Brutus and Cassius's partisans, he doubled the reward, only for saving their lives.[8] The death of the two men enabled Sextus to enlist a considerable number of suddenly unemployed legionaries. Several officers who survived Philippi sought refuge with Sextus as well, notably among them Staius Murcus, commander of the Caesaricides' fleet, whose men and ships came to be added to the naval force Sextus had constructed in early 43. Domitius Ahenobarbus, for his part, went from presiding over the Adriatic to setting himself up as a warlord; Velleius describes him as the chief of his own faction (fig. 5.1).[9]

FIGURE 5.1. Denarius struck in honor of Cn. Domitius Ahenobarbus Imperator

We do not know the details of the decisions that led to Antony being given responsibility for operations in the East, but they were taken between late 42 and early 41. According to our sources, Octavian went back to Italy while Antony entered upon what is sometimes called his oriental period. Cassius Dio devotes only a few lines to it. "Following the battle at Philippi," he says, "Mark Antony came to the mainland of Asia, where he levied contributions upon the cities and sold the positions of authority; some of the districts he visited in person and to others he sent agents."[10] Then he met Cleopatra in Cilicia and, as schoolbooks have long made a point of insisting, at once fell in love with her—a cliché that fails to capture the complexity of the situation.

Antony was not only the true victor at Philippi and a more experienced commander than Octavian; unlike Octavian, he had firsthand knowledge of the East. In 57, as a young cavalry officer serving under Aulus Gabinius, proconsul of Syria, he had established friendly relations with the Hasmoneans of Judaea and with the priestly dynasty of Comana in Pontic Cappadocia.[11] Furthermore, he had mastered Greek, indispensable in dealing with kingdoms and cities that had borne the heavy burden of taxation under Brutus and Cassius and feared the prospect of new exactions.

Antony could not avoid imposing taxes, however; without enough money to pay his soldiers he could not respond to the provocations of the Parthians. We will see in what follows that one of the Parthian commanders was the renegade Labienus, who was no doubt rallying men and raising funds for his cause. The legions most loyal to Antony were stationed in Macedonia, Italy, and Gaul; troops in the East were less reliable, consisting for the most part of veterans of the armies of Brutus and Cassius. Antony sought to assemble a trustworthy force close to hand. For this purpose, he recruited a certain number of Roman officers from the opposing camp at Philippi whose military and administrative experience might prove to be very valuable to him. One such man was Quintus Dellius, known to history for his changeable loyalties; having betrayed Dolabella, promising Cassius he would kill his former commander, he went on to become Antony's official historian. Antony sent Dellius to Egypt, ordering him to summon Cleopatra to Cilicia.

The situation in the East was well summarized almost a century ago by the historian Mario Attilio Levi. Describing the state of mind of non-Romans on the eve of Philippi, he remarks:

> All the factual circumstances, even if they are contradicted by theories, and by a formalistic and exclusionary mentality that has only grown over the centuries, combined to bring about a new political order; . . . the local problems of the different parts of the empire were reflected in turn through the prism of the civil wars. . . . The new political consciousness and the new mentality to which it gave rise a few decades after the end of the Mithridatic Wars were one of the clearest signs of the emergence of a new conception of the Roman state, which already for several decades had been violently asserting itself through legionary action, chaotic, tumultuous, unaware of its own purposes. . . . Through force, violence, and oppression, with the aid and obedience to their power of friendly states such as Rhodes and Cappadocia under Ariobarzanes, the Caesaricides imposed the bloodiest and most oppressive tyranny of the Hellenistic world in the name of freedom in Rome. They refused to concede to these peoples, whose culture they had themselves profoundly nourished,

> the most elementary civil rights, including the right to political participation, however subordinate, in the civic life of the state into which they were to be integrated. The conservative ideals that had inspired the Caesaricides in Rome, Republican tradition, and hatred of military tyranny were reduced to the triumphant application of the ways and means of publicans and usurers with regard to subject peoples.[12]

Antony was anxious in the first place to obtain the support of the Greek cities, particularly Athens, which for the Greeks constituted a cultural and religious point of reference and symbolized their ancient grandeur and the liberty that the Romans, at least nominally, had conceded to their cities. On the model of a Hellenistic benefactor (*euergetēs*), Antony made donations to the principal cities and sanctuaries and paid for the restoration of various monuments; furthermore, he tended to show leniency regarding judicial disputes where, in his capacity as governor, he was called upon to arbitrate. This policy earned him honorific titles, such as "Philhellene" and "Philathenian"; in Athens, a Panathenian festival was held in his honor.[13] Subsequently it was said that the Athenians had sought Antony's clemency, but it could be had only in exchange for a payment of a thousand talents.[14]

On leaving Greece, Antony entrusted the Balkans to the proconsul Lucius Marcius Censorinus, whom he charged with repressing raids by certain chiefdoms that were formerly allied with Brutus. Antony was careful not to underestimate the machinations of these peoples, which must have reminded him of his earliest military experiences, some twenty years before, when his uncle Gaius Antonius Hybrida had tried, with paltry results, to reestablish order in Macedonia. Antony went on to Asia Minor, which had greatly suffered under the occupation of the Caesaricides. His diplomatic skills enabled him to repair relations with the largest communities, oppressed by the requisitions of Brutus and Cassius and unwilling to furnish Rome with any additional tribute; the first order of business was to compensate those cities that had resisted and had endured the harshest exactions. The league (*koinon*) of Lycian cities was granted a fiscal exemption, and the reconstruction of

Xanthus encouraged; Rhodes and Athens were given islands in the Aegean.[15]

The Augustan version of events later described the triumvir as passing through the province of Asia with an entourage of artists and musicians. Antony did in any case manage to attract the favor of its people, who fondly remembered his brother Lucius, quaestor and then interim governor between 50 and 49, who had been honored as a patron of the cities of Pergamum, Thyatira, and Ephesus, in the last place having protected the Temple of Artemis from the rapacity of publicans, the dreaded Roman tax collectors.[16] Antony therefore found himself in a position to profit from Lucius's popularity; the warm recollection that the cities of Asia retained of him is not contradicted by the many passages in the *Philippics* where Cicero professes to be shocked by his exploits as a gladiator (more precisely, as a *murmillo*), capable of fiercely executing an opponent in the arena at Mylasa, in Caria. In fact, the participation of Roman knights in such contests was fairly common; even senators enthusiastically took part in gladiatorial combat, in such numbers that in 38 it was officially prohibited, at least in public spectacles.[17] What Cicero saw as evidence of the violent and barbarous character of the detested Antony's brother testifies instead to the increasingly integrated nature of Greek and Roman customs in the Greek cities of Asia Minor.

Some Roman soldiers who had fought in the armies of Brutus and Cassius (such as Cassius's brother Lucius) found asylum in the sanctuary at Ephesus. Antony granted them pardon, with the exception of two men whom Appian calls Petronius and Quintus; the first was a conspirator of the Ides of March, the second a soldier, more probably an officer, serving under Dolabella at Laodicea, who had betrayed his commander to Cassius.[18] The suppliants at the Temple of Artemis also included Arsinoë IV, Cleopatra's younger sister; taking advantage of the right of asylum granted to those who took refuge in sanctuaries, she was welcomed by a priest of Artemis called Megabyzes.[19] Furthermore, in imitation of the style of Hellenistic royalty, earlier borrowed by Pompey, Antony was pleased to be honored as a prince. One city was given the name of Antoniopolis; Eumeneia in Phrygia was rebaptized Fulvia, in honor of his wife.[20] This is attested by a coin issued by the city, with a picture of Fulvia on the reverse, struck at the direction of the magistrate Zmertorix, son of Philonides—a sign of the importance of Galatians in these territories.

Socrates of Rhodes, author of a work on the civil wars of which only two fragments have come down to us, says that Antony, after a sumptuous and drunken celebration in Athens, ordered that henceforth he be proclaimed as a "new Dionysus" in all the cities of Greece.[21] Indeed, an Athenian inscription dating to 39/38 refers to Antony with this title (already adopted by Ptolemy XII of Egypt), also mentioning the Panathenian festivals associated with his name that accompanied assumption of the office of gymnasiarch, who bore the expense of certain public services (liturgies). This very prestigious responsibility involved the organization of religious ceremonies and sporting contests, as well as the provision of oil for the athletes.[22] Antony also managed and funded public banquets, the liturgy of *hestiasis*.[23] During this period he maintained close relations with notables to whom he had granted Roman citizenship, such as Marcus Antonius Aristocrates, and showed favor to freedmen, such as Marcus Antonius Theophilus and Marcus Antonius Hipparchus, father and son, all three from Corinth. The senior Hipparchus is mentioned by Pliny the Elder in the same breath as two of Sextus Pompey's pirates, Menas (Menodorus according to Appian) and Menecrates.[24]

In Ephesus, Antony's proclamation as a new Dionysus presented him with the occasion for a triumphal entry. Plutarch, reflecting on the frenzy his procession inspired, was led to point out a contrast recalling once again the opposition between Apollo and Dionysus: "While at Rome [Octavian] was wearing himself out in civil strife and wars, Antony himself was enjoying abundant peace and leisure, and was swept back by his passions into his wonted mode of life."[25] The strife in this case was connected with the question of discharged soldiers. Lucius Antonius, with Fulvia's support, had attacked Octavian for favoring his own veterans to the detriment of those of Antony and, of course, of the cities that were obliged to bear the cost of their resettlement. Negotiations failed, inaugurating a new episode of civil war. Lucius and Fulvia enjoyed the backing of the senatorial aristocracy, which sought to restore the republican order—an apparently paradoxical alliance motivated by fear of Octavian's increasingly hegemonic ambitions and of the atmosphere of terror that, on the strength of his authority as triumvir, he had caused to reign in Rome.

Antony's attitude toward the situation in Italy was rather ambiguous. There had been no choice but to accept a political compromise that gave him a free hand in the East, where Rome's prestige was threatened by the Parthians. Now, in order to reconfigure the regional balance of power, he looked back to the examples of Pompey and Caesar. Appian traces Antony's itinerary through the province of Asia and beyond, which saw him pass through Phrygia and Mysia, Galatia and Cappadocia, Cilicia and Coele-Syria, then Palestine, Ituraea, and the other regions of Syria.[26] According to Plutarch, whose sources in this connection are quite hostile to Antony, kings were prostrating themselves at his feet and queens were offering themselves to him—this last probably an allusion to his affair with Glaphyra, mother of Archelaus Sisines, then a child, whom a group of nobles associated with the family of the high priests of the temple state of Comana installed as king of Cappadocia, the legitimate successor of Ariobarzanes III, Ariarathes X, having been eliminated by Cassius.[27] Octavian mocked Antony's liaison in a few vulgar verses, making reference also to Fulvia.[28]

Antony was well aware that the geopolitical stability he had reestablished would remain precarious so long as the Parthian problem was not resolved. It was in order to respond to the dangerous advance of Parthian forces that he concluded an alliance with the sovereign of the wealthy and powerful kingdom of Egypt, the fascinating Cleopatra VII. One must not be fooled by ancient authors who portray Antony and Cleopatra as a sort of diabolical couple. Given the nature of the sources they drew upon, any judgment about Antony's personality is bound to be arbitrary. I do not venture to propose a new interpretation of his career, except to say that the myth of the "last prince of the Greek East" needs to be put into perspective. The life of Mark Antony cannot be reduced to his relations with the Greek world, and still less to the scarcely defensible presumption of a grandiose destiny bound up with conquest of the East. Modern historians have been unduly influenced by Augustus's later version of events, interpreting Antony's oriental maneuvers as evidence of a determination to form a new empire, a sort of alternative to the *imperium Romanum*.

Like all the great generals of the Republic, of course, Antony possessed a range of experience and enjoyed a field of action commensurate with his talents and his ambition. Ultimately, however, his policy did not diverge from the one devised by the principal architects of Roman imperialism. His task as a triumvir was to strengthen the alliance with Egypt, a commercial and strategic power whose capital, founded by Alexander the Great, played a primordial role in what Immanuel Wallerstein, inspired by Fernand Braudel, later called a world-empire, of which Rome was not yet the absolute center. Moreover, even if the situation in Italy was changing, Antony well understood that he had to remain in the East to consolidate his position there. Parthia was a key aspect of this calculation. As Plutarch succinctly put it, when Antony summoned Cleopatra to Tarsus, "he was getting ready for the Parthian war."[29]

By the time of the Alexandrian war in 47, as we have seen, the queen had entered into an affair with Caesar, by whom she had a son that same year, nicknamed "little Caesar." Mother and child are represented on a rear wall of the Temple of Hathor at Tentyris (present-day Dendera), founded in 54 by Ptolemy XII and still under construction during Cleopatra's reign (fig. 5.2). The accompanying inscription displays the hieroglyphic titles borne by "her son, the son of Ra, master of the crown, Ptolemy who is called Caesar (*ksyrs*), he of life everlasting, beloved of Ptah and Isis, the god Philopator-Philometor." The mention of Caesar in the cartouche is therefore revelatory. Antony, who may have seen Cleopatra on his first visit to Egypt (around 56, during the campaign under Gabinius), certainly crossed paths with her in Rome prior to her return to Alexandria after the Ides of March.

Their interview at Tarsus, in Cilicia, took place in the autumn of 41 just after hostilities had broken out in Italy, as Antony learned from envoys. Tarsus had been a victim of Cassius's vengeance. Antony granted it liberty and immunity from exactions, and those inhabitants who had been sold into slavery were released.[30] Following the example of Caesar, Antony crowned a number of local potentates and confirmed them in

FIGURE 5.2. Depiction of Cleopatra and Ptolemy XV Caesar

their rule, as in the case of Tarcondimotus, the chieftain of Upper Cilicia, who had coins struck in his own image bearing the epithet *Philantonios* and went on to support Antony against the Parthians.

The pact between the triumvir and the queen was sealed by a banquet that Cleopatra hosted with a view to impressing her new ally. Plutarch briefly describes the dinner, which followed an extraordinary demonstration of royal pomp, contrasting Egyptian luxury and refinement with the "meagerness and rusticity" of Antony's reception the following day. Cleopatra had sailed up the Cydnus (now Tarsus Çayı), the river that connects Tarsus with the sea, "in a barge with gilded poop, its sails spread purple, its rowers urging it on with silver oars to the sound of the flute blended with pipes and lutes"—a spectacle that gave rise on all sides to the rumor that "Venus was come to revel with Bacchus for the good of Asia."[31] Socrates of Rhodes reports that Cleopatra gave two banquets in honor of Antony and his entourage, at which they were served by Black slaves; the gold drinking vessels were inlaid with gems, the walls hung with purple tapestries sewn with threads of gold; for roses alone, which were braided to form a covering for the floors of the banquet rooms, she had spent a talent.[32]

The point of all this was not primarily to astound a rather boorish lot of roughneck soldiers, but to make a show of the wealth and power of Egypt. Lucan later devoted a long passage of *The Civil War* to a description of the banquet in Alexandria that Cleopatra had prepared for Caesar, at which he learned to "squander the wealth of a plundered world."[33] Hellenistic kings before her had entertained in enormous halls accommodating dozens of guests for public banquets, where they could manifest their generosity, often after a private audience; the symposium proper took place in the evening, following the dinner, for the benefit of a restricted circle that typically included court dignitaries, notables, and occasionally intellectuals. Drinking parties were not invariably held in the palace; some were held on royal boats, floating palaces, in effect. All these forms of entertainment were part of the tradition of eurgetism.

The meeting at Tarsus was first and foremost a diplomatic conference, but the human aspect must not be neglected: At twenty-eight years of age, Cleopatra was at the height of her beauty, and Antony was smitten. In the course of their time together, immortalized by Plutarch and subsequently destined to enjoy great literary and cinematographic success, from Shakespeare to American films, the queen conceived twin children. Rome did not object to the relationship with Cleopatra, which had no legitimacy under Roman law and therefore did not call into question Antony's marriage with Fulvia. The political and diplomatic implications of the liaison were of greater moment. There can be no doubt that Cleopatra seduced Antony, as much by her feminine charms as by her royal charisma. But it is necessary to keep in mind the aspect that mattered most in the eyes of Romans: Once again, as in the case of his affair with Glaphyra, Antony was imitating Caesar, well known for his escapades with queens. That he had made the dictator's former mistress his concubine can only have whetted his ambition; just the same, the view propagated by his enemies, of a weak man blinded by his passion for Cleopatra, needs to be qualified. On this view, the triumvir of the East had renounced his identity as a Roman and become a Hellenistic prince consort, and in so doing had undone two centuries of conquest and undermined the prestige of Rome in the minds of the friendly rulers that some historians call incorrectly "client kings." The agreement with Egypt depended, of course, on acceding to certain demands made by Cleopatra, who insisted that various nuisances be gotten rid of, notably among them Arsinoë, killed in Ephesus by a hired assassin; even so, Antony spared Megabyzes, the priest of Artemis who had given shelter to the queen's sister and rival.[34] Arsinoë's supposed tomb has conjecturally been identified with an octagonal monument on the Curetes Way in Ephesus, a street named after the priestly class associated with the cult of Artemis.

Antony's first oriental campaign was not yet over; he still had to visit Syria. Paying homage to the memory of Dolabella, he passed through Laodicea, to which he granted liberty and immunity. He also pardoned those Hebrews who had compromised themselves by siding with Cassius, in the name of their former friendship with Caesar, and conferred honors on both the high priest, Hyrcan, and the governor, Herod, the most powerful political figure in Judaea. The reorganization of Syria is attested by Antony's official correspondence, transcribed by Josephus. The following letter was sent to the inhabitants of the prosperous Phoenician city of Tyre, who, at the time of Cassius's governorship, had seized territory and other property belonging to the Jews. In this communication, as in ones addressed to other cities, Antony describes himself as *autokratōr,* the Greek term that translates the Latin *imperator,* meaning "victorious general" but which was understood in the East as having the sense of "ruler."

> "Statement of Marcus Antonius, Imperator, one of the triumvirs appointed to govern the republic. Whereas Gaius Cassius in the late rebellion seized a province which did not belong to him, and after occupying it with armed forces, plundered it and our allies, and forced the surrender of the Jewish nation, which was a friend of the Roman people, we, therefore, having overcome his madness by our arms, do establish order by our edicts and decisions in the territories plundered by him, so that they may be restored to our allies. And whatever was sold belonging to the Jews, whether persons or possessions, shall be released, the slaves to be free, as they were originally, and the possessions to be returned to their former owners. And it is my wish that whoever disobeys my edict shall be brought to trial, and if such a person is convicted, it shall be my concern to prosecute the offender in accordance with the seriousness of his act."
>
> In the same way he also wrote to the people of Sidon, Antioch, and Aradus. Now we have cited these documents in a suitable place, for they will be proofs of our statements concerning the thoughtfulness which the Romans showed for our nation.[35]

Since disagreements persisted, Antony went to Tyre and bloodily subdued Herod's opponents. By means of this policy he attracted further support in the East, enabling him to set about restoring to Rome the prestige that it had lost.

Antony's journey brought him finally to the edge of the desert. He launched an attack on the merchant city of Palmyra, an important staging point for caravans headed to the East.[36] For his Roman horsemen this was an opportunity to perfect their raiding skills, possibly drawing upon the experience of their Ituraean allies. In this case, however, their objective was not limited to seizing booty and taking slaves; they sought also to obtain, by terror, the support of communities situated on the borders of the areas of influence of the two powers. According to Appian, this attack was not as effective as the Romans had hoped. The Palmyrenes, having been informed of it beforehand, succeeded in carrying their merchandise across the Euphrates, and Antony's cavalry came back empty-handed. No matter. Even if it was only a provocation, this show of force—the first such display in the region since the battle of Carrhae—served as a warning to the Parthians on the other side of the desert: The Romans, with Egyptian support, were prepared to launch military action against them. It also put Octavian on notice: Whereas Antony was ready to put Caesar's grand plan into effect, the schemes of the son of *Divus Iulius* were hobbled by obstacles at home and abroad in the persons of Lucius Antonius and Fulvia, Sextus Pompey, and Lepidus; for harmony to be restored, Apollo still could not do without Dionysus.

6

The Advent of a Golden Age

"JUNO VESTA minerva Ceres Diana Venus Mars / Mercury Jupiter Neptune Vulcan Apollo"—Thus in the *Annals* did Ennius enumerate the twelve deities that watch over the Roman people. The context is the Punic invasion of 217 BCE, when a sumptuous meal was offered to them as part of a propitiatory ceremony, the lectisternium.[1] The six goddesses and six gods, collectively known as the "harmonious divinities" or "councillor-gods" (*consentes dii*), were memorialized by gilded statues erected near the Forum in Rome.[2] They were also the subject of an impious bit of theater contrived by Octavian as part of a private dinner he gave, with the host evidently playing the role of Apollo.[3] This performance, sharply criticized by Mark Antony, among others, cannot be dated with precision. It took place sometime during the long famine when the chain of supplies intended for Rome was disrupted by the needs of the armies and, above all, the maritime blockade instituted by the fleet of Sextus Pompey, alias Neptune.

According to a spiteful tradition, Lepidus, consul at the time of the Philippi campaign, was prepared to negotiate with Sextus; probably this was a rumor spread by Antony and Octavian to cast doubt on his loyalty to his triumviral fellows, though the possibility cannot be excluded that negotiations did take place.[4] Meanwhile, in the Adriatic, Domitius Ahenobarbus was making his influence felt as a warlord, whereas Staius Murcus had chosen to put himself at Sextus's service. Sextus Pompey's countervailing power, supported by the survivors of Philippi (including various senators), crucially affected the course of events in 41–40, notably the series of military operations constituting what is commonly called the Perusine War.

The conquest of the city of Perusia (present-day Perugia) in early 40, followed by an exemplary massacre of three hundred senators and equestrians, marked the definitive victory of Octavian and his generals over Lucius Antonius, Fulvia, and a number of experienced commanders, notably among them Ventidius Bassus, Asinius Pollio, and Munatius Plancus. More generally, the situation in Sicily had repercussions for Italy as a whole and the western provinces. In early 41, Transalpine Gaul was subject to the authority of the proconsul Quintus Fufius Calenus, a veteran of the Gallic Wars. Octavian's legate Carrinas was in charge of Hispania Ulterior, a region that had yet to be wholly pacified; six legions, under the command of Salvidienus Rufus, had been sent to Spain, but they were stopped at Placentia (Piacenza), where Antony held sway, through the action of his legates Ventidius Bassus and Asinius Pollio, who were responsible for the settlement of discharged soldiers.[5]

The experience of the civil wars had shown the importance of alliances contracted with African sovereigns as well. It must always be kept in mind that friendly kingdoms had lives of their own and were not mere pawns in the game of Roman politics. Strabo summarizes a fragmentary text due to a certain Iphicrates, perhaps the author of a military manual, about a campaign conducted by King Bogos (Bogud, brother of Bocchus II, both of whom we encountered earlier) in the land of the "western Aethiopians." Here, according to Iphicrates, were found

> camelopards, elephants, and the *rhizeis* [rhinoceroses?] as they are called, which are like bulls in their form, but like elephants in their manner of living and their size and their courage in fighting. And he speaks of serpents so large that even grass grows on their backs; Bogus, the king of the Maurusians, when he went up against the western Aethiopians, sent down to his wife as gifts reeds like those of India, of which each joint held eight choenices [about a gallon and a half], and also asparagus of similar size.[6]

Lucius Antonius instructed Bogud to cross the Strait of Gibraltar and attack Carrinas, who was still in Spain with his troops, to prevent him from sending them to Italy.[7] It was possibly on this occasion that the king pillaged Gades and the Temple of Hercules/Melqart, where the same priests who had predicted that Caesar would rule the world now found themselves deprived of animals for sacrifices, on account of the long siege.[8]

Further to the east, in the Roman provinces of Africa, Lucius instructed Sextius to take back command of the troops that he had recently handed over, by Lucius's order, to Fuficius Fango, who rejected Sextius's summons and assembled an army composed of veterans of Caesar's campaigns as well as "a large crowd of Africans, and other men sent by the kings."[9] Defeated by Sextius and abandoned by his Numidian allies, Fango committed suicide in a moment of despair.[10] By early 40 Sextius governed both African provinces with the aid of four legions.

Antony spent the winter of 41–40 in Alexandria, where messengers brought him news of the situation in Italy. According to Appian,

> [Cleopatra] gave him a splendid reception, and he spent the winter there without displaying the insignia of command and wearing the clothes and leading the life of a private person. He did this either because he was in a kingdom ruled by someone else, in a sovereign city, or because he was treating the winter as a holiday. He certainly set aside his worries and his commander's retinue and wore the square-cut Greek cloak instead of his native one, and the white Attic sandal also worn by the Athenian and Alexandrian priests, which they call a *phaecasium*. His only excursions were to temples or gymnasia or the discussions of scholars, and he spent his time with Greeks, in deference to Cleopatra, to whom he particularly devoted his stay in Alexandria.[11]

In attributing vices and defects of character to him that were unworthy of a Roman, Appian helped to strengthen the unsympathetic legend that had grown up around Mark Antony.

During the year 40, the queen gave birth to twins, children by Antony, who were named Alexander Helios and Cleopatra Selene. Plutarch frequently mentions the queen, her charms, and her talent for flattery.

In a passage emphasizing the "sweetness [of] the tones of her voice," Plutarch adds a further detail of fundamental importance:

> Her tongue, like an instrument of many strings, she could readily turn to whatever language she pleased, so that in her interviews with Barbarians she very seldom had need of an interpreter but made her replies to most of them herself and unassisted, whether they were Ethiopians, Troglodytes, Hebrews, Arabians, Syrians, Medes or Parthians. Nay, it is said that she knew the speech of many other peoples also, although the kings of Egypt before her had not even attempted to learn the native language, and some actually gave up their Macedonian dialect.[12]

Living in what amounted to a Greco-Roman empire from the administrative point of view, where mastery of the two tongues was sufficient to almost any purpose, Plutarch knew Greek and got by well enough in Latin, but knowledge of so many barbarian tongues did not impress him at all; his point in mentioning it was simply to observe that the queen's intellectual ability was exceptional by comparison with the other Ptolemies, who were no longer capable even of understanding their original language. Like Mithradates VI before her, Cleopatra dispensed with interpreters.[13] The shrewdest Romans, beginning with Antony himself, respected this talent.

When winds were favorable Antony sailed to Greece. There he met Fulvia, who had just left Italy, having decided against taking refuge, together with her children, with Sextus Pompey, to whom Julia, the mother of Antony and Lucius, and other important persons had gone after the taking of Perusia.[14] Sextus's relations with Antony were equivocal, however, and he thought it prudent to send Julia on to him in Greece. Antony, for his part, thought it prudent to send an eloquent message to Sextus, assuring the new Neptune that in the event he went to war against Octavian he would treat Sextus as an ally.[15]

After a stormy meeting with her husband in Athens, Fulvia fell ill. Antony continued on his way to the Adriatic with a small army and a fleet, sailing first to Corcyra (Corfu) and from there to Italy.[16] Five legions under the command of Salvidienus Rufus were dispatched by

Octavian to prevent him from disembarking. Salvidienus Rufus, who had just been given the governorship of Gaul, now resolved to defect, offering to work in concert with Antony. In the interval Antony had reached an agreement with Sextus Pompey, hoping to further undermine the position of Octavian, whose popularity had fallen sharply on account of the expropriation of land for the settlement of discharged soldiers and the shortages caused by the war against Sextus. Antony therefore moved to install garrisons in southern Italy, encircling Brundisium, while Sextus enlarged his sphere of influence, occupying Sardinia and Corsica; Menodorus (or Menas, as Plutarch and Cassius Dio call him), a freedman of Pompey and formerly a pirate in the eastern Mediterranean, now harassed the governor of these islands, Marcus Lurius, and captured an admiral named Helenus, probably a Cilician like Menodorus, who had been freed by Octavian.[17]

Neither Octavian nor Antony had any interest in pursuing the conflict, however; both needed to take steps to ensure that the situation, chaotic since the fall of Perusia, did not become aggravated to the point that the morale of their troops was adversely affected. Between August and September, they managed to find common ground. It was said that their soldiers refused to fight one another, and that the diplomacy of the representatives of the two men was particularly skillful (the accounts transmitted by our sources were undoubtedly revised and corrected after the fact). The understanding between Antony and Octavian made it possible to further diminish Lepidus's influence and to get rid of the weakest and least fortunate military commanders.

Responsibility for the Perusine War was assigned to Fulvia, who in the meantime had died at Sicyon, a port on the Gulf of Corinth, and to Lucius Antonius, of whom we hear nothing more (perhaps he had been sacrificed for political reasons). It seems very probable that after the death of his wife and his brother, Antony found it convenient to encourage the belief that they alone were responsible for this latest episode of civil war. Be that as it may, he was chiefly interested at this point in preparing for the campaign in the East, for which he needed soldiers and, above all, financial support. It was necessary to do everything possible to avert a Parthian invasion, which would upset the equilibrium that with great effort had been reestablished after Philippi.

In preliminary talks with Octavian's envoy Lucius Cocceius Nerva, who had earlier been appointed as an ambassador to Antony when he was still in Phoenicia, Antony complained that Octavian had taken the Gallic provinces away from him, confiding them to Salvidienus Rufus following the death of Fufius Calenus.[18] If he was to be able personally to supervise the forthcoming campaign, however, so that the glorious conclusion he hoped for it would be assured, Antony had no alternative but to give up his provincial governorship; even so, he succeeded in taking revenge on Salvidienus, whose treachery in offering to come over with his legions to Antony's side he revealed and who was subsequently put to death, depriving his rival of his best general. As a reward for denouncing Salvidienus, Octavian placed his troops under Antony's command and assigned them to Asia.[19]

One wonders whether Salvidienus had contemplated seizing power, confident that his military experience would enable him to prevail. In the event he was found guilty of *crimen maiestatis*, for he had made an attempt not only on Octavian's life but also on the security of the Roman people. The Lex Titia provided for capital punishment in the case of those who tried to assassinate a triumvir. The harshness of Salvidienus's sentence probably reflected the dismay of the Senate at the thought that a member of the equestrian class who had been designated consul for the year 39 might be immune from political reprimand; the senators were mainly intent, however, on deterring generals from usurping power with the support of the legions that had been confided to them. Octavian later did his utmost to justify the execution of his former friend, making him into a symbol of treason—and a warning to all aspiring warlords.

Antony, a more capable diplomat, had managed to rally Domitius Ahenobarbus to his cause. Worn out by the war in the Adriatic, in connection with which he had lately encountered opposition from Asinius Pollio, then serving as consul, Ahenobarbus made his way to Venetia after Perusia and from there went on to Illyria, taking the city of Salona;

on finally disembarking in Italy, at Brundisium, his troops saluted Antony as *imperator*.[20] The pact subsequently concluded there, urged by advisors such as the Etruscan Gaius Cilnius Maecenas, was sealed by dinners that each of the two triumvirs held for the other.

Cassius Dio once again makes a point of criticizing Antony's taste for the exotic: while the entertainments sponsored by Octavian were "in military and Roman fashion," the ones offered by Antony were in "Asiatic and Egyptian style"—evidently an allusion to the banquet at Tarsus, which nonetheless did not prevent the two men from consolidating their alliance with a political marriage, the Senate having authorized Octavian's sister, Octavia, who had just lost her husband, Marcus Claudius Marcellus (consul in 50), to marry Antony before the end of the customary period of mourning.[21] New measures of amnesty (in the root sense of the term) were agreed upon as well, for it was necessary once more to forget the horrors of civil war, as well as to rapidly come to an agreement with Sextus Pompey in view of the deteriorating situation in the East, where Syria had been occupied by the Parthians and Asia Minor now found itself threatened.

Already the effects of the Parthians' operations had made themselves felt in Judaea. Antigonus II, the successor of Aristobulus II, had taken power in Jerusalem, where he executed Herod's brother Phasael and cut off Hyrcanus's ears, this last an act that prevented Hyrcanus from holding the office of high priest, for under Hebraic law a priest could be neither maimed nor mutilated. In Alexandria, Herod ignored Cleopatra's attempts to dissuade him from leaving and went on to Brundisium, narrowly escaping shipwreck, to seek assistance from Antony, who looked with favor upon his request and promised to confer upon him the title of King of Judaea.[22] Apparently without consulting Lepidus, Antony and Octavian proceeded to draw up a new distribution of provincial authority, with Antony retaining control over all the territories to the east of the Adriatic and Octavian now overseeing the affairs of all those to the west with the exception of Africa, which was left to Lepidus.

Henceforth we hear nothing of Sextius, who, like Lucius Antonius, vanishes from the historical record that has come down to us. The line of demarcation between the respective spheres of interest of the two triumvirs passed through Scodra (present-day Shkodër, in northern Albania), on the border separating Macedonia from Illyria.[23] Octavian's de facto appropriation of Gaul was therefore ratified de jure by the treaty of Brundisium. The new governor of Gaul was very probably Agrippa, whom Appian mentions in connection with his later "sparkling victory over the Gauls of Aquitania."[24]

After Brundisium, Octavian was obliged to turn his attention once more to Italy, stricken by war and famine. It was just then that the triumvirs set about restructuring the Senate, which had lost a good many members on account of the war and the proscription lists of 43. Citizens from the lower orders who could be counted on to support the triumviral claim to authority were elected by fiat, raising the number of senators to a thousand. Never in the whole of its history had the Senate been so overcrowded and so discredited, and yet for all that it did not cease to function as a deliberative body.

On the occasion of Antony's marriage to Octavia, in Rome, the triumvirs gathered to consider further measures, among them the appointment of a consul of foreign extraction.[25] As we have seen, the naming of a suffect consul made it possible to reward the new officeholder while at the same time weakening the authority of incumbent magistrates, who could be replaced for a very short period. One of the two beneficiaries in this case was Lucius Cornelius Balbus, an aristocrat of Hispano-Phoenician origin (born in Gades) who had obtained Roman citizenship from Pompey. A member of the equestrian order, he was a confidant of Caesar and had managed his affairs in Rome during the last civil war. Caesar appreciated his talents not only as a military administrator (he had served as *praefectus fabrum* in Gaul) but also as a civil servant and a political intermediary. But Balbus was the first Roman citizen of foreign descent to be raised to the consulship. The nomination of a man of his social standing must have seemed scandalous to the senatorial class, but the triumvirs were determined to perpetuate this practice, which marked the beginning of a slow process of importing wealthy naturalized citizens into government at the highest levels.

Before resuming his activities in the East, Antony received Herod and approved his request for aid. Herod's royal appointment was then ratified by the Senate in Rome, in the presence of Antony, Octavian, and Herod himself. Antony had succeeded in persuading the Senate to approve Herod's consecration as King of Judaea by means of an irresistible argument: Herod was an indispensable ally in the campaign against the Parthians.[26] The motion to crown Herod was brought by the praetors, Marcus Valerius Messalla Corvinus (a participant in the negotiations at Brundisium) and Lucius Sempronius Atratinus, who praised the nominee and "brought accusations against Antigonus, whom they declared an enemy, not only because of the first offense he had committed against them but because he had received his kingly title from the Parthians, thus showing no regard for the Romans."[27]

Domitius Calvinus, consul for the year 40 whom Balbus had replaced, was sent to Spain, and his colleague Asinius Pollio to Macedonia.[28] It was to Asinius that Virgil dedicated the fourth *Bucolic*, a glorification of an imminent golden age that would witness the birth of a boy, the son of a Roman, heralding the advent of peace. The identity of this anonymous *puer* has been variously attributed: a son of Pollio, a child conceived by Octavia or by Scribonia, Octavian's wife, or simply a symbolic figure. Christians later interpreted the poem as a prophecy of the coming of Jesus. I myself incline toward a more exotic solution, namely that the child was Alexander Helios, the son of Antony and Cleopatra. Virgil was not yet at this point a supporter of Octavian; like Pollio, he sided with the Antonians. Antony's military skill would presumably have been passed along to the boy, permitting him to dominate the world, after having been elevated to the great *honores*, the Roman magistracies.

As for Lepidus, one must not underestimate his role. The history of this period as we have it from our sources is usually read as a sort of cold war between Antony and Octavian, the third triumvir having practically disappeared from the scene between 40 and 36. Lepidus had nonetheless been given control of Africa, with six legions at his disposal, to which he added the four belonging to Sextius without notifying Antony, who had need of them in the East. Unaware of Lepidus's deception, Antony sent his legate Gaius Furnius, an old loyalist of Pompey the

Great who transferred his allegiance to Antony and who had fought alongside Lucius Antonius during the Perusine War, to bring them back from Africa for service against the Parthians.[29]

Furthermore, Lepidus could count on the support of Roman citizens resident in the provinces, in this way creating new friendly rulers in the third part of the *oikoumenē*; indeed, it was thanks to him that a number of Sittius's former partisans, who had remained in control of Cirta with a relative degree of autonomy that was to last until 42, were able to obtain Roman citizenship. Until this time, in the African provinces, few people bore the *nomen gentilicium* Iulius or Sittius. Under Lepidus, we start finding a good number of *Aemilii* in local onomastics: In the city of Thibilis alone, in eastern Numidia, sixty-five citizens with this name are attested. Evidently, Lepidus had not given up hope of recovering territory with the help of an African clientele. In the meantime, he looked to attract new settlers from among the native population, discharged veterans, and Italians dispossessed of their lands by triumviral colonies.

Sextus Pompey had no intention of giving in at this point. The Roman people had responded favorably to Antony's marriage, taking the cordial relations between Antony and Octavian as a hopeful sign for themselves, but their impatience with famine and taxes was no less great for that. Riots threatened the lives of the triumvirs, and soldiers had to be sent in to quell the violence.[30] New measures regarding veterans (who Cassius Dio says were sent to the colonies) held out the prospect, however remote, of domestic tranquility.[31] An accord with Sextus was nonetheless essential. The first talks were held on the island of Aenaria (Ischia), between the triumvirs' representatives and Sextus's emissary, Lucius Scribonius Libo; the triumvirs then came down to Baiae, and Sextus finally arrived to take part in the conference, which took place on a boat anchored near Cape Misenum.

This was the summer of 39. Sextus, disregarding the counsel of Menodorus and Staius Murcus (Murcus he later had killed), ended up obtaining extremely favorable terms from Antony and Octavian:

> The war between them was finished, and trade was to proceed unhindered everywhere; Pompeius was to remove all garrisons he had in

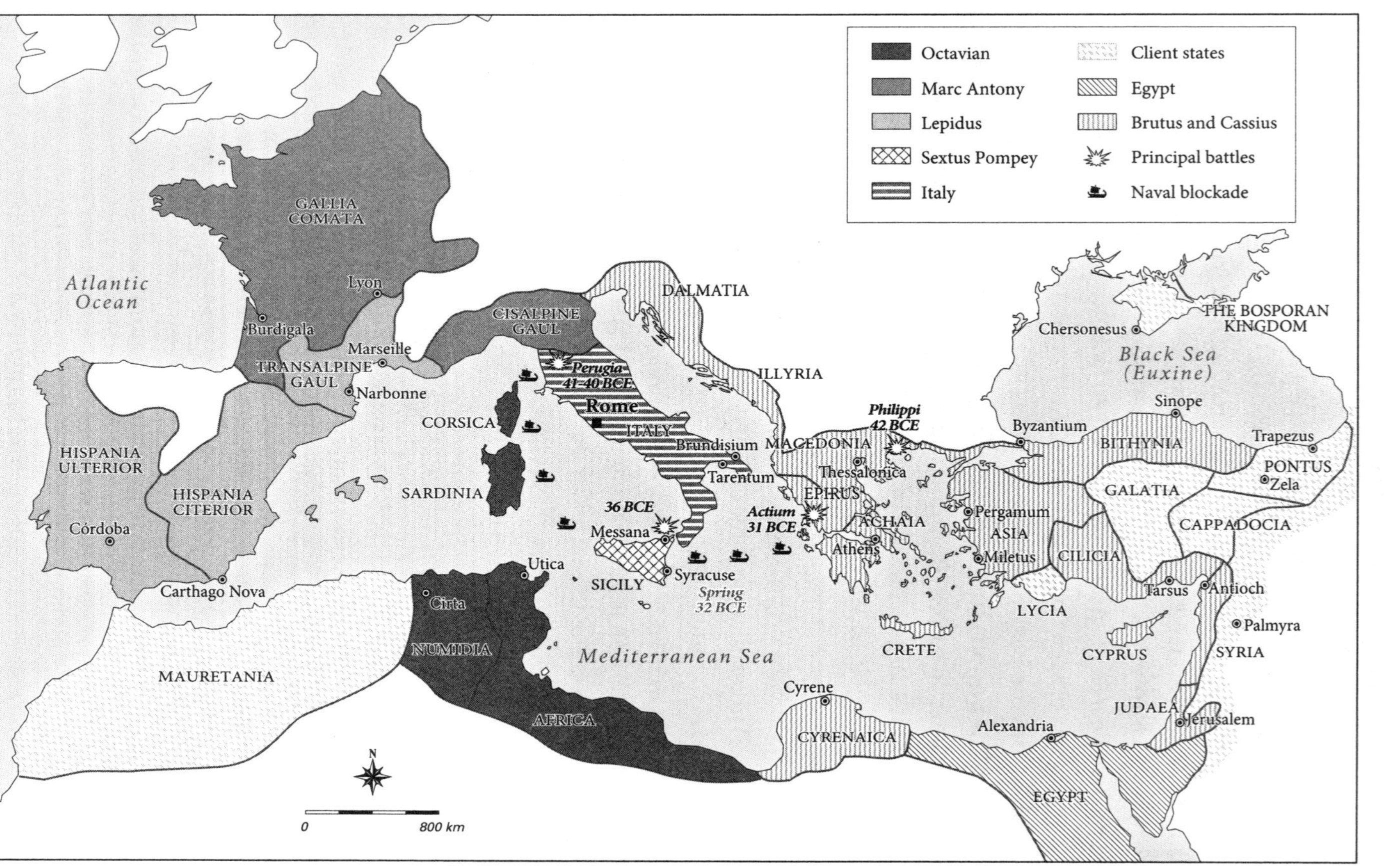

MAP 4. The Mediterranean during the triumviral period

> Italy, and no longer take in runaway slaves or blockade the Italian coast with his ships; he was to have authority over Sardinia, Sicily, and Corsica, and any other islands then in his possession, as long as Antony and Octavian had authority over the other territories; he was to send to Rome the grain that had long been required of these places to pay in tax; in addition he was to have the Peloponnese.[32]

These operational concessions permitted Sextus freedom of maneuver on the seas between Corsica and the Peloponnese for a period of five years; at the end of this term, he would share the consulship with Octavian. New matrimonial agreements completed the preceding ones. Exiled "republican" citizens (except for those of Caesar's assassins who were still alive and whose exile was permanent) would be able to recover a quarter of the properties that had been taken from them, and they would have the right to hold public office; as for slaves who had deserted, they were to be freed. Cassius Dio describes the atmosphere of rejoicing among the Romans who witnessed the drafting of these compacts; the leaders, for their part, embraced and then entertained one another on ship and shore. Antony and Octavian thus acknowledged Sextus's power.

To be sure, they had no intention of respecting these arrangements for any longer than was necessary, but for the moment, they had no choice but to comply, or at least to appear to comply. The peace with Sextus would lift the blockade in the Tyrrhenian Sea and allow supplies once more to reach Italy and, still more importantly, Rome, where the position of the triumvirs, on account of the famine, was now nearly untenable. The new concord was bound to be temporary; Menodorus, whom Appian describes as a diabolical counsellor, described the Pact of Misenum as merely a truce (*anochai*).[33] In particular, Sextus was slow to realize that the Peloponnese was a poisoned chalice, for Antony again demanded from him payment of all the taxes that had formerly been imposed there and that were still in arrears; in the end Sextus balked, refused to accept the territory, and went on to violate the conditions of the treaty, adding to the number of his ships and enlisting new crews. Gradually the blockade was reinstituted. The triumvirs, in order to appease the Italians and to divert attention from their own violation of the treaty, spread rumors accusing Sextus of commanding a fleet of pirates and fugitive slaves.[34]

At all events, the Pact of Misenum gave the triumvirs at least a brief respite. Octavian went to Gaul, presumably to inspect the colonies of veterans beyond the Po (where he installed trusted lieutenants in place of Antonians), but also to tamp down the unrest that Agrippa's troops had been unable to still. Antony, for his part, concerned himself once more with affairs in the East and the conduct of operations against the Parthians.[35] Cassius Dio maliciously claims that Antony went to Greece for the purpose of "satisfying his desires," but in reality it was to raise the money needed to finance the eastern campaign.[36] He also had to keep an eye on the Balkans, where Illyrian peoples threatened the security of Macedonia: The Parthini, former allies of Brutus, were obstructing access to the strategic junction of Dyrrachium, and the Dardanians were constantly making incursions. It was also necessary to monitor the movements of the Dacians (we do not know whether Burebista was still alive); during his stay in Greece, Antony drew up a plan of attack with the new proconsul, Asinius Pollio.[37]

Antony spent the winter in Athens with Octavia, who had recently given birth to a daughter, known as Antonia Minor. An altar was dedicated to her parents in the Agora; the inscription identifies them as "benefactor gods."[38] Cassius Dio speaks of a sacred marriage with Athena (Octavia, as it may have been supposed), for which Antony extracted from the Athenians a dowry of a million drachmas.[39] In Athens, as he had done in the winter of 41–40 in Alexandria, Antony set his official duties aside:

> [He] merely look[ed] over the reports sent from the armies, once again adopting the simple life of a private citizen in place of military command, wearing the square-cut pallium and the Attic shoe, and with no crowd at his doors. He would go out, in similar manner, without the insignia of his office, accompanied by two friends and two attendants, to the discussion and the lectures of the public teachers. He took his meals in the Greek fashion, exercised with Greeks, and

> enjoyed their festivals in Octavia's company: for he was very much in love with her too, being quick to fall in love with women.

Once more this moment of relaxation was only temporary. Appian goes on to say that

> [W]hen winter came to an end, he was a different person: he changed his clothing again, and with his clothing his whole appearance. Immediately his door was crowded with standards and officers and bodyguards, and fear and apprehension were everywhere. Embassies were received which had previously been told to wait, and lawsuits were decided, and ships were launched, and all other preparations were put in motion.[40]

Antony's forces having been enlarged and strengthened, in other words, the moment had come to quit his winter quarters. It is quite true that Antony loved excess. Even so, as triumvir and *autokratōr*, he knew how to manage, and, if need be, to endure extreme adversity. Virgil's golden age had only begun.

7

The *Imperium* Strikes Back

IN 1930 the Austrian philosopher Otto Neurath, a member of the Vienna Circle, resolute exponent of the unity of the sciences, and a keen student of statistical analysis, created a method of pictorial statistics that came to be known as International System of Typographic Picture Education. Commonly referred to by its acronym, Isotype (International System of Typographic Picture Education), it formed the basis of an atlas of human societies that attached great importance to demography. Neurath's map of the world at the time of the birth of Christ, in the thirties of the first century BCE, rather accurately describes in visual terms the state of the world when the triumvirate, reinvigorated by the treaty of Brundisium, found itself in a position to test its strength against the Parthian Empire. Neurath plainly overestimated the extent of the territories controlled by Rome: Germania remained free, and the Balkans and the Iberian Peninsula had by no means been subjugated. Even so, his map neatly summarized the situation that had developed in the aftermath of the conquests of Alexander the Great, which marked the end point of Hellenistic geography. Between Parthia and China lay a number of kingdoms and chiefdoms of traditionally nomadic peoples. The Parthians dominated the Caucasus; in the main part of Anatolia, they shared power with Rome.

The problems at the heart of the Roman Empire were connected with a reconfiguration of alliances on its eastern borders. Deiotarus had died an old man in 40, the same year as Attalus of Paphlagonia, another former beneficiary of Pompey's new order.[1] According to Cassius Dio,

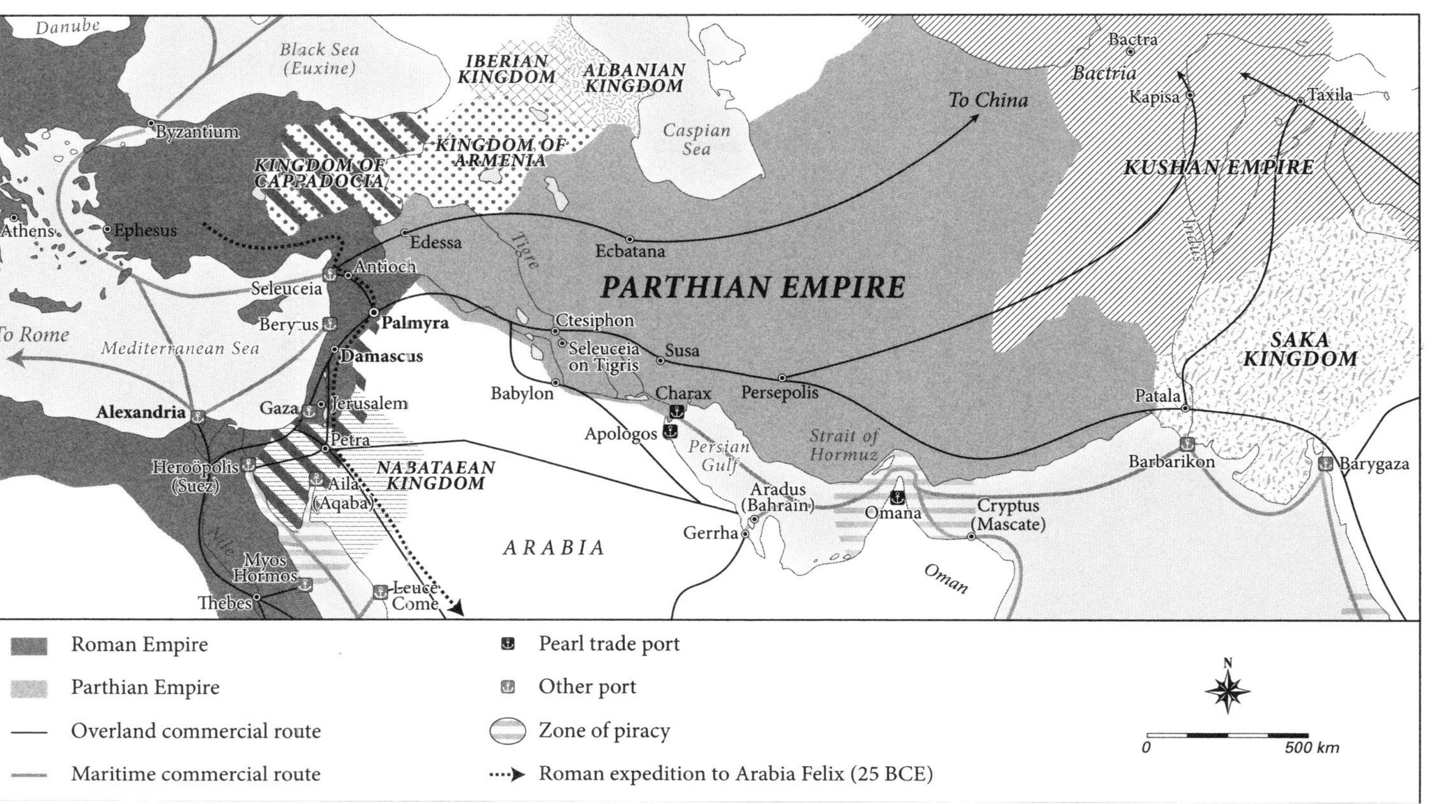

MAP 5. The Parthian Empire

FIGURE 7.1. Silver drachma of Artawazd II

Antony entrusted these territories to "a certain Castor," whom some identify with the historian Castor of Rhodes, others with the son of the Galatian chieftain who had brought the charge of conspiracy against Deiotarus—his own grandfather—at his trial in Rome in 45. Amyntas, formerly secretary and adviser to the Galatian king, was given Pisidia. The southeastern coast of the Black Sea was assigned to Darius, son of Pharnaces and grandson of Mithradates VI.[2] Cyprus, which could rely on the support of the Egyptian fleet, was confided to a freedman of Caesar, Gaius Iulius Demetrius.[3]

In eastern Anatolia the situation was more complicated. Cappadocia had not been fully subdued, and Antiochus of Commagene did not seem to be much opposed to the arrival of the Parthians; indeed, he came to their aid.[4] Moreover, the Parthians could depend on the backing of Artawazd of Armenia (fig. 7.1), whose father, Tigran the Great, had made sure that his son would receive an international, which is to say Hellenistic, education; Plutarch credits Artawazd with authorship of tragedies, orations, and historical works.[5] But his Greek learning did not necessarily incline him toward Rome and the Western world; after all, his familial affinities drew him closer to the Parthians, to whom he was bound by matrimonial alliance after the Roman defeat at Carrhae, when his sister married the crown prince Pakur, known to us as Pacorus. In the course of the wedding festivities, in obedience to the wishes of the philhellenic host, a scene from the *Bacchae* of Euripides was performed in which Dionysius induced a group of frenzied Theban women to tear apart their king Pentheus, hostile to Dionysian rites, having made them believe in their Bacchic delirium that he was a mountain lion. Pentheus's head was carried off by his mother Agave. At Artawazd's banquet, one of the actors, a Greek from Caria who played the role of Agave, gave new meaning to the terrible scene by spontaneously seizing the head of Crassus, which had just been brought to the king.[6] Not long thereafter, in 50 or so, apparently to demonstrate his neutrality toward Rome, Artawazd promised his son in marriage to Deiotarus's daughter.[7]

The Parthians nonetheless managed to profit from this state of affairs, holding the Romans at bay until a propitious opportunity presented itself for taking the offensive. One of the commanding officers of their campaign, which began in 40, was Quintus Labienus. According to Cassius Dio, it was Labienus who had persuaded King Orodes to launch an attack against Roman Syria, taking advantage of the dissension among the triumvirs: "For he declared their armies were either destroyed utterly or impaired, while the remainder of the troops were in a state of mutiny and would again be at war; and he accordingly advised the king to subjugate Syria and the adjoining districts, while Caesar was busy in Italy with Sextus and Antony was indulging his passion in Egypt."[8]

Dio says that Labienus was confident of success, certain that he would be able to convince the garrisons in the territories under Roman domination to cooperate, directly or indirectly. Here, then, yet another Roman warlord had emerged to complicate the situation facing Antony and Octavian. Our sources overstate Labienus's role in the Parthian expedition. Quite obviously, he was not the commander in chief, only one of several generals subject to the orders of Pacorus, who was not without military experience, as it happens, having himself occupied Syria in 51 and attempted another invasion in late 45. In the present instance he moved to assert control over Phoenicia to begin with, and then over Judaea, in concert with the Parthian satrap Barzaphranes. The Parthians could also count on assistance from Lysanias, son of Ptolemy of Ituraea, recently deceased, and from the Arab ruler Malichus. In spite of resistance from Herod and his brother Phasael, Jerusalem was taken and

FIGURE 7.2. Silver denarius bearing the image of Quintus Labienus

placed under the authority of Antigonus the Hasmonean. Herod fled with his family and an escort of soldiers to Idumaea, repelling attacks not only from the Parthians but also from Jewish partisans of Antigonus.[9] He then sought aid from Malichus, unsuccessfully, since the Parthians had prevented Malichus from receiving Herod.[10] The final objective was the conquest of Syria. Until now the Parthians had been unable to overcome Roman resistance. On this occasion, however, they had an exceptional asset in the person of Labienus, a master of Roman tactics and, what is more, sure of his ability to persuade his compatriots to change sides.

If Labienus, in the eyes of the Parthians, was no more than an auxiliary general, a coin from his personal mint betrays the scale of his ambition: on the recto, his portrait, showing him with a short beard and the legend Q[*uintus*] *Labienus Parthicus imp*[*erator*]; on the verso, a warhorse outfitted with a saddle and cuisses, an indispensable part of the armor of Parthian cavalry (fig. 7.2). His beard contrasted with that of Brutus, which was long and unkempt, in the manner of the philosophers; Labienus's style was a sign of mourning, in memory of his father Titus, the Pompeian commander who was killed in 45 during the battle of Munda, where he had fought valiantly against Caesar. One cannot help but be reminded of the beard worn by Sextus Pompey, who is shown on coins bearing his image in mourning for his father and his brother Gnaeus, both of whom likewise died in Spain.

The message of these coins was aimed neither at the Parthians nor at the cities of Syria or Anatolia. It was addressed to Latin-speaking soldiers, formerly supporters of Brutus and Cassius, whom Antony had enlisted for his garrisons in Syria because of their knowledge of the territory. Many of them defected to the Parthians, and all the more readily since Labienus had also thought to resort to psychological warfare, for example by shooting arrows with pamphlets attached to them into the enemy camp. The confusion this tactic created in Antony's garrisons permitted Pacorus to occupy all of Syria. In a pitched battle, Labienus's horsemen defeated the army of the legate Decidius Saxa, who was forced to take refuge at Antioch, fleeing from there to Cilicia. Labienus set off in pursuit and succeeded in capturing him and putting him to death.[11] Thirteen years after Carrhae, a Roman army had once more been vanquished, and the standards collected from the battleground, in addition to those that had been confiscated, further added to Rome's dishonor.

The question arises whether Labienus should be regarded as a renegade or instead as the last military leader of the Caesaricides. According to Plutarch, the native Parthian generals officially proclaimed him "Parthian *imperator*."[12] If that is so, Roman soldiers would have found it difficult to serve under him. To be sure, we cannot exclude the possibility that the Parthians had welcomed their new comrade by acclamation. Plutarch's source was probably thinking of the legend on his coinage, *Q[uintus] Labienus Parthicus imperator,* which can be translated as "Quintus Labienus of Parthia, victorious general," a sort of Lawrence of Arabia avant la lettre. We saw earlier that Antony, in his Greek correspondence, described himself as *autokratōr,* the equivalent of the Latin *imperator,* an acclamatory epithet. Labienus did the same, but from the point of view of Roman tradition, which probably goes back to Livy, he was "acting directly contrary to [this tradition], in that he took his title from those whom he was leading against the Romans, as if it were the Parthians and not his fellow-citizens that he was defeating."[13]

The view popularized by Plutarch only strengthened the image of Labienus as a renegade, in the fashion of the dishonorable survivors of Carrhae, Italians from Apulia and the territory of the Marsi in the Apennines, to whom Horace alludes in a poem composed around 23: "[They] have remained alive in disgraceful wedlock with barbarian wives, . . . have grown old in the army of the enemy whose daughters they have married."[14] A passage in Justin's *Epitome of Pompeius Trogus* best explains the nature of this war: Pacorus had concluded an alliance with Labienus (*Pacoro duce inita cum Labieno societate*).[15]

Antony had cultivated the support of local aristocrats and, in particular, of orators who could both mobilize their fellow citizens and use their diplomatic talents to win over other cities. From Strabo, however, we know that there were limits to the persuasive powers of this fifth column:

> For while the other [cities], since they were without arms and inclined to peace, yielded to Labienus when he was coming against them with an army and an allied Parthian force, the Parthians by that time being in possession of Asia, yet Zeno of Laodicea and Hybreas, both orators, refused to yield and caused their own cities to revolt. Hybreas also provoked Labienus, a [young man] who was irritable and full of folly, by a certain pronouncement; for when Labienus proclaimed himself Parthian Emperor, Hybreas said, "Then I too call myself Carian Emperor." Consequently, Labienus set out against the city with cohorts of Roman soldiers in Asia that were already organized. Labienus did not seize Hybreas, however, since he had withdrawn to Rhodes, but he shamefully maltreated his home, with its costly furnishings, and plundered it. And he likewise damaged the whole of the city.[16]

Antony also counted on the loyalty of dynasts whom our sources on the whole consider to have been brigands, among them the Cilician Tarcondimotus and the Phrygian Cleon, from Gordion (a village at the time of his birth), who launched a guerilla attack against Labienus's tax collectors and later was rewarded by control of a district in Phrygia.[17]

Rome's counterattack against the rival empire was delayed by the course of events in Italy, which had occupied the attention of Antony and his best generals for so long. After Brundisium, Antony sent

Ventidius to the East, where he had no trouble repulsing Labienus's forces. Labienus, notwithstanding his titular status as a Parthian general, had at his command only Roman troops and a certain number of recently recruited native soldiers; he was stunned by the size of Ventidius's army and the suddenness of its approach.[18] Antony had not been inactive in the meantime, as some authors claim. A fair idea of the size of the forces he had entrusted Ventidius with may be had by considering that in 38 his successor, Gaius Sosius, inherited a corps of eleven legions of infantry and six thousand horsemen, these in addition to Syrian auxiliaries—roughly the same number of soldiers whom Crassus had assembled for his expedition in 54/53.[19] These legions were no doubt partly comprised of auxiliary units: Florus says that Crassus had eleven legions at his disposal, as against the seven mentioned by Plutarch; auxiliaries, often overlooked by ancient sources, here again surely played a considerable role.[20] One of the commanders of these auxiliary troops was a man Josephus refers to as Machaeras ("Sword" in Greek), but who was probably called Machares, like the minor king of Cimmerian Bosporus at the time of Lucullus's expedition.[21]

Caesar's former lieutenant had mastered the art of surprise and had no difficulty driving Labienus out of Asia Minor.[22] The theater of operations then moved into the mountains between Cilicia and Syria. Ventidius managed to avoid the advance of the Parthian cavalry, unlike Crassus, whose army had been crushed on the Mesopotamian desert plain. Remaining on the high ground, he profited from the self-assurance of the enemy horsemen, who, underestimating his forces, climbed the hill at dawn to attack him, without waiting for Labienus. The routed Parthians retreated into Cilicia; Labienus's men, demoralized by the flight of the barbarians, had no will to fight. Learning from deserters of Labienus's plan to make an escape under cover of darkness, Ventidius set an ambush for his troops, killing many of them and winning over others to his side, now that they found themselves abandoned by their leader.[23] Cassius Dio, who relates these events, probably relied on Livy's account, adopted also by Frontinus, who summarizes Ventidius's strategy thus: "Keeping his own men in camp on pretense of fear, [he] caused the Parthians and Labienus, who were elated with victorious successes, to come out for battle. Having lured them into an unfavorable situation, he attacked them by surprise and so overwhelmed them that the Parthians refused to follow Labienus and evacuated the province."[24] Labienus, having disguised himself, went into hiding in Cilicia but later was captured by Demetrius, seemingly in the waters around Cyprus, from which he had departed for Syria, still occupied by the Parthians.[25] Ventidius had Labienus killed.[26] Henceforth, there was only one Roman adversary standing in the way of the triumvirs: Sextus Pompey.

With Labienus's death, Ventidius regained control of Asia Minor, instructing his lieutenant Poppaedius Silo to occupy the mountain pass that separated Cilicia from Syria. But the Parthians, under the command of the general Phranapates, defended the pass and repelled Silo's attack, almost killing him. Cassius Dio, probably following Livy once again, relates that Ventidius, with his customary skill, came to Silo's rescue and struck down Phranapates together with many other enemies; Strabo says that the battle took place at the top of a hill called Trapezōn; Frontinus says that Ventidius sent a very small detachment of troops to draw the Parthians in, at which point infantry and cavalry waiting in ambush in an adjacent valley came forward and slaughtered them, not sparing Phranapates.[27]

The rest of the Parthian army, under the command of Pacorus, crossed the Euphrates and retired to its winter quarters in Upper Mesopotamia, allowing Ventidius to retake control of Syria and Judaea. Josephus suggests that Antigonus had bribed Ventidius, and after him Silo; and that Antony, through his envoy Dellius, had convinced the two of them to support Herod, who had disembarked at Ptolemais (Acre).[28] Antigonus did in fact give money to Ventidius, in his capacity as governor, and so by way of tribute, just as his rival Herod, then recognized as the ruler of Idumaea and Samaria, had done.[29]

Ventidius was therefore free to turn his attention to the Parthian campaign, employing a very subtle stratagem that involved duping a certain prince of Cyrrhestica called Channaeus (or, less probably, Pharnaeus). Channaeus, as he knew, was playing a double game. He persuaded Channaeus to believe that he feared the Parthians would take a lowland route downstream across the Euphrates, rather than go across the mountainous territory near the Zeugma of the Euphrates controlled by the kingdom of Commagene, as they customarily did. Through Channaeus he also deceived Pacorus, who took the longer route, permitting Ventidius to regroup his forces, no longer having to worry about fighting on the plain, where the Parthian horsemen would have had a better chance of prevailing. Thanks to this deception, Ventidius was able to move his army into Cyrrhestica and set up camp outside the city of Gindarus (now Jinderes in Arabic, Cindirēsē in Kurdish), a highland Strabo described as the "acropolis" of Cyrrhestica and "a natural stronghold for robbers," whose strategic importance had recently been confirmed in the course of military operations in Syria.[30]

While Pacorus's army spent more than forty days marshaling materials and constructing a bridge over the Euphrates, the Romans took advantage of the delay to consolidate their forces in place, three days before the Parthians arrived.[31] Ventidius emerged victorious from the third and final battle of Gindarus; there were twenty thousand dead, and Pacorus, though he fought like a lion, was slain. His head, impaled on a pike, was paraded throughout the cities of Syria to terrorize the population, but also to visit upon Pacorus the treatment he had meted out to Crassus's son Publius. By this victory, then, Ventidius had avenged the shame of Carrhae. Following his defeat the Parthian sovereign, Orodes, is said to have gone mad from grief; he abdicated in favor of his son Phraates IV, who shortly thereafter murdered his father, his thirty brothers, and even his own son.[32]

Ventidius, like Caesar, had marvelous good luck (*incredibile felicitate*, in Florus's phrase).[33] His victory over the Parthians on 9 June 38, the fifteenth anniversary of the battle of Carrhae, could not help but strengthen Antony's position. The violence of the civil wars had not caused the rout of Crassus's army to be forgotten, but finally Rome had taken its revenge. Ventidius himself had no interest in carrying on the fight against the Parthians. Antony's jealousy is sometimes mentioned in this regard, but there were practical reasons for Ventidius's disinclination: Not only did order need to be restored in Syria and neighboring provinces, it was necessary above all to punish disloyal allies, such as Antiochus, who had offered refuge to Parthian survivors.[34]

Responsibility for continuing military operations in the East therefore fell to Antony. The Senate, acting on the recommendation of the triumvirs, granted Ventidius the right to celebrate a triumph "over the mountainous region of the Taurus and over the Parthians."[35] On 27 November of the same year, he entered Rome to mark the first Roman victory over these people. Sallust, an inveterate Caesarian and member of the Italian urban moneyed class, delivered the oration in his honor—a ceremony that no doubt scandalized the aristocratic class, which despised Ventidius on account of his humble origins, looking down on him as a coarse provincial soldier who as a young man, it was maliciously said, had plied the degrading trade of mule driver.[36] When he died, the mule driver was nonetheless entitled to a public funeral.[37]

8

Mare Nostrum

A LARGE NUMBER of the triumvirs' victories were due to Caesar's former lieutenants. One thinks in particular of Ventidius Bassus in the East and of the proconsul Gnaeus Domitius Calvinus in Spain, the Far West. The Alps, subjugated in 41 by Lucius Antonius, posed relatively few problems, but Spain required Rome's sustained attention. Since the second century Roman armies had had difficulty bringing the Hispanic peoples under their control, notably in the mountainous districts, as the tower of Sant Martí Tentellatge, midway between Barcelona and Andorra, attests. The coins that Calvinus caused to be struck at Osca (Huesca) testify to the intensity of the fighting in this region; we know of only one episode, which throws into relief the commander's iron discipline.

After his lieutenant had been ambushed by the Cerretani, a people of Northern Iberia, and subsequently abandoned by his troops, Calvinus administered an exemplary punishment to the centurions and the soldiers of two centuries (units consisting of one hundred men), who were submitted to the penalty of decimation, every tenth randomly selected soldier being put to death. Calvinus subsequently led his army to victory and was acclaimed imperator. Cassius Dio tells us that the cities of Spain gave him gold in the form of crowns (*aurum coronarium*), an exaction used to pay for the cost of his triumph, but also of reconstructing the Regia, the administrative building of the pontifex maximus in the Forum, destroyed by fire.[1]

Returning to Rome, Domitius Calvinus organized the triumphal procession, spending a part of his tribute on the ceremony itself. An inscription on a marble statue base found on the Palatine Hill near the Arch of Titus celebrates one of his offerings, financed *ex manibieis*, which is to say thanks to the booty taken from vanquished enemies.[2] The *fasti triumphales Capitolini* record the date of Calvinus's procession as 17 July 36—evidence that he had been in the province for two years.[3] The scale of these operations should not be minimized, then, for they must have involved a territory larger than the central area of the Pyrenees, with the purpose of preventing Sextus Pompey from regaining lands in Spain. It may have been at this time, if not before, that Octavian recruited for his personal bodyguard Iberian warriors from Calagurris (Calahorra, in Rioja Baja), who remained in his service until Antony's defeat.[4] We do not know whether Antony was still escorted by his Ituraean archers; be that as it may, it is clear that Octavian constantly sought to imitate him.

Further north, in Gaul, Agrippa's army had pressed on beyond the Rhine. Cassius Dio remarks that he was the second Roman (the first was Caesar) to cross the Rhine for military reasons.[5] This campaign was not intended to be one of conquest, of course, but rather to suppress a revolt by the eastern Gaulish cities, supported by transrhenane peoples. Nevertheless the symbolic dimension of the crossing of the river, inspired by Caesar's example, must not be neglected. Caesar had crossed the Rhine on two occasions, in 55 and 53. In his commentary he proudly described the bridge, constructed from local timber in only ten days, whose pilings were arranged in opposing pairs, on the one side leaning forward in the direction of the river's current and on the other slanting back against it.[6] Renaissance architects greatly admired this design for embodying the ideals of *utilitas* and *firmitas*; what is more, by virtue of this achievement, Caesar had shown himself to be the equal of the great conquerors of the past who had reached the limits of the *oikoumenē*. Agrippa's crossing therefore could not have gone unnoticed; no other feat in the two years of his campaign surpassed it. Virgil does not expressly mention Agrippa, either in the tenth *Bucolic* or the first *Georgic*, but his evocations of the Rhine are eloquent.[7]

Unlike Ventidius, however, Agrippa renounced a triumph he would have been entitled to celebrate in 37, the year of his consulship, and contented himself with receiving "triumphal honors"—the solemn ceremony known as an ovation, a less extravagant commemoration of military victory of the sort that Octavian had recently permitted himself at Philippi.[8] According to the official version, Agrippa did not wish to make a proud display at a moment when Octavian had just suffered a naval defeat at the hands of Sextus. Appian recounts the misfortunes of Octavian's admirals, Gaius Calvisius Sabinus and the defector Menodorus, vanquished by enemies and storms; more than half of Octavian's fleet had been lost. Agrippa prudently settled for the consulship, for he was a very young *homo novus*, scarcely twenty-seven years old; had he claimed a triumph for himself, conservatives would have been extremely displeased. More than this, he was well aware that Antony and Octavian were ready to cooperate in ridding themselves of overly ambitious commanders, as they had done in the case of Salvidienus Rufus earlier. There was no more room for aspiring warlords. Glory was better left to the triumvirs.

The spoils of Agrippa's campaigns in Gaul, in addition to the booty brought back from Spain by Domitius Calvinus and the ships promised by certain cities in Aquitania that had fallen to Agrippa, made him an indispensable part of the campaign against Sextus Pompey.[9] His talents as an organizer proved to be no less valuable. A military port was constructed under his supervision near Cape Misenum, the *portus Iulius*; probably also another in Gallia Narbonensis, at Forum Iulii (Fréjus).[10] Until now Agrippa had not been entrusted with a command on the seas, where he was soon to demonstrate his talent as an admiral. But even this was not enough to satisfy Octavian. He needed to reach an agreement with Antony.

In the meantime, in Africa, Lepidus continued to pursue the policy of Romanization. By virtue of his prerogatives as pontifex maximus, he undertook a program of demolition on the site of the ancient city of Carthage to purify the new colony of all traces of malediction. This made it possible to reestablish Carthage as a commercial center capable of competing with the trading posts of Mauretania and Roman Numidia and to reassert its primacy within a territory where Punic identity was still embraced in indigenous cities tolerated by the Romans, perhaps with the aim of emphasizing their inferior legal status. Lepidus therefore had to deal with security problems while at the same time seeking to consolidate his power in the new municipalities. An inscription from the colony of Thabraca (Tabarka), honoring the city's triumviral patron, attests his third imperatorial acclamation.[11]

At about the same time, Bocchus II of Mauretania had profited from the rivalry between Antony and Octavian to take possession of the domains of his brother Bogud, a protégé of Antony.[12] He also took advantage of the revolt of the city of Tingis (Tanger) against Bogud, which allowed him, no doubt with Lepidus's support, to reunify the Moorish kingdom. Later, in aid of the last campaign against Sextus Pompey, Bocchus mobilized an auxiliary corps of five thousand Numidian horsemen.[13]

Antony, for his part, was preparing his eastern campaign while at the same time taking steps to ensure that it would not add to the burdens of the local population. In 39, in the province of Asia, the triumvirs forbade Roman legionaries from imposing forced labor on the residents of Aphrodisias and Plarasa or confiscating property.[14] Ventidius had driven back the Parthians and avenged Crassus, but the triumvir of the East aimed at much more than that, hoping finally to carry out Caesar's plan. While Octavian was assembling his fleet, Antony was organizing his army and working to strengthen Rome's position in Asia Minor. There was no risk of another invasion there, for Antony once again controlled Commagene, having joined with Ventidius after the campaign against the Parthians to subdue the king, Antiochus. The Romans laid siege to Samosata, the capital of Commagene; Herod, in spite of serious internal disturbances in the kingdom of Judaea, took part in this assault.

Antony then concluded a treaty with Antiochus. Our sources, which are highly unsympathetic to Antony, undervalue the significance of his victory, treating it as nothing more than an attempt to limit the extent of Ventidius's glory and to appropriate the wealth of Antiochus's kingdom.[15] But one must not overlook the strategic importance of Commagene and the junction on the edge of the Euphrates, at the Zeugma, the main point of access to Mesopotamia from the northwest. Antiochus's prestige is evident in the famous tomb-sanctuary he had caused to be constructed in honor of himself and his ancestors atop Mount Nemrut. A relief from another sanctuary, on the site of Arsameia on the Nymphaios, shows the king with a divinity whom the Armenians called Vahagn, likened by the Greeks to Heracles (fig. 8.1).

FIGURE 8.1. Depiction of Antiochus of Commagene and Vahagn

In Syria, Ventidius's successor Gaius Sosius carried on his policy of pacification. Strabo, in a fragment of his *Historical Commentaries*, transmitted by Josephus, says that

> when Antigonus was brought to Antioch, Antony beheaded him. He was the first Roman who decided to behead a king, since he believed that in no other way could he change the attitude of the Jews so that they would accept Herod, who had been appointed in his place. For not even under torture would they submit to proclaiming him king, so highly did they regard their former king. And so he thought the disgrace would somewhat dim their memory of him and would also lessen their hatred of Herod.[16]

The decapitation of Antigonus gave the region's kings, major and minor alike, pause for reflection.

Our sources concerning Antony's policy toward the Hebrews highlight Herod's activities and those of Roman military leaders, but willfully downplay Egypt's role in reasserting control over this troublesome region. It is true that the precious logistical and material support furnished by Cleopatra was by no means disinterested; indeed, the queen gained possession of a part of the territories ruled by the Nabataean king Malichus I, who on this occasion had adopted a benevolent attitude toward the Parthians. At about this time, too, Antony put Lysanias of Ituraea to death on the ground that earlier he had aided Pacorus.[17] Cleopatra insisted also on having Idumaea, which covered southern Palestine, but Antony left it under the jurisdiction of Herod, a native of the region. On returning to Jerusalem, Herod ordered a citadel to be built, to which he gave the name "Antony's fort."

Having thus resolved some of his problems in the East, Antony went back once more to Italy in the spring of 37 for the purpose of meeting with Octavian, who had sent his faithful adviser Maecenas to welcome him. Antony had also maintained contact in the meantime with Lepidus and Sextus Pompey. He arrived in Greece with a fleet of three hundred ships, an impressive display of force.[18] Going on from there to Italy he did not land at Brundisium, for Octavian had indicated that their talks would be held at a place between Metapontum and Tarentum.[19] As at

Brundisium two years earlier, in 39, negotiations lasted for several weeks. The two triumvirs ended up agreeing to prolong their alliance, and the triumvirate was renewed for a second term of five years. Our sources do not say whether Lepidus had sent an intermediary, but he kept control over Africa and its coastal waters; moreover, Antony assented to the marriage of his daughter Antonia Major (born in 39) with one of Lepidus's sons.

In exchange for two legions to be employed in the war against the Parthians, Antony placed at Octavian's disposal a naval contingent for use against Sextus Pompey, who had been stripped of his offices as a consequence of the annulment of the Pact of Misenum. Octavian and Antony concluded a matrimonial agreement of their own, whereby Antyllus, the elder son of Antony and Fulvia, on reaching adulthood would marry Julia, the daughter of Octavian and Scribonia, also born in 39. As for Octavia, who had been at Corcyra when she was pregnant with Antonia Minor (promised, in turn, to Domitius Ahenobarbus), she was sent back to stay with her brother in Italy. Finally, Octavian received one hundred forty ships from Antony's fleet, this against a promise to send him ten thousand Italian legionaries for his expedition against the Parthians.

Antony now hastened to cross the Adriatic, appointing as admiral Titus Statilius Taurus, consul suffect that year in replacement of Agrippa's colleague Lucius Caninius Gallus, Antony's nephew by marriage.[20] Menodorus defected once again; Calvisius Sabinus was held responsible for this latest betrayal and replaced by Agrippa. The former pirate having departed, Octavian's senior officers were all Romans. His strategy consisted in opening three fronts with a view to encircling Sicily. While Lepidus was crossing the Strait of Sicily with seventy warships and many others carrying legionaries, Statilius Taurus set off from Tarentum with a fleet of one hundred thirty vessels. But the decisive offensive depended on Octavian's grand fleet, comprised of roughly four hundred ships, not only triremes but also powerful quinqueremes and hexaremes; the crews had been trained at the port of Baiae, in Campania. Officially the fleet was under the command of Octavian, but the officer who was actually in charge, the real mastermind of the operation, was Agrippa.

On 1 July 36 the ships of Octavian and Agrippa set sail for Sicily. From his base at Messana, Sextus made plans to prevent the triumviral fleets from landing. To hold back Lepidus, one of his legates, Lucius Plinius Rufus, dropped anchor at Lilybaeum (present-day Marsala), where he is mentioned in at least one inscription; other units were stationed near the island of Cossyra (Pantelleria). The advance of the Roman forces was arrested by bad weather: Statilius Taurus had to turn back to Tarentum, whereas Lepidus's fleet was shattered by the storm. Only Agrippa managed to limit his losses. Octavian was inclined to postpone the expedition until the following year, but Agrippa persuaded him to attack. Statilius Taurus eventually set off again in the direction of Tauromenium (Taormina) on the east coast, and Lepidus finally succeeded in landing and occupying western Sicily, laying siege to Plinius Rufus's stronghold at Lilybaeum, prompting Sextus to send his lieutenant Tisienus (or Titisienus) Gallus to Plinius's aid.

Agrippa stationed himself with a hundred or so ships off the island of Stromboli. His idea was to attract the larger part of the enemy fleet, making it easier for Lepidus's and Octavian's ships to disembark their troops. A first battle took place in the waters off the coast of Mylae (Milazzo), in mid-August 36, but Sextus countered Agrippa's maneuvers. Octavian's troops, having landed in Tauromenium, came under strong attack, and after having lost a number of ships crossed the Strait of Messana (Messina) to join up with Agrippa's forces at Tyndaris (Tindari).

Sextus's fleet, under the command of the admirals Papias and Demochares (Menecrates had died some time before), numbered some one hundred sixty ships; Agrippa's, augmented by a few captured enemy vessels, about one hundred thirty. Lepidus and Gallus, for their part, had set an eastern course from Lilybaeum, looking to join their respective allies at Mylae. In late August or early September, probably on 3 September, the decisive battle took place on the waters between Mylae and a small port called Naulochus, whose name in Greek means "a place offering safe anchorage." Here for the first time the instrument of war called a *harpax* was used. According to Appian, it was Agrippa's invention:

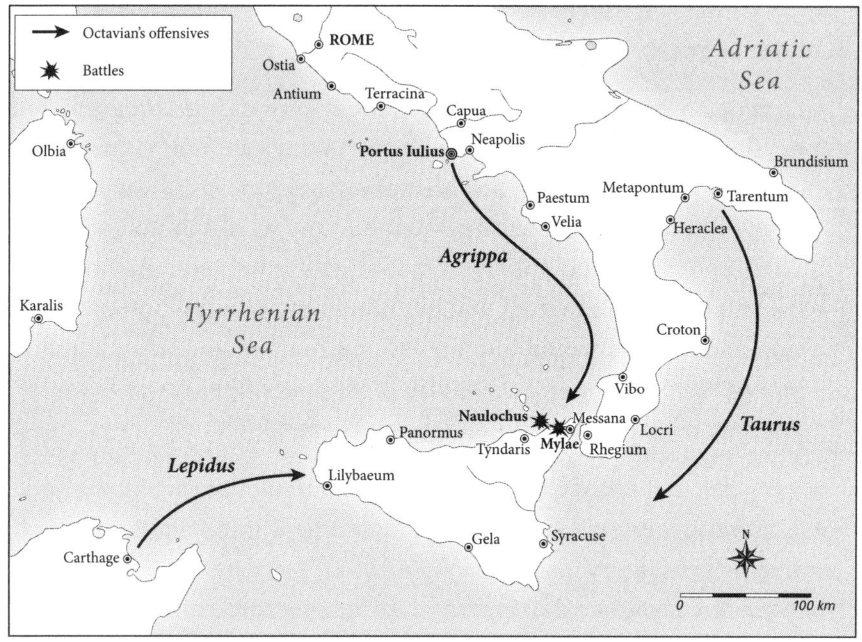

MAP 6. The campaign against Sextus Pompey

> Agrippa devised [a machine] called the "grab," a piece of wood five cubits long encased in iron and having rings at each end. To one of these rings was attached the grab itself, a curved piece of iron, to the other numerous ropes, which [mechanically] pulled in the grab after it had been fired from a catapult and had hooked an enemy ship.[21]

By means of this device, Agrippa was able to restrict the room for maneuver of his adversary, most of whose ships were smaller and less well equipped to launch attacks than his own.

The two fleets sailed side by side, but because Sextus's formation was more compact, Agrippa's ships were able to surround it. When he saw that Sextus's force was in difficulty, Agrippa launched the decisive attack. Only seventeen ships succeeded in escaping. Sextus himself managed to flee. After having plundered the wealthy temple of Juno Lacinia, near Croton (present-day Crotone), he made his way through safe waters to the Greek island of Lesbos, where, in 49, when he was young, his father had left him in the care of his mother during the war against Caesar.[22] Appian remarks:

> Octavian neither pursued [Sextus Pompey] nor ordered others to do so. This may have been because he was taking care not to encroach on someone else's jurisdiction, that of Antony; or else he was waiting to see what would happen and how Antony would behave toward Pompey to have an excuse for a dispute if this proved unlawful (for it had long been suspected that because of their love of power Octavian and Antony would quarrel with each other once they had removed the others); or, as Octavian himself said later, it was because Pompey was not one of his father's murderers.[23]

Sextus's defeat marked the end of his domination of Sicily and the end of his naval power. Strabo reports having seen in Rome a pirate chieftain named Selurus, known as the "son of Aetna" since he roamed around the volcano at the head of an army; he was captured and brought to Rome, where he was torn to pieces by wild beasts in the Forum.[24] We do not know if Selurus was involved into Sextus Pompey's operations, but Octavian had an interest in restoring order to prevent the revolt of the Sicilian cities, punished for having supported his enemy. The citizens of Tauromenium were exiled, and a few years later a Roman colony was founded on the town's site.

Another collateral effect was the fall of Lepidus. Owing to his naval victory, Octavian was able at last to settle accounts with someone who was a great nuisance to him, who had (at least according to the Augustan version transmitted by Cassius Dio) continued to negotiate secretly with Sextus, who commanded twenty-two legions of infantry and a certain number of horsemen, laid claim to Sicily, and was even ready to exchange Africa for it.[25] With Lepidus now effectively exiled, Octavian was able to convince his soldiers to come over to him. Although Lepidus was deprived of his *imperium*, he nonetheless retained his senatorial dignity and the office of pontifex maximus. Under close surveillance, he withdrew to Circeii (now San Felice Circeo, between Rome and Naples), where he lived long enough to see Augustus consolidate his power.

On returning to Rome, Agrippa was entitled to a very special honor, the gold naval crown (*corona navalis*), ornamented with miniature prows; the victorious sailors were awarded crowns made from olive branches. Octavian, for his part, received unprecedented honors, among them the erection of a gilded statue, placed atop a rostral column. The inscription at the base of the column reads: "Peace long disturbed by civil discord he restored both on land and sea."[26] Later, having become Augustus in the meantime, he looked back and said, "I freed the sea from pirates. About thirty thousand slaves, captured in that war, who had run away from their masters and had taken up arms against the republic, I delivered to their masters for punishment."[27] This passage in the *Res Gestae* alludes to the Sicilian War against Sextus Pompey; the mention of slaves may well concern the crew members of Sextus's warships, since he had in fact welcomed fugitives and slaves. The situation seemed favorable to putting an end to fratricidal struggles at long last. Octavian ordered that the written records of these years of conflict be burned and declared that the time was at hand, once Antony had returned from the East, to terminate the state of emergency that had brought the triumvirate into being.

PART III

The End of a Republic

9

Antony's Eastern Campaign

IN SPITE of the victory over the Parthians, Rome had not quite regained its former prestige; nonetheless, its deterrent power was greater than it had been. Sextus Pompey, despite a substantially reduced naval capability, remained hopeful of taking revenge. Antony was finally able to prepare for his eastern campaign, while the provincial governors of the Eastern provinces set about restoring peace to territories exhausted by war and chronic insecurity. Responsibility for Bithynia and Pontus, and for patrolling the Black Sea, was given to a senior admiral, Domitius Ahenobarbus. Strabo notes that the governors of these parts had neglected to protect merchant shipping against attacks by pirates in squadrons of slender light boats called *kamarai* by the Greeks. Supported by a segment of the local population, the brigands profited from their knowledge of the territory to hide their vessels, which they put to sea whenever crews could be taken captive and then sold into slavery if their families were unwilling or unable to pay a ransom. "In those places which are ruled by local chieftains," Strabo says, "the rulers go to the aid of those who are wronged, often attacking and bringing back the [*kamarai*], men and all. But the territory that is subject to the Romans affords but little aid, because of the negligence of the governors who are sent there."[1] By contrast, he notes, traces were still to be found during this period, on the Crimean Peninsula, of long wars waged by Scythian "nomads," who lived not by robbery, but depended instead on the tributes they demanded from the local population, and went to war only in the event that their demands were not met.[2]

Antony implemented a policy for controlling the East first devised by Pompey and Caesar, a skillful mixture of diplomacy and military aggression. After the treaty of Tarentum, for reasons that escape us, he decided to put an end to the dynasty of Mithradates VI in Pontic Cappadocia, replacing Darius, the ruler whom he himself had crowned, by Polemon, who had no association with the local aristocracy. Darius's brother, Arsaces, tried to reclaim his territories but found himself besieged in the fortress at Sagylium by Polemon and Lycomedes, high priest of Comana Pontica, to whom Antony seems to have granted a royal title.[3] At about the same time the throne of Galatia was given to Amyntas; Castor II, Deiotarus's grandson, who had succeeded him after his death in 40, either died or was gotten rid of, and Paphlagonia was offered to Castor's son, Deiotarus Philadelphus.[4]

Antony had entrusted the province of Asia to Gaius Furnius, a very competent military officer and administrator. Now that the horrors of the war against the Caesaricides were no more, and the exactions imposed by Labienus had been lifted, the cities of Asia were beginning to recover their former prosperity. In Ephesus, Antony had to ask forgiveness for his impiety in respect of the Temple of Artemis, whose sacred boundaries he had violated in ordering the murder of Arsinoë; he therefore caused the perimeter within which one could seek asylum to be enlarged, thus creating a very considerable area of immunity that moreover might serve the interests of his protégés.[5] Antony cultivated ties with local aristocrats, who in at least one case seem to have been family relations: Pythodorus of Tralles, the exceedingly wealthy president of the league of cities of the province of Asia, had married one Antonia (the daughter of Gaius Antonius or, more probably, Lucius Antonius).

Antony's adversaries made much of the fact that he had appointed the apparently least suitable members of his entourage to assist him in reorganizing the East. Anaxenor, a citizen of Magnesia on the Maeander and an immensely popular figure of the stage, was named tax collector for four cities in Asia and equipped with an armed escort. His fellow citizens honored him with the priesthood of Zeus Sosipolis (savior and protector of the city) and two statues, one in the agora and the other, in bronze, in the theater (Strabo, who visited Magnesia, made a point of noting grammatical errors in the inscription borne by the second of these), and compensated him as a public benefactor.[6] Plutarch, ever the moralist, mentions a clique of artists, including "cithara players like Anaxenor, flute players like Xanthus, one Metrodorus, a dancer, and such other rabble of Asiatic performers."[7] The fact of the matter, however, is that artists, particularly the most gifted and acclaimed, played an important role in shaping relations between the cities of Asia Minor; from the fourth century onward they had often been employed as ambassadors on account of their celebrity.

Some cities were punished, such as Heracleia Pontica, where Antony established a Roman colony; the rest of the city was placed under the authority of the Galatian Adiatorix.[8] A fragment from the historian Memnon of Heracleia mentions the attempts of a notable named Brithagoras to attract the favorable notice of "Gaius Caesar" (Octavian), in "the hope of restoring his fellow citizens to the condition of free people"; he was therefore sent on a mission to Rome, where "the *autokratōr*, which is to say the triumvir, treated him in such a way as to give him to understand that his request would meet with his approval."[9]

In the meantime, Sosius was occupied restructuring the administration of the province of Syria and the part of Cilicia that had been confided to him. According to Octavian's version of events, he had deliberately "accomplished nothing worthy of note" to avoid arousing Antony's jealousy.[10] A large part of Cilicia was under the control of Cleopatra, who had also obtained Cyprus, Phoenicia, Coele-Syria, Ituraea, and Arabia Nabataea.[11] Officially, of course, all these additions to her dominion embodied the unanimous will of the triumvirs. In Cilicia, the city of Tarsus had particularly suffered from military campaigns; a prominent figure called Boethus, who, after the battles of Philippi, had composed a poem in honor of Antony, was named to the office of gymnasiarch. In Strabo's view he was as bad a citizen as he was a poet. Accused of having misappropriated the olive oil meant for the gymnasiums, Boethus was brought to trial before Antony but escaped punishment owing to his extravagant flatteries.[12]

It was also necessary to compensate those Greeks who had fought in the triumviral forces. A long Greek inscription found near the ancient city of Rhosos (present-day Arsuz, on the Gulf of Alexandretta) comprises a series of texts dating to sometime between 42 and 30. The second of these describes the honors awarded to the admiral (*nauarchos*) Seleucus in accordance with a law of 42, the Lex Munatia Aemilia. Seleucus acquired Roman citizenship, which was also granted to his parents and his descendants, as well as total immunity, including exemption from tax on property, and a series of legal privileges.[13] Probably Seleucus had commanded one of the ships delivered by Antony to Octavian for the war against Sextus Pompey; having earlier been on the wrong side, he might have been considered a pirate like Menodorus, who subsequently redeemed himself through services rendered to Octavian and likewise became a Roman citizen, joining the equestrian order. Seleucus may have returned to Rhosos at the helm of one of the seventy ships that Octavian had given to Antony, which were used to track down Sextus.[14]

Finally, one must not underestimate the consequences of the practice, increasingly common under Antony and Octavian, of offering benefits (such as Roman citizenship) to foreigners who made contributions of great value. Pompey and Caesar had helped to popularize this policy, overcoming strenuous opposition from hard-line conservatives, but because of the triumvirs' extraordinary powers it was now more easily put into effect, with the additional provision that the new Roman could keep his native citizenship.

Antony went to Syria, asking Cleopatra to join him there, and recognized under Egyptian law the twins to whom she had given birth, Alexander Helios and Cleopatra Selene, whose education was entrusted to a certain Euphronios.[15] In this way, without his lawful marriage with Octavia having been annulled, he enjoyed in the eyes of the people of Alexandria prerogatives in every way identical with those of a Ptolemy, which is to say those of a pharaoh or king. Nevertheless he was virtually ignored in the rest of Egypt, a sign that in the eyes of the priests his status was not sanctioned by tradition. In those parts of the East falling within the Roman-Egyptian orbit, coins circulated bearing portraits of Cleopatra and Antony that communicated the official character of their union (fig. 9.1). Henceforth it was said, and widely believed, that the city

FIGURE 9.1. Coin struck in honor of Antony and Cleopatra, 34 BCE

of Antioch modified its system of chronological calculation, which until then had been based on the Pompeian era; and yet this new era, whose first year began on 1 September 37, bore the name, not of Antony, but of the queen of Egypt.

Cleopatra's marriage with Antony inaugurated a new phase in her reign. At the time of their wedding the couple conceived another child, who was born in 36 and called Ptolemy Philadelphus. Their union, which had no sanction under Roman law, was meant chiefly to enhance their charismatic appeal, on both sides. For the Egyptians it had special importance because it constituted a sacred marriage (*hierogamia*) inspired by the deities Isis and Serapis (whom the Greeks likened to Aphrodite and Dionysus). It imbued Antony with the charisma necessary to win acceptance for his military authority, while at the same time strengthening the power of Cleopatra and her reign among not only the Egyptians but also the Macedonians and the Greeks. According to one Hellenistic tradition, the powers of a female sovereign, even one as energetic and determined as Cleopatra, were limited. A queen (*basilissa*) was considered to be such only in her capacity as wife or mother of the ruling *basileus*, in this case her son Ptolemy XV, also known as little Caesar. Cleopatra's sacred marriage with Antony therefore helped to consolidate the religious basis of her authority. Furthermore, it must not be forgotten that a temple of Isis and Serapis had been dedicated at Rome in 43, in accordance with the will of the triumvirs.[16]

A maneuver of this sort could not have passed unnoticed, and Octavian was certainly informed of it. The possibility cannot be excluded that he and Antony had reached an agreement on this point during their negotiations at Tarentum. Antony's marriage with Octavia nonetheless remained strong. To the Roman mind, the principal value of conjugal relations resided in *concordia,* a circumstance that corresponded perfectly to this union; the legitimate wife looked after her husband's affairs and, above all, helped to manage any difficulties that might arise in his relationship with a brother-in-law. Today an arrangement of this kind would be regarded as a marriage of convenience, but in ancient Rome the situation was altogether different.

The liaison between Antony and Cleopatra was dictated by political considerations. Anyone who wished to govern the East had to adapt himself to the local traditions of government, resisting the temptation to exert direct control in favor of an imperialist hegemony aimed at supervising local balances of power and collecting taxes. Oriental governors had the title of king, and even the least powerful among them possessed a religious charisma that assured them of their subjects' loyalty and the submission of nobles to their will. Rome had every interest in preserving this state of affairs, and all the more as the Parthian threat had once again upset the equilibrium established by Pompey, making it necessary to strengthen economic ties with Egypt and its influential queen, in this way reemphasizing the bipolarity between Rome and Alexandria that had characterized the entire Hellenistic period. This is precisely what Caesar had in mind before his death. For the time being at least, Antony saw no reason not to carry on with the plan he had devised, interrupted by civil war, to lay claim to the dictator's political legacy (and, in Asia Minor, that of Pompey). Cleopatra's vigor and her charismatic hold over her people made her an important ally for Rome. Unlike the other Ptolemies, she possessed a remarkable talent for diplomacy, which, in the East, proved to be of paramount importance.

A relief from Praeneste (today Palestrina, a city built around a sanctuary located some twenty-five miles east of Rome), dating from the

FIGURE 9.2. Drachma bearing the image of Phraates IV

second half of the first century BCE and conserved in the Vatican Museums, depicts officers standing on the bridge of a bireme of the Hellenistic type; a crocodile lounging on the prow has been interpreted as a reference to Octavian's war against Cleopatra and to the battle of Actium, but more probably it represents an Egyptian ship under the command of Antony (shown seated above the crocodile).

In the meantime, in 37, Orodes II died shortly after having abdicated in favor of his son Phraates (Frahāt) IV (fig. 9.2), who was accused of assassinating him. Pompeius Trogus later described Rome's new enemy in this fashion:

> So he immediately killed his father, as if he was unwilling to die; and he also slaughtered all his thirty brothers. Nor did the murders end with the brothers. For when he saw himself hated by the nobles because of his ongoing atrocities, he, so no one else should be appointed king, gave orders for his adult son to be killed.[17]

When Phraates then ordered that the nobles be eliminated, an aristocrat named Monaeses (Manēč) took refuge with Antony, who is said to have given him three cities in eastern Syria, Larissa, Arethusa, and Hierapolis.[18] Antony may have sought in this way to buy off Monaeses, having heard of Phraates's violent succession; he may even have promised to reward him with the kingdom of the Parthians.[19] But since Monaeses did not belong to the royal dynasty of the Arsacids, he would have had a hard time establishing his authority, even in the event of a Roman victory; it is therefore difficult to credit this account, due to Cassius Dio. Dio goes on to say that Monaeses was sent by Antony in the company of envoys to Phraates for the purpose of getting back the standards captured from the legions of Crassus and Decidius Saxa, together with any surviving soldiers who had been taken prisoner.

However this may be, Antony needed an official pretext for attacking the Parthians. The death of Pacorus had avenged that of Crassus and his son (Crassus's other son, Marcus Crassus junior, was now the governor of Crete and Cyrenaica), but the question of standards and prisoners remained open. We have already seen that Horace (who was writing when the negotiations between Augustus and the Parthians had not yet been concluded) had reproached these soldiers for having taken barbarian wives and fighting in the ranks of their fathers-in-law. It has been suggested that prisoners from Carrhae were deployed as frontier guards on the eastern border of the Parthian Empire with Han China, but this seems improbable.

Antony now set about laying the groundwork for a campaign in the Caucasus, where he could count on the support of Polemon in Pontic Cappadocia and of Archelaus in inner Cappadocia. His main interest was in reestablishing friendly relations with Artawazd of Armenia, who seemed to have proposed a change of strategy to Crassus, in 53, recommending that he pass through Armenia, instead of going to Mesopotamia, where he would have risked disaster. The fact remains that the king had been obliged to reconsider his position and to repudiate the pact of friendship imposed by Pompey on his father Tigran. Over the centuries, the kingdom of Armenia had hesitated between Rome and Parthia; some modern historians have anachronistically likened it to a modern buffer state. Here we will be better off listening to Tacitus, who remarked that

> Armenia, whose national character since ancient times [*ambigua gens ea antiquitus*] has been no less ambiguous than the geopolitical situation of the country itself, since with a wide extent of frontier coterminous with our own provinces, it stretches inland right up to

> Media; so that the Armenians lie interposed between two vast empires, with which, as they detest Rome and envy Parthia, they are too frequently at variance.[20]

Antony placed matters in the hands of his legate Canidius Crassus, whose activity is summarized by Plutarch thus: "Left by Antony in Armenia, [he] conquered that people, as well as the kings of the Iberians and Albanians, and advanced as far as the Caucasus."[21] Plutarch goes on to say that Canidius was "a man of the greatest influence with Antony."[22] Formerly Lepidus's legate in Gaul, and then Asinius Pollio's legate in Cisalpine Gaul, he was one of the staunchest Antonians. We do not know a great deal about Canidius. He was appointed suffect consul in 40, and it is certain that he conducted his first campaign in the Caucasus before the beginning of Antony's expedition in 36. According to Cassius Dio, Canidius's operations took place under the consulship of Lucius Gellius Publicola and Marcus Cocceius Nerva, which is to say in 36, in late winter, between January and March. He vanquished the king of the Iberians of the Caucasus, who inhabited the central and eastern parts of present-day Georgia, and made him a Roman ally; Dio calls him Pharnabazus (Parnavaz), a name that goes back to the founder of the Iberian dynasty. Pharnabazus agreed to support Canidius against Zober, king of Caucasian Albania.[23]

This means that Antony must have made the same arrangement with Artawazd of Armenia, having in all likelihood had to defeat the king in battle to have his support, which took the form of light cavalry supplemented by six thousand horses in full armor (the same number he had supplied Crassus with earlier) and seven thousand infantrymen; what is more, according to Strabo, Antony relied on him for tactical advice.[24] If, as Cassius Dio says, the operations against the Iberians and the Albanians took place in early 36, it is probable that the campaign against the Armenians, following Artawazd's submission, had taken place in 37, just after the victory over the Parthians and the offensive in Commagene. Armenian auxiliaries thus came to be added to the other troops furnished by allied kings, who together reinforced some sixty thousand legionaries and "Iberian and Celtic" auxiliaries; if, as seems altogether likely, the Iberians in this case were from the Caucasus, rather than Hispania, the Celts might have been Galatians sent by Amyntas. Plutarch tells us that this army struck terror throughout Asia as a whole, as far as the borders of the Parthian Empire.[25]

According to a tradition originating very probably with Livy, Antony had planned to march through Mesopotamia, but since this territory was closely surveilled, he took Artawazd's advice and attacked Media Atropatene, which was ruled by another Artawazd who had gone over to Phraates's side.[26] There is no need to suppose that this amounted to a strategic diversion on Antony's part; his main concern, in accepting the plan of attack that Artawazd recommended to Crassus earlier, no doubt was simply not to repeat the error Crassus had made. Moreover, Livy's summary of Antony's eastern campaign makes it clear that he invaded Media belatedly, for he had been delayed by his revels with Cleopatra and had postponed his departure.[27]

Plutarch, for his part, says that, after having sent Cleopatra back to Egypt, Antony went to Armenia via Arabia and Osrhoene.[28] In reality, he had had to shore up his position in Syria. Florus, in a passage reproaching Antony for his reckless ambition, seems to confirm this itinerary: "But such was the exceeding vanity of the man that, in his desire for fresh titles of honor, he longed to have the Araxes and the Euphrates inscribed beneath his statues, and, without any pretext or design and without even a pretended declaration of war, just as if it were part of the art of generalship to attack by stealth, he left Syria and made a sudden attack on the Parthians."[29] These two rivers marked the boundary between the *imperium Romanum*—comprising Roman provinces and friendly kingdoms—and the Parthian Empire and its tributary kingdoms. Plutarch asserts that Antony, rather than spend the winter in Armenia, moved at once to attack Media; in other words, he relied on the same advantage of surprise that had assured Caesar's success and allowed Ventidius to prevail over Labienus and the Parthians. Plutarch says nothing of this, dwelling instead upon the fatigue of his soldiers, who had just completed a march of some eight thousand stadia (one thousand miles or so); additionally, they were obliged to transport heavy siege machines, among them an enormous battering ram, on three hundred wagons.[30]

An account of Mark Antony's campaign was composed by his lieutenant Quintus Dellius, fragments of which are found in Strabo.[31] In one fragment Dellius says that the Armenian capital of Artaxata was separated from the summer residence of the Median kings, in the city of Gazaka (present-day Gəncə in Azerbaijan), by a distance of two thousand four hundred stadia (three hundred miles).[32] Strabo says that the royal winter palace was in the citadel of Vera; Plutarch and Cassius Dio speak of a city that they call respectively Phraata and Praaspa, home to the king's spouses.[33] Plutarch and Cassius Dio furnish rather detailed descriptions of the campaign; Justin reports that there were fifty thousand Parthian horsemen, only four hundred of whom were "free men," which is to say belonging to the minor nobility (*āzād*).[34]

Antony, having placed the army's equipment and two legions under the authority of his lieutenant Oppius Statianus, supported by the auxiliaries supplied by Polemon, launched an attack against Vera. He seems not to have wanted to use siege engines in this case. In the meantime, Artawazd had returned to his kingdom, enabling the Parthians and the Medians to overwhelm Statianus's forces. Equipped themselves with the equivalent of two legions, they killed Statianus, took Polemon prisoner, and destroyed the idle siege engines.[35] Antony tried in vain to react. The Parthians, relying on their preferred tactic of making raids against the enemy rather than commit themselves to a pitched battle, were astonished by the discipline of the Roman troops, who, though they routed their adversaries in the end, killed very few of them.[36] Antony, having at this point reestablished discipline by means of very severe punishments, including the decimation of two cohorts, proceeded to lay siege to Phraata/Praaspa.[37]

King Phraates, seemingly fearing the defection of Artawazd of Armenia, sent envoys to Antony, who in turn dispatched an embassy to him. Phraates, seated on his golden throne, twanging his bowstring, received the Roman delegation with undisguised disdain. Antony decided to retreat, but it is hard to agree with Cassius Dio that this was proof of cowardice and naivete: "Antony was both alarmed at the king's haughtiness and ready to believe that a truce could be secured if he himself should shift his position; hence he withdrew without destroying any of his instruments of siege, just as if he were in friendly territory."[38] In reality, he had no choice.

Beset by the formidable Parthian archers, Antony's troops had succeeded in neutralizing them by employing a famous defensive tactic, the tortoise (testudo) formation: "They were contending in full armor against unprotected men, men prepared against men off their guard, heavy infantry against archers, Romans against barbarians. All the survivors immediately retired and no one [pursued] them thereafter."[39] It has often been said that, by means of this expedition in the East, Antony sought to follow in the footsteps of Alexander the Great. The stress laid on the superiority of Roman combat techniques, however, seems to show his determination to appear above all as a Roman military commander, on the model of Caesar and Pompey. For the first time, a Roman army, deprived of its oriental auxiliaries, used the testudo tactic to overcome enemies who had crushed Crassus.

Antony's desire to imitate Alexander did not go beyond a claim of divine descent from Heracles and Dionysus; Antony's army, by contrast, did not lose its Roman identity. As for Antony himself, he was not indulging his appetites at Cleopatra's court by this point, nor did he have any interest in offending the sensibilities of his officers or of his Italian soldiers. It would in any case have been unwise on his part to allow his army to be seen for what it really was, namely, the multiethnic contingent of a Roman-Egyptian coalition whose mission was to consolidate the geopolitical entity that he had conceived with Cleopatra. For propaganda purposes, the triumviral legionaries were meant to be Crassus's avengers, bent on recovering the honor lost at Carrhae. Anyone who regards Antony as the last Hellenistic prince has neglected to consider his bond with his soldiers.

Another proof of the traditional Roman manner that Antony cultivated is to be found in the reasons for his retreat to Armenia, reported by Livy. According to Strabo and Plutarch, the Romans took a route recommended by a Mardian guide. Living between Armenia and Media, the Mardians (or Amardians) were inclined to side with Rome, whether from fear of reprisals or owing to a political calculation. Velleius Paterculus and Florus give another version of the story, in which a Roman legionary, taken captive at Carrhae, honorably replaces the apparently more trustworthy Mardian guide.[40] This soldier, on making his way to the Roman camp by night, enabled Antony to avoid calamity by pointing out to him a safe passage through the woods. "A survivor from the disaster of Crassus dressed in Parthian costume rode up to the camp," Florus relates, "and having uttered a salutation in Latin and thus inspired trust by speaking their language, informed them of the danger that was threatening them. The king, he said, would soon be upon them with all his forces; they ought, therefore, to retreat and make for the mountains, though, even so, they would probably have no lack of enemies to face."[41]

Neither of these versions has any very solid historical foundation, of course. But the story of the providential prisoner had an emotional appeal that could not help but please Roman families whose members remained prisoners of the Parthians. Anecdotes of this sort served to reinforce the image that Antony wished to give to his campaign. He had resisted the Parthians thanks to Roman tactical superiority; and the idea that his guide was a survivor of Carrhae allowed him to present himself as a worthy heir to the republican tradition. In a sense, Antony felt it necessary to perpetuate a traditional military sensibility, as Caesar himself had done—a sensibility that, in the name of Romano-Italian values, scorned everything that departed from tradition, considering it to be foreign and barbarian.

This may seem to be at variance with Antony's passion for the Hellenistic style and his oriental posturing. But at a time of profound change, political figures found it difficult to behave consistently; and authors who recorded recent events had trouble keeping things straight. Plutarch, for example, corrected the information in his source by relying on common sense, speaking of a *Mardos* rather than a *Marsos*; Horace says that among the Italians in Crassus's army there was a contingent of Marsi, natives of the tail end of the Apennines, in the present-day Abruzzo region, fearsome warriors who two generations earlier, in the Social War of 91–89, had valiantly battled the Romans in defeat.

Notwithstanding the manifest failure of his expedition, Antony was acclaimed *imperator* for the third time, by his soldiers in the course of their retreat. Plutarch maintains that no general of the period had assembled an army "more conspicuous for prowess, endurance, or youthful vigor."[42] This unhappy campaign had nonetheless ended with heavy human losses, between twenty and thirty thousand men, legionaries and auxiliaries included. After a difficult passage through the mountains of the southern Caucasus, Antony was obliged to spend the winter in Armenia and accept the aid of Artawazd, whom he suspected of prevarication. Cleopatra's wealth permitted him to pay his troops; no doubt this is why he set out for Egypt.[43] But he was not yet done with the Armenian king.

10

End of the Young Pompey, Wars of the Young Caesar

WHILE ANTONY was fighting in Media Atropatene, Sextus Pompey had gone to Asia; the governor there, Gaius Furnius, who had been a friend of the elder Pompey, did not openly attack him, for Sextus seemed ready to surrender to Antony. According to Appian, who devotes the final part of *The Civil Wars* to Sextus's last days, "when he heard that Antony had been defeated—and rumor exaggerated what had happened—his hopes once more revived, either of succeeding Antony, if he was dead, or of sharing power with him when he returned; and Labienus, who had overrun Asia not long before, was constantly on his mind."[1] Sextus sent ambassadors not only to Antony but also to the kings of Thrace and Pontus, as well as "to the Parthians, in the hope that for the rest of their war against Antony they would enthusiastically welcome a Roman general, especially a son of Pompey the Great."[2]

The king of the Thracians was probably Cotys VII, son of Rhascupolis/Rhescuporis; as we saw in connection with the battles of Philippi, his father and uncle had played a sort of double game. By contrast, it is difficult to believe that Sextus, who looked to court other dynasties of the Black Sea, would have sought the aid of Polemon, even if he had been released by the Medes. As for the envoys sent to Phraates, they never reached their destination. Captured by Antony's men, they were brought to Alexandria, where the triumvir introduced them to the ambassadors he had received from Sextus. Antony pretended to believe that Sextus was acting in good faith but instructed the quaestor Marcus Titius, one of his lieutenants in the eastern campaign, to advance against him with an army and a fleet.[3] Titius, a nephew of Munatius Plancus, had a score to settle with Sextus, whose commander Menodorus (or Menas) had taken him captive in 40. Sextus had spared him on account of his friendship with Titius's father, who had been proscribed by the triumvirs; for Titius now to take up arms against him he considered to be the height of ingratitude and determined him to go to war. According to Cassius Dio, Titius was an ambivalent character, an ambitious outsider who, at the time of his capture by Sextus's admiral, "had got together some ships in the interest of his own supremacy"—in short, yet another aspiring warlord.[4]

When Antony understood the belligerent intentions of Pompey's son, he mobilized additional forces against him under the command of the Galatian Amyntas and Domitius Ahenobarbus, the latter of whom had lately thwarted an attempted assassination or kidnapping of his person by a certain Curius, a member of his entourage, whom Sextus had won over to his cause. Sextus then elected to go on the offensive, occupying Lampsacus, which allowed him to control the Hellespont (now the Dardanelles) with his fleet. Striking out from this base, he attacked the port of Cyzicus by land and by sea, unsuccessfully in the event. With the support of the inhabitants of the region, bled dry by Roman exactions, he then attacked Furnius's camp and went on to seize Nicomedia and Nicaea. In the meantime cavalry reinforcements had arrived from Italy (Appian calls attention to the role played by Octavia, who was then in Athens, as an intermediary); Sextus tried to buy their allegiance, but the men he sent to persuade them with gold were intercepted by the governor of Macedonia.[5] Just then, too, Sextus found himself caught in a pincer movement, seventy ships having come from Sicily, on the one hand, and, on the other, Titius's forces having recently arrived from Syria. The generals and senators who until this point had remained loyal to Sextus (among them Gaius Cassius Parmensis, the last of the Caesaricides) now rallied to Antony's side.

Pursued by Furnius, Titius, and Amyntas, Sextus burned his ships and followed an overland route into Bithynia with the intention, it was said, of seeking refuge in Armenia. Appian does not seem to believe this, but the suggestion is by no means absurd; after all, Pompey the Great had allowed Artawazd's father, Tigran, to keep his kingdom.[6] To pass from Bithynia into Parthian-controlled territory, Armenia was almost an obligatory stage, and one moreover that would have served Antony's interests by enabling him to accuse Artawazd of betrayal, which is to say of trying to sabotage his eastern campaign. In a chapter worthy of the sort of declamation taught in schools of rhetoric, Appian purports to reproduce a dialogue between Furnius and Sextus, talking to each other on opposite banks of an unidentifiable river in Bithynia or perhaps Phrygia. Furnius had summoned Sextus to hand himself over to Titius. But Sextus refused to grant this honor to an ingrate, "a man of [no] distinction at all." When Sextus tried to surrender to Furnius and Furnius refused, he said that he was prepared to hand himself over even to a non-Roman, Amyntas.

Ultimately, it was the Galatian cavalry that overcame the resistance of Sextus's troops. Sextus did in fact surrender to Amyntas, but in the end he was slain by Titius, at the age of forty.[7] Appian summarizes the matter thus: "After the death of Pompeius, Antony conducted a second campaign against Armenia, and Octavian attacked the Illyrians, who were plundering Italy, some of whom had never been subject to Rome, while others had revolted during the civil wars."[8] In other words, the only two generals whose inspirational leadership could rival that of Antony and Octavian were no longer a threat, Lepidus having been sidelined and Pompey the Younger eliminated. The stage was now set for putting Caesar's old plan into effect, only with this change in strategy: Instead of a single expedition consisting of consecutive campaigns, two fronts were to be opened at the same time.

The idea of a divide between East and West was now an accomplished fact. Hyginus Gromaticus, writing in the early second century CE, remarks in his treatise *On the Establishment of Boundaries* that "the divine Augustus, after having brought peace to the whole world, gave land to the armies who had fought under Antony and Lepidus as well as to the soldiers of his own legions, settling some in Italy, others in the provinces."[9] Hyginus is evidently referring to the beginning of the Principate, in 27, but this situation was already a reality in 36, after the political downfall of Lepidus. In agreement with Antony, who had obtained the fleet that allowed him to settle his differences with Sextus Pompey, Octavian had given up the idea of going to Africa. He therefore sent in his place Titus Statilius Taurus, suffect consul in 37, who, after having pacified Sicily, was appointed proconsul of the two African provinces. His military feats won him a triumph *ex Africa*, celebrated in 34.[10] Immediately afterward, Statilius Taurus took part in Octavian's Illyrian campaign.

We have already noted the strategic importance of the Balkans, a vulnerable region that had suffered greatly during the course of the civil war between Caesar and Pompey. And yet we do not know a great deal about the political organization of a territory inhabited by peoples without a history, as they might be spoken of today. A few years earlier, at the time of the Perusine War, Lucius Marcius Censorinus fought against the Dalmatians, and after him Asinius Pollio.[11] Appian, in the short book he devoted to Illyria, notes that the Thracian-Illyrian people living to the north of Macedonia whom the Romans called Pannonians were called Paeonians by the Greeks.[12] Our earliest information about the Pannonians comes from one of Appian's principal sources, Augustus's autobiography, a work in thirteen books that recounts his wars up until the Spanish campaign of 25.[13]

Antony had not managed to recover the standards lost by Crassus's army. Octavian, by contrast, got back the ones left to the Dalmatians by Gabinius in 48—a further proof of his military skill and energetic leadership, by contrast with Antony's commanders, whose failure was said to be a sign of his rival's indolence (*apraxia*).[14] This was an important element of Augustus's propaganda. In the *Res Gestae*, he made an inventory of the standards recovered under his Principate, from west to east: "From Spain, Gaul, and the Dalmatians, I recovered, after conquering the enemy, many military standards which had been lost by other generals. The Parthians I compelled to restore to me the spoils and standards of three Roman armies, and to seek as suppliants the friendship of the Roman people."[15] The armies humiliated by the Parthians were those of Crassus in 53, of Decidius Saxa in 40, and finally of Mark Antony in 36;

their standards were recovered in 20. We do not know who had left them behind in Spain and Gaul, but Appian (here following Augustus) says that the loss of the ones gotten back from the Dalmatians was due to Gabinius.[16]

Dalmatia, as we noted earlier, comprised a group of Illyrian chiefdoms, whereas Illyria was a Roman province, not from an administrative point of view but in the sense that it formed a quite sizable area of military operations extending from the territory of the Salassians, in the western Alps, to Scodra, the line of demarcation that marked off the zone of Octavian's authority from that of Antony, on the border of the province of Macedonia. The young Caesar could count on the support of four loyal lieutenants: Agrippa, Marcus Cicero the Younger, Statilius Taurus, and the infamous Menodorus, now a member of the Roman equestrian class and a full-fledged citizen.

Menodorus's past as a freedman of Pompey having been forgotten, he could now dine at the same table as Octavian.[17] This is the first attestation of a procedure called "restitution of birth" (*restitutio natalium*), still more extraordinary than the "restitution of juridical integrity" that a magistrate was empowered to grant a citizen who had fallen into disgrace, for example, because he had been taken prisoner. Caesar had applied this latter measure rather liberally on behalf of his protégés. His heir, perhaps by exploiting the exceptional powers granted to the triumvirs by the Lex Titia, succeeded in rehabilitating Menodorus, who, at least theoretically, could henceforth even hold a public office. After all, Menodorus had been enslaved and then freed by Pompey the Great: He well deserved the right to enjoy unrestricted liberty, which furthermore contributed to his credibility as a naval commander; that he should have been raised up to the rank of equites was justified on practical grounds, for Roman soldiers would not gladly have served under someone having the status of a freedman.

According to Appian and Cassius Dio, the strategy devised by Octavian called for multiple attacks, both by land and by sea. Some of his most trusted lieutenants were veteran admirals, such as Agrippa, Statilius, and, of course, Menodorus. The Romans had prior experience in waging war against Illyrian pirates. To control the northern Adriatic, it was necessary to engage with the fleet of the Liburnians, a people who made use of a particular type of light boat (*liburna* in Latin) that permitted rapid maneuvering among the islands off the Dalmatian coast. Appian, having considered all the information available to him regarding the history of the Balkans before Octavian's campaigns, could not conceal his puzzlement: "It seems to me . . . that there were other Illyrian peoples subject to Rome in the early period, besides the ones I have already mentioned. How this came about, I do not know. For Augustus wrote about his own achievements, not those of other people."[18]

A historical reconstruction is difficult, all the more as the situation in the Balkans had changed after the disappearance of the Dacian king Burebista from the geopolitical scene. Our only source is a passage in Strabo, who rapidly summarizes events discussed earlier in his lost historical work, without, however, supplying any chronological context. Strabo reports that Burebista was deposed by plotters before the Romans arrived to launch a campaign against him; whether he was killed, imprisoned, or banished, Strabo does not say. At the time of his death, the empire of the Getae was divided into in four parts (Strabo gives no further details), later extended to five; at all events, "such divisions are temporary . . . and vary with the times."[19]

Burebista's successors failed to maintain the unity of his empire. Without him, the Balkans no longer represented a real threat to the Roman order, but incursions by Balkan peoples were nonetheless dreaded in Illyria and Roman Macedonia. Additionally, there was a strategic problem, for Octavian's operations were directed not only against peoples who lived in lands beyond his own area of control. We do not know what orders Antony gave to the governor of Macedonia, and it is perhaps not by chance that our sources tell us nothing about his identity.

However this may be, the military campaigns of 35–33 laid the groundwork for the expansion of Roman authority to include the future provinces of Pannonia and Dalmatia. In Cisalpine Gaul, Octavian continued to apply Caesar's policy, seeking to highlight his more or less notable conquests and his victories over a number of more or less important peoples—Carni, Taurisci, Iapodes, Segestani, and so on. Were

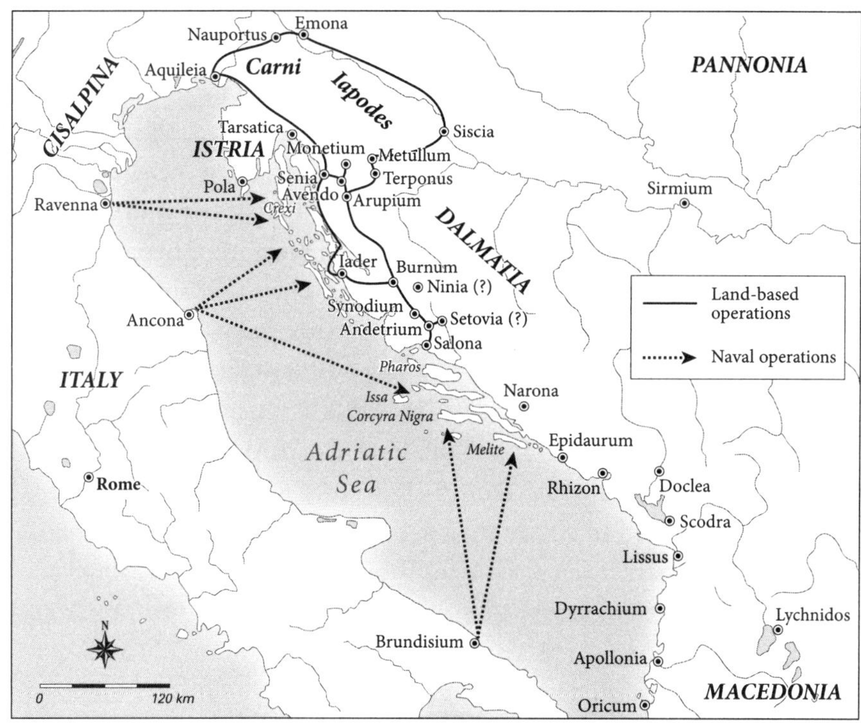

MAP 7. Octavian's Illyrian war

these peoples really a menace to the Roman order? Their movements did, of course, interfere with commerce; and while Rome could rely on the free passage of goods through certain Adriatic ports, these were enclaves within hostile Illyrian territory. Appian gives large estimates of enemy forces, but, even allowing for his tendency to exaggerate, the figure of one hundred thousand Pannonian warriors seems not unreasonable.[20] The term "Illyria" is used in Appian's account to designate the region as a whole, but he names its peoples individually. Livy says that three major ethnic groups resisted the Roman invasion: Iapodes, Dalmatians, and Pannonians.[21]

Octavian's triumph (the first of the three triumphs celebrated in 29, after the end of the civil wars) was recorded as a single victory, over Illyria/Dalmatia. Appian describes the vigor of a youthful triumvir, in contrast to Antony's indolence, ready to defend Italy against the presumed threat posed by the peoples of the Alps and the Balkans. Foremost among those "giving him particular trouble" were the Salassi, who inhabited present-day Aosta Valley in northwestern Italy and controlled considerable deposits of gold. They inhabited "the high Alps, difficult mountains to climb, with a narrow and steep path up to them. Because of this they were independent, and imposed tolls on those who traveled through their territory." Subjugated by Caesar and forced to pay tribute to Rome, the Salassians profited from the troubles that arose after the Ides of March. Prior to Octavian's campaign, this region had been under the authority of Antistius Vetus, who in 45 had fought under Caesar in Syria against Caecilius Bassus and then had gone over to the side of Caesar's assassins; after Philippi, the triumvirs pardoned him. For two years he blockaded the Salassians. Gaining control of the Alpine passes, he finally managed to cut off their supplies of salt.[22] This operation is usually said to have taken place at the beginning of Octavian's campaign, which is to say from late 35 to early 34, but nothing prevents us from assigning it an earlier date, shortly after the operations of Lucius Antonius, which had earned him a triumph in 41.

Pacification of the Alpine territories was complete only in 25, two years after Augustus had established the Principate. Strabo, describing the Alps, says that "when the Salassi were powerful, they [possessed gold mines], just as they were also masters of the passes. . . . Until quite recently, indeed, although at one time they were being warred upon by the Romans and at another were trying to bring to an end their war against the Romans, they were still powerful, and, in accordance with their custom of brigandage, inflicted much damage upon those who passed through their country over the mountains; at any rate, they extracted from Decimus Brutus, on his flight from Mutina, a toll of a drachma per man."[23]

After the departure of Antistius Vetus, the Salassians regained control of their territories. They drove out the Roman garrisons and stockpiled a good amount of salt. At the time of Octavian's campaigns, they had to confront Messalla, the former proscript who had joined the triumvirs and who played a fundamental role in the treaty of Brundisium. Strabo relates that "when Messalla was wintering near their country, he had to pay for wood, cash down, not only for his firewood but also for the elm-wood used for javelins and the wood used for gymnastic purposes. And once these men robbed even Caesar of money and threw crags upon his legions under the pretext that they were making roads or bridging rivers."[24] Finally, Messalla "starved them into submission."[25]

On the eastern front, it remained to carry on Caesar's work. For even if his commentary on the Gallic Wars is principally devoted to recounting the campaigns conducted against Gauls, Germans, and Britons, one must not underestimate the strategic importance of Cisalpine Gaul, where Caesar's lieutenants had to keep a watchful eye on the Adriatic coastal arc. In 54, Caesar had to intervene personally, but this was not enough. In 52, when he was busy fighting Vercingetorix, some barbarians (probably Iapodes) had attacked the ports of Aquileia and Tergeste, where Roman citizens had settled. This area was the least secure of the Alpine region, having to be defended against invasions by neighboring Celtic populations who coveted the merchandise coming from the eastern coast of the Adriatic, for example the excellent olive oil produced in Istria. In 51 Caesar was obliged to send a legion, commanded by Titus Labienus, "to protect the colonies of Roman citizens [in Cisalpine Gaul] and to prevent the occurrence of a disaster, through a raid of barbarians, similar to that which had occurred the summer before to the men of Tergeste, who had been overwhelmed by a sudden assault of Illyrian brigands."[26] Octavian, for his part, aspired to incorporate the Istrian peninsula into Cisalpine Gaul, now an Italian territory. An inscription due to Octavian attests the construction of ramparts and towers, a sign of the transformation of the village of Tergeste into a Roman colony. The inscription is fragmentary, but a Renaissance copy gives Octavian his full dignity; since 38 he had borne the praenomen of *imp[erator]*, to which there came to be attached the patronymic *divi filius* (son of the divinized [Caesar]).[27]

The Alps now formed the frontier of Italy, which entailed the granting of Roman citizenship to all the inhabitants of the Peninsula. Some indigenous peoples nonetheless remained second-class citizens, as in the case of the Carni and the Catali, who were assigned (*adtributi*) to Tergeste; their affiliation, dating to the city's creation as a Roman colony by Caesar, did not entitle them to exercise all the rights reserved for citizens. No doubt they participated in the productive and commercial activity of the territory, but they played a subordinate role in the process of Romanization, as did other local communities situated on the boundaries of Roman Italy. Their status seems to have approximated that of what we would call today an ethnic minority.[28] The persistence of this condition may have been a collateral effect of the establishment of the colony of Tergeste: Its occupation by Roman settlers was surely not free of violence, and it is probable that resistance was not extinguished until the arrival of Octavian's army.

If Appian is to be believed, the young Caesar attributed great importance to the campaign against Metulum, the capital of the Iapodes, whose inhabitants possessed an arsenal of Roman-made artillery, recovered from Decimus Brutus when he took flight.[29] This account seems implausible, however, since, as we have seen, Decimus Brutus had been abandoned by his men at a place on the opposite slope of the Alps from Metulum, which was located to the north of the present-day village of Josipdol, in Croatia. The city was surrounded and then taken by a Roman force commanded by Agrippa and the young Cicero; Appian also mentions a certain Lupus, Octavian's bodyguard (*sōmatophylax*), an office equivalent to the Latin "scout" (*speculator*), and another person, identified again only by his cognomen, Aviola. Another important lieutenant, Fufius Geminus, was put in charge of Pannonia at the end of the campaign.[30] And, inevitably, Menodorus.

The inhabitants of Metulum were finally induced to open their gates to the Romans, but on being ordered to lay down their arms, they shut up their wives and children in the council building before setting it on fire and then fought desperately to the end. The destruction of their capital persuaded the rest of the Iapodes to submit to Octavian. After his departure a neighboring chiefdom, the Poseni, rebelled, but the revolt was put down by Marcus Helvius, who put its leaders to death and sold the others into slavery.[31]

For the Roman legions of the period, a bloody episode such as the fall of Metulum was by no means unusual. Cicero, in 51, during his proconsulship in Cilicia, had taken the strongly fortified town of

Pindenissus after two months of laying siege to it, an operation involving a series of massacres that won him the title of *imperator*.[32] This accolade meant little or nothing to him, at least by comparison with the political feats that he hoped to accomplish and, above all, with the triumph that the Senate was to deny him. What Cicero's son, a senior officer under Octavian, did at Metulum is unknown to us. Octavian himself, in spite of his wounds (to the right leg and both his arms), "immediately scrambled onto the tower with his insignia of rank, to show that he was alive and well, and avoid any confusion arising from a report of his death."[33] This exploit attracted no notice, because even though Metulum was the largest of the Iapodes's cities, it was no less obscure than Pindenissus—this by contrast with the cities of the East, where Mark Antony sought to imitate Caesar, if not also Alexander the Great. Strabo, describing the Iapodes, says that "their cities are Metulum, Arupini, Monetium, and Vendo. Their lands are poor, the people living for the most part on spelt and millet. Their armor is Celtic, and they are tattooed like the rest of the Illyrians and the Thracians."[34]

The campaign continued in Pannonia. The Pannonians had at their disposal a rather large military force, one hundred thousand men of fighting age, but politically they were divided. According to the summary of Augustus's autobiography given by Appian, he did not fail to describe the customs of enemy peoples, possibly having been influenced in this respect by the ethnographic descriptions frequently found in Caesar's commentary on the Gallic Wars. The Pannonians did not live in towns, he reported, but in the countryside or in villages. Their communities were formed of family clans and, unlike the Gauls and the Germans, they neither recognized the authority of local chieftains nor met in representative councils. By contrast, because of their complete knowledge of the land, which was covered with forests, they were able to harass invaders using guerilla tactics.[35] Cassius Dio, who governed the region at the beginning of the third century CE, described their "barbarous" way of life:

> [The Pannonians] lead the most miserable existence of all mankind. For they are not well off as regards either soil or climate; they

> cultivate no olives and produce no wine except to a very slight extent and a wretched quality at that, since the winter is very rigorous and occupies the greater part of their year, but drink as well as eat both barley and millet. For all that they are considered the bravest of all men of whom we have knowledge; for they are very high-spirited and bloodthirsty, as men who possess nothing that makes an honorable life worthwhile. This I know not from hearsay or reading only, but I have learned it from actual experience as once their governor.[36]

They were nonetheless crushed by the Romans with brutal efficiency. Octavian conducted his operations in the land of the Segestani, a Pannonian people whose capital, Segestica (Siscia in Latin, today Sisak), was a fortified town situated at the confluence of the Kupa, Sava, and Odra Rivers. Control of this strategic position permitted the Romans to attack the Bastarnae and the Dacians, weakened by the death of Burebista. Appian, again following Augustus, says that the nobles of the city had accepted the Roman occupation and gave their children in surety, but that the common people, finding the prospect of a Roman garrison intolerable, had closed the gates of the town.

In response to this, mindful of the example of his adoptive father, the young Caesar had a bridge built over the Sava and marshaled an array of siege machines. A river battle ensued in which Menodorus met his death; the demise of an able but unreliable commander seems to have comforted the ambitious Agrippa. After a month, Segestica capitulated. According to Appian, Octavian wished to spend the winter in Rome, but that was impossible, apparently because of an attempted revolt by the Segestani and, more than this, because of the need to punish the Dalmatians.

Cassius Dio says that Octavian did in fact go back to Rome but postponed the triumph he had already been granted, and adds this very striking detail: "In emulation of his father he had set out to lead an expedition into Britain also, and had already advanced into Gaul after the winter in which Antony (for the second time) and Lucius Scribonius Libo became consuls, when some of the newly-conquered people and Dalmatians along with them rose in revolt."[37] Is this information trustworthy? Would Octavian, in his desire to imitate Caesar, really have thought to conquer Britain, something his adoptive father had not managed to do? The possibility cannot be excluded, of course, all the more as Antony, as we shall see in the next chapter, had partly compensated for his failure in the East by imprisoning Artawazd of Armenia.

While Octavian concerned himself with military affairs in the western sector of his campaign (operations in the Alps continued under the direction of Messalla), Agrippa made repairs to the Aqua Marcia aqueduct and helped to improve the drainage of the city of Rome. To implement these measures, Agrippa, already elected to the consulship in 37, had been named aedile two years later, a step backward in the senatorial sequence of offices (*cursus honorum*). An aedile, responsible for urban infrastructure and public entertainments, occupied a magistracy without *imperium* whose prerogatives were less important than those of a praetor or a consul. Nevertheless, a capable administrator was needed to handle a delicate situation that was liable to provoke unrest.

The last phase of the campaign was concentrated on the coast of Dalmatia, though no doubt it began before 33; reconstructing its history and the circumstances under which it was conducted is difficult.[38] In a place now called Tasovčići in Bosnia and Herzegovina, to the north of ancient Narona, a monument was found honoring Octavian's conquest of Sicily. The dedication, engraved on a cippus, probably dates from the beginning of the new campaign, having been composed by the brothers Gaius Papius Celsus and Marcus Papius Kanus.[39] As in the case of Salona, Narona (today the village of Vid, near Metković) seems to have been granted the status of a Roman colony toward the end of Octavian's campaigns. Be that as it may, attention had to be drawn to the young Caesar's military successes, beginning with the retaking of Sicily, and all the more as the Antonian Gaius Sosius, in celebrating his triumph in Judaea, had chosen the date of 3 September 34, the second anniversary of Agrippa's victory in the battle of Naulochus in 36.[40] Sosius also planned to construct a temple in honor of Apollo, very probably with the intent of showing that Octavian did not have a monopoly on this god.

Unlike the Pannonians, the Dalmatian peoples were united around a leader, Versus, whose troops included twelve thousand elite warriors. Versus had set up his headquarters in the stronghold of Promona, near the present-day village of Tepljuh in Croatia, "a mountainous location, surrounded by sharp ridges on all sides that look like the teeth of a saw."[41] After having driven back another army that had come to the aid of the besieged population of Promona, Octavian's men massacred a third of Versus's occupying force inside the walls of the town. The others were able to flee and managed to gain entrance to a citadel in the mountains owing to the negligence of a Roman cohort stationed at the gates. Octavian took them prisoner, then severely punished those of his soldiers who had abandoned their post, putting every tenth man to death and executing two centurions; wheat was prohibited to the remaining soldiers, who for the rest of the summer were forced to subsist on a diet of barley.

At sea, Statilius Taurus battled the Liburnian pirates off the coast of Melite (Mljet) and Corcyra Nigra (Korčula). The people of these islands were either killed or sold into slavery, and the Liburnian fleet was seized for future use by Octavian and Agrippa. On 1 January 33, Octavian, now beginning the final year of his second triumviral mandate, assumed his second consulship (with Lucius Volcacius Tullus), only then at once, the same day, to resign this office; he was replaced by Lucius Autronius (or Antonius) Paetus, the first in a series of suffect consuls appointed over the course of the year. The third and last year of the Illyrian campaign found Octavian determined to be done once and for all with the Dalmatians, now weakened by supply shortages, and to recover Gabinius's standards. In this he was wholly successful: The capitulation of the Dalmatians led to the surrender of other enemies in the region.

Gabinius's standards were to be dedicated in the Portico of Octavius (not to be confused with the Portico of Octavia), a second-century construction near the newly refurbished Circus Flaminius. Appian, echoing the Augustan account, claims that Octavian subjugated all of Illyria, but he is mistaken: Certain communities, as he himself says, were stricken by disease and therefore did not give hostages, as was customary for this type of treaty, "but they too appear to have been subdued later."[42] By contrast, Octavian took advantage of the death of Bocchus II in 33 to incorporate Mauretania (which, according to Cassius Dio, the king had bequeathed to Rome) in the provincial system, thereby further increasing his power.[43]

11

The Inimitable Life of Alexandria

ANTONY'S FAILURE in 36, by diminishing his prestige in Rome, had weakened his position in relation to Octavian. The two triumvirs nonetheless continued to respect their agreements; indeed, Octavian sent Antony troops so that he could resume his campaign in the East, where the focus of attention was now the kingdom of Artawazd of Armenia. In the meantime, Antony's relationship with Cleopatra had taken on a new dimension. The couple had formed a Dionysian religious association of so-called Inimitable Livers that sponsored refined and extravagant drinking parties in which a circle of initiates sought perfection in a sort of drunken sobriety.[1] The anecdotes that have come down to us are chiefly concerned with the intemperance of this form of elite amusement, without seeking to understand the reasons for it. The search for perfection on the part of the Inimitables was sanctioned by the code of Egyptian royalty, according to which a monarch's charisma derived from a capacity to detach himself or herself from the common run of mortals to approach the divine.

Antony was at pains to cast his indisputable enthusiasm for banquets and wine, for which his enemies had always criticized him, in a positive light. In the court life of Alexandria these symposia were endowed with a prestige far superior to what was customary in the Greek world, to the point that they constituted the supreme example of an oriental liturgy of mystical drunkenness. It is not by chance that Antony, shortly before the battle of Actium, wrote a book "on the subject of his own drunken habits" (*de sua ebrietate*).[2] His detractors in Rome made him out to be a morally dissolute lush, but in the eyes of the Alexandrians he appeared to be a new Dionysus and, above all, a new Alexander.

While officially he remained Rome's representative in the Egyptian capital, Antony affected the style of a Hellenistic sovereign. It was said that he had offered to the library of Alexandria the two hundred thousand volumes conserved in the library of Pergamum, its great rival.[3] Octavian's former teacher, Apollodorus, who in 44 had gone back to his native land, pleading old age (sixty-one years) and illness, almost surely played a role in the seizure of these volumes.[4] Antony also ordered the plunder of works of art: Three colossal statues of Zeus, Athena, and Heracles, attributed to the great sculptor Myron, were removed from the sanctuary of Hera at Samos.[5] No doubt this was by way of punishing the city, which, around 38, had requested the privilege of liberty from Octavian.[6] Here again he indulged his habitual fascination with exotic arms; often, in place of the Roman sword, he wore in his belt an oriental dagger (*akinakēs*), alluding to his expeditions beyond the Euphrates. It was also said that he called his headquarters a royal residence (*basileion*), in preference to the traditional Latin term, *praetorium*.[7]

Plutarch quotes the testimony of a contemporary Greek physician, Philotas of Amphissa, which he had from his own grandfather, Lamprias. Philotas (who was still practicing medicine at Delphi toward the end of the first century) saw the "inimitable life" as nothing more than an excuse for overeating and overdrinking, with a corresponding waste of food, to say nothing of the vain display of gold and silver on the tables.[8] But these excesses, which later were a source of inspiration to certain decadents in the modern era, represented only one aspect of what amounted to an ideological program. As he had done earlier in Rome, Antony surrounded himself with Greek intellectuals—notably the scholar Alexander Polyhistor, the historian Nicolaus of Damascus, and the orientalist Timagenes of Alexandria—who, among other things, helped to disseminate his propaganda and, along with Dellius, carried out diplomatic missions on his behalf.

Antony and Cleopatra were not the only adepts of the inimitable life; there was also the very young Antyllus (born in 47), Antony's first son with Fulvia. The boy gave dinner parties to which he invited his friends in addition to members of the court, among them Philotas, at the time his personal physician. Plutarch relates one such episode, where the young man—imitating the generosity of his father and grandfather—made a gift to Philotas of all the silver cups on the table to reward him for a witticism that reduced an annoying guest to silence.[9] According to Plutarch, Antyllus wore the *toga virilis* only after the battle of Actium, and therefore, even if he was sixteen years of age or so, he was still technically a child.[10] It was his rank that permitted him such precocious sociability, though it seems to have been in keeping with the conventions of royal life in Alexandria; indeed, at the court of a Hellenistic king, pages (who, among other duties, served the king at table) began their apprenticeship at the age of fourteen. If, like his father, Antyllus deviated from Roman ancestral custom (*mos maiorum*), it was less owing to arrogance and impiety than to an attraction to Hellenistic traditions and a desire to assimilate them.

The inimitable life was interrupted by Antony's new eastern campaign. In the winter of 35, Antony had asked for the hand of the daughter of Artawazd of Armenia, so that he might marry her to his six-year-old son, Alexander Helios, but the king refused to go to Egypt.[11] Later that year Octavia set out from Rome to the East with a convoy bearing gifts for officers and "friends," clothes for soldiers, and beasts of burden. It stopped in Athens, where Antony was preparing once more to attack the Parthians.[12] Pro-Augustan sources suggest that Cleopatra tried to prevent Antony from carrying out his plan, but the reality is that a changing geopolitical situation had made it necessary for him to profoundly modify his strategy. Antony's target was now Armenia. He concluded a new alliance with Artawazd of Media, who, in turn, took advantage of it to recover territories that formerly had belonged to Media Atropatene, having probably been conquered by the father of Artawazd of Armenia, Tigran the Great.[13]

In the spring of 34, Antony marched as far as Nicopolis, near the Armenian frontier, and sent his legate Dellius to confer with the Armenian king. When Artawazd refused his request for an interview, Antony marched onward to Artaxata, the Armenian capital, and eventually persuaded the king to come to his camp, whereupon he arrested him.

Antony then "led him around [unfettered] to the various forts where the king's treasures were deposited, in the hope that he might secure them without a struggle; for he professed to have arrested him for no other purpose than to levy tribute upon the Armenians for the safeguarding of the king and to maintain his sovereignty. [But] the keepers of the gold would pay no heed to the king, and the Armenian citizens who bore arms [which is to say the nobles] chose Artašēs [Artaxes], the eldest of his sons, king in his stead."[14] Although Artašēs tried to resist the Romans, he was soon obliged to seek refuge among the Parthians. Antony, having occupied the whole of Armenia, left behind a rather substantial garrison and sent a great amount of booty, together with the royal prisoners (Artawazd, his wife, and their other children), to Alexandria.[15]

The Romans also plundered the temple of Anahit, an Iranian deity whom the Greeks called Anaitis or Artemis Persica. Her shrine, located at Erēz (present-day Erzincan) in western Armenia, was known to the Romans; Lucullus's troops, and then Pompey's, had already visited it, but apparently without any larcenous intent.[16] According to Pliny, sacrilege in the present instance was limited to stealing the massive golden statue of the goddess. It was said that the deity blinded, paralyzed, and finally killed the soldier who was the first to profane her sanctuary, but in fact Augustus had occasion a few years later in Bononia to dine with this man, now a prosperous veteran, and learned that he was eating his meal off of one of the goddess's legs. The legionaries, ignoring the curses heaped on desecrators, had very probably divided up the spoils, with Augustus's future host, perhaps a centurion—one of the first, in other words, to storm the temple—claiming part of the goddess's statue for himself. What happened next is readily imagined: After melting down his share of the gold, the man returned home and, having taken advantage of his untraceable wealth to enter the equestrian order, found himself in a position to entertain the *princeps* with a feast worthy of his rank. Presumably he would have avoided using gold plates in order to forestall awkward comparisons with the sumptuous banquets that Antony, his former commander, held in Alexandria.[17] This, at any rate, is the Roman version of the story.

The Armenian historian Moses of Khoren (Movsēs Khorenats'i) says that Artawazd resolved to take up arms against Antony for having seized the territories of southern Armenia ("Mesopotamia"), and for this purpose raised a very large army of soldiers from Atropatene and fighters from the mountains of the Caucasus, Albania, and Iberia. In his first attack on Mesopotamia he vanquished the Roman force, but Antony reacted fiercely and, "roaring like a lion," massacred the entire enemy army and took Artawazd prisoner, offering him as a gift to Cleopatra together with the spoils of war.[18] According to Cassius Dio, Artawazd was brought to Alexandria "in golden bonds."[19]

The occupation of Armenia consolidated Antony's position in the East, where he was increasingly preoccupied by Octavian's intrigues. Since the death of Sextus Pompey, it had become clear to Antony that the marginalization of Lepidus set a dangerous precedent. Octavian, during sessions of the Senate and in public speeches, sought to defend himself, saying that "he had deposed Lepidus from office because he was abusing it, and as for what he had acquired in war, he would share it with Antony whenever Antony, on his part, should share Armenia with him."[20] Cassius Dio says that Octavian had been secretly conspiring with the Armenian king against Antony, and that he begrudged Antony his triumph.[21] Dio's opinion of Antony was influenced not only by Augustan historiography but also by his misogyny, as may readily be seen from what he has to say about Cleopatra. And yet, though he was convinced of the necessity of monarchical government, he could not help but regard matters unfavorably:

> The Roman people had been robbed of their democratic form of government, but had not become a monarchy in the strict sense of the term; Antony and Caesar still controlled affairs on an equal footing, having divided by lot most of the functions of government between them, and though nominally they considered all the rest as belonging to them in common, in reality they were trying to appropriate it to themselves, according as either of them was able to seize any advantage over the other. But afterwards, when Sextus had now perished, the Armenian king had been captured, the forces that had

> warred upon Caesar were quiet, and the Parthians were stirring up no trouble, these two turned openly against each other, and the people were actually reduced to slavery.[22]

Once more, the Parthians had realized that the Romans were going to fight among themselves yet again.

Antony, having returned to Alexandria as a conqueror, arranged for a *pompē*, a solemn royal parade that, albeit different from the Roman triumph, could be compared to it in its spectacular aspects. In order to discredit the triumvir, Plutarch says "he had triumphed," that is, he had celebrated a triumph—a typically Roman ceremony that took place only in the city of Rome.[23] Artawazd and his family were paraded in golden chains through Alexandria; to the great displeasure of Cleopatra, who treated them very harshly afterward, they refused to render homage by prostrating themselves before her.[24]

Coins were struck bearing the effigies of Antony and Cleopatra and the legend *Antoni*[*us*]. *Armenia devicta* ("Antony. Armenia has been subjugated").[25] But Octavian (who claimed a half-share of the spoils) reproached Antony for having captured Artawazd by means of a ruse, a major violation of accepted diplomatic procedure that tarnished the reputation of the Roman people.[26] In other words, though Artawazd was a prisoner, he could still be considered the legitimate king; furthermore, his children (we know the names of two sons, Tigran and Artawazd), having been brought to Rome as hostages, could be used against Artaxes. For the moment, however, Armenia, deprived of its king, had effectively come within the Roman-Egyptian orbit, destined to be ruled by Antony and Cleopatra's eldest son, Alexander Helios. Once installed on the throne, Alexander was to marry Iotapa, daughter of the king of the Medes, with Armenia Minor, bordering the Euphrates, being entrusted to Polemon. For the first time in their history, the Armenians were forced to pay tribute to Rome.[27]

After this victorious campaign, Antony seems at first glance to have adopted a still more scandalous, if not actually dishonorable, attitude toward Rome. In the autumn of 34, at a public ceremony in the gymnasium of Alexandria, he celebrated the sharing of the territories he had promised Cleopatra. Before an immense crowd, he placed "on a tribunal of silver two thrones of gold, one for himself and the other for Cleopatra," and from the height of his authority as consul proclaimed Cleopatra and her son by Caesar, Ptolemy XV (Caesarion), associate kings of Egypt, Cyprus, Libya, and Coele-Syria. His own children, Alexander Helios and Ptolemy Philadelphus, still very young, were also granted the title of king: Alexander's authority encompassed Armenia and Media, as well as "Parthia, when he [will] have subdued it"—in the context of Antony's overall plan, the invasion was only partly underway at this point; Ptolemy was granted Phoenicia, Syria, and Cilicia. The children's clothing and headgear evoked the proud displays of the Macedonian empire, Alexander being dressed as a Mede, crowned with an oriental tiara, and his brother as a Macedonian, his head covered with a *kausia* (the same beret worn by Afghans still today) surmounted by a diadem, the ornamental symbol of royalty. Cleopatra, for her part, as she was now in the habit of doing on public occasions, wore a robe sacred to Isis. "And when the boys had embraced their parents, one was given a bodyguard of Armenians, the other of Macedonians."[28]

Like Alexander before him, Antony was recasting the past in such a way as to stress the geopolitical implications of his donations. Are these to be understood as genuine gifts aimed at constituting a Roman-Egyptian federation? The detail of the dual bodyguard of Macedonians and Armenians calls our attention to the theatrical aspects of the ceremony orchestrated by the inimitable couple. The role of the Armenian soldiers, intended to protect Alexander, the newly anointed "king of kings" who now ruled over their sovereign Artawazd, as well as his homonymous rival, Artawazd of Media Atropatene, is readily seen. With regard to the Macedonian troops, the message is no less clear: The territory entrusted to his younger brother, formerly disputed by the Ptolemies and Seleucids, was a domain of the old kingdom of Alexander the Great. The Seleucid Empire being no more, the Macedonian heritage fell to Cleopatra.

The political motivations for the liaison between Antony and Cleopatra, it bears repeating, must not be underestimated. Antony needed to establish a less unilateral and, above all, less arrogant relationship that

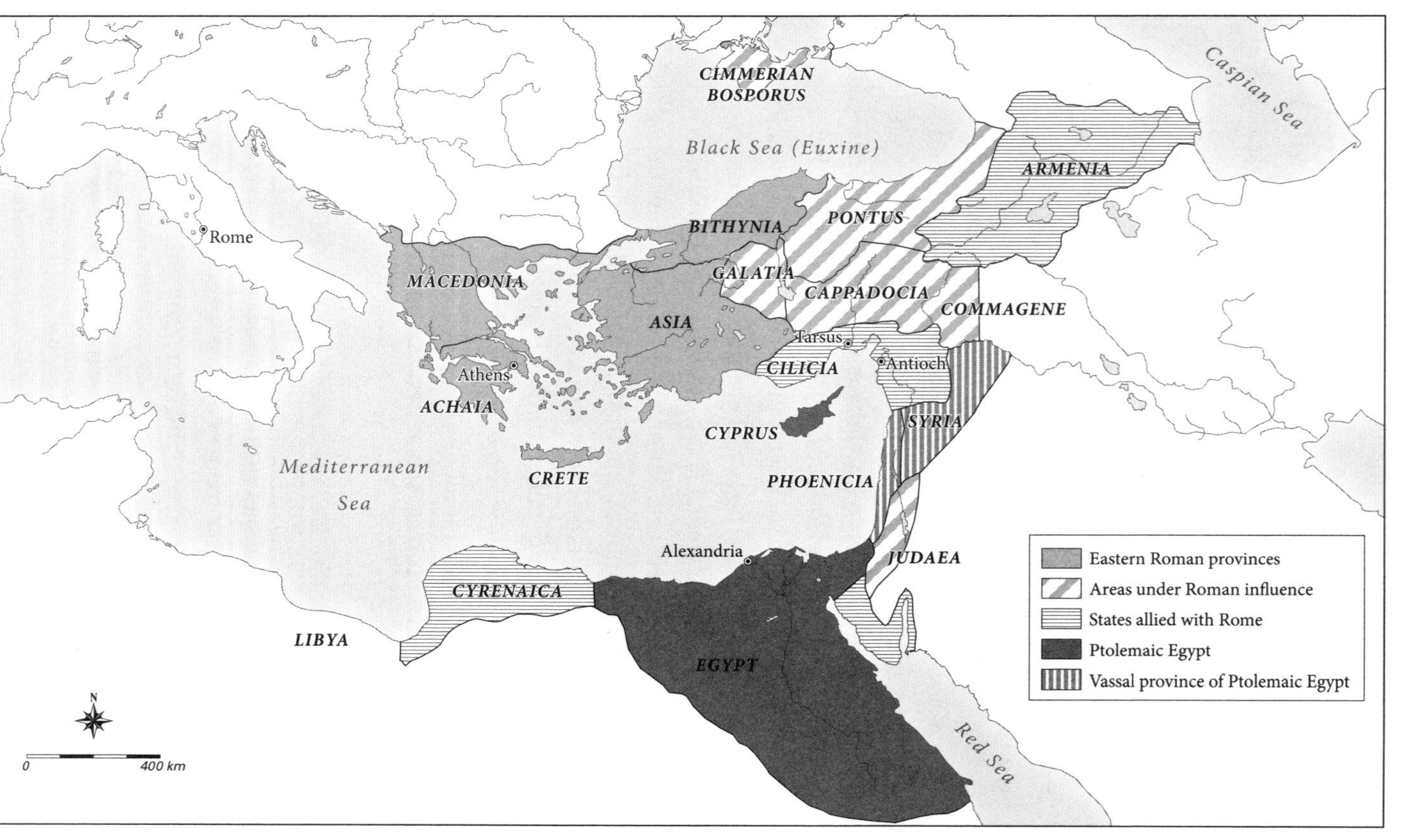

MAP 8. The donations of Alexandria

recognized the economic power of Egypt and its sovereign influence, in this way recalling the outstanding fact of the Hellenistic world, namely, the bipolarity that obtained between Rome and Alexandria for more than two centuries. Caesar had perfectly understood the necessity of reestablishing an international order founded on two centers of power, one at either end of the Mediterranean. Antony now undertook the campaign he had envisioned, with a view also to making himself Caesar's political heir (and, in Asia Minor, the heir to Pompey).

Criticism of Antony bore chiefly upon the nature of his union with Cleopatra and its legitimacy. For students of Roman law, the crux of the matter is to be found in a famous passage of Suetonius, who cites a letter to Octavian, blunt and familiar in tone, in which Antony tried to reach at least a temporary understanding, in the hope of staving off a final rupture: "What has made such a change in you? Because I am humping the queen? She is my wife."[29] The term *uxor,* meaning "wife," obviously poses a problem. To preserve its primary meaning, some commentators have interpreted it in the broader sense of "concubine." It suffices then to reformulate the last element interrogatively, so that the passage reads: "What has made such a change in you? Because I am humping the queen? Is she my wife, perhaps?"

But none of this is enough to explain why some scholars continue to take at face value arguments that originally were advanced as part of the disinformation campaign against Antony. Probably this is because Antony is difficult to like. Octavian was more ruthless, and often more cruel—this much they are prepared to admit; but Antony, they say, was principally responsible for the death of Cicero, the defender of republican values. Even today, Western historians have a hard time making sense of Antony's taste for oriental culture. Anthony Pagden, in his impressive survey of conflict between East and West since the ancient Greeks, ends up conceding that "much of Marc Antony's 'Orientalism' is the fabrication of subsequent Augustan propaganda, enthusiastically endorsed by Lucan and then by Plutarch."[30] And yet this acknowledgment is apt to go unnoticed, so often is the conventional view of the man recapitulated.

Here again it bears repeating that Antony's career cannot be understood solely in terms of his preoccupation with exotica; still less can it be explained on the basis of the scarcely provable assumption of a grandiose destiny to conquer the East. Modern historians, under the influence of the Augustan vulgate, have for the most part interpreted Antony's maneuverings as a personal initiative aimed at forming a new empire, an alternative to Rome. Like all the great *imperatores* of the Republic, he possessed a breadth of experience and enjoyed a field of action commensurate with his talents and his ambition. Nevertheless his policy did not depart in any essential respect from the one pursued by the principal architects of Roman imperialism.

In early 32, the second term of the triumvirate having just come to an end, the Roman-Egyptian alliance began to take a turn that displeased Octavian, who felt that Antony, by officially recognizing Caesar's marriage with Cleopatra, had sought to make their son ("little Caesar") the dictator's legitimate heir. However this may be, the modus vivendi between Octavian and Antony was bound sooner or later to fall apart. In the wake of the defeat of 36, the victory over Armenia had restored Antony's fortunes; going back as far as the battle of Mutina, in 43, he had demonstrated an ability to turn apparently hopeless outcomes to his advantage. Mutual recrimination between the two men intensified.

Antony complained that Octavian had failed to properly compensate him for his support of the campaign against Sextus Pompey. Octavian, for his part, appealed to patriotic feeling in disapproving of Antony's alliance with Egypt, forgetting that it was only a continuation of the policy that Caesar himself had pursued until the end of his life. Octavian's propaganda depicted Antony as a man wholly subservient to Cleopatra, his judgment impaired by wine and drugs, neglectful of his proper role as Rome's representative in Egypt, ready even to move the capital to Alexandria. Mindful of the civil war between Pompey and Caesar, Antony sought, unsuccessfully, to gain control over Italy; in the eyes of the Romans, then, he came to be seen as a tyrant and a public enemy, all the more as his oriental allies had not rendered any great assistance. The time for settling accounts had finally come. Earlier, in Rome, gangs of children, identifying themselves as Antonians and Caesarians, had clashed in the streets for two days.[31]

12

The Oath of All Italy

IN THE meantime, war not yet having broken out, Antony and Octavian sought to strengthen the resolve of their supporters by means of propaganda campaigns based on rumors and even prophecies.[1] Whereas Antony called attention to the humble origins of his rival, Octavian was concerned to deny Caesar's affair with Cleopatra and, above all, the claim that "little Caesar" was his legitimate heir.

At all events it is clear that Antony's partisans made the same error as Pompey, who, after Caesar had crossed the Rubicon in early 49, left Rome, calling upon the consuls and senators loyal to him to do the same. The consuls for 32, Sosius and Domitius Ahenobarbus, left with a group of senators (some three hundred out of a thousand), whom Antony had summoned to gather in Ephesus as a sort of alternative Senate for the purpose of declaring war against Octavian, counting on the aid of his allies: "[A]ll the kings, dynasts, tetrarchs, nations, and cities between Syria, the Maeotian Lake [present-day Sea of Azov], Armenia, and Illyria had been ordered to send or bring their equipment for the war."[2]

Then, having set out for Athens, he officially repudiated Octavia. Nothing could have suited Octavian better, for now he could accuse Antony of serving Egyptian interests; in the interval, he set about assembling the forces of Italy and the Roman West. Later, in the *Res Gestae*, recalling his declaration of war against Cleopatra and Antony, Augustus described it as a war conducted in the first place with the support of "the whole of Italy" but also of "the provinces of the Gauls, the

Spanish, Africa, Sicily, Sardinia."[3] In other words, this was a war of West against East, and all the more since, with the end of the triumvirate, the assignment of new governors, done by drawing lots, had yet to be determined.

In insisting on the central role of Italy, Octavian put pressure on the people, the army, and minor provincial notables whom he had won over in the course of directing his military operations. Virgil, in the *Georgics*, his poem on agriculture composed a few years earlier, sang the praises of the Peninsula by comparison with the opulent but dangerous regions of the East. This was the revenge of the West, and especially of Italy, whose glory knew no rivals, neither India, nor Bactria, nor Media "with its groves, land of wondrous wealth."[4]

The moment had come to throw one's support behind the man who seemed likeliest to emerge triumphant. Preparations were now being made for a war against Cleopatra, but in reality it was the civil war that was about to resume. We noted earlier that Appian's account began with the Gracchi and ended with the demise of Sextus Pompey in 35; the events of the five years following were described in the second part of this work, lost to us.[5] Historiographical tradition regards Octavian's last war as having been waged against Egypt, whereas Augustus, again in the *Res Gestae*, declares that he put an end to the civil wars.[6] What was at stake in the war against Egypt was the survival of the last Hellenistic kingdom. Victory would permit Octavian to revise history, so that Rome no longer imitated Alexander, having eradicated his political heritage.

Octavian's scheming provoked Antony to make a countermove that proved to be fatal. The pretext for declaring war had been furnished by Munatius Plancus and his nephew Titius, the assassin of Sextus Pompey. These two men, who had authenticated Antony's last will and testament, set sail to Italy and, once arrived in Rome, revealed to Octavian the contents of this document, which Antony had deposited at the Temple of Vesta. Octavian unlawfully seized the document and publicly revealed its provisions, most damagingly with regard to a future sharing of the territories of the East in the form of donations to Cleopatra's children, who, being considered to have obtained Roman citizenship, became his authentic heirs. Theoretically, these arrangements in no way encroached upon the *imperium* of Rome, for they concerned foreign kingdoms, but they permitted Octavian to malign Antony as a traitor and a renegade in the eyes of the Senate. Antony was declared a public enemy and stripped of his offices and all his property.

The opening of Antony's will, no matter that it was illegal, turned out to be effective. Some of Antony's supporters who had begun to have doubts about him following his failed campaign against the Parthians four years earlier now had an excellent reason to save face by changing sides. One such person was Messalla. Proscribed at the beginning of the triumvirate, he hastened to place his talents as a panegyrist and propagandist at Octavian's disposal. His pamphlets were devoted not only to denouncing the slanders put about by Antony, but also to casting his management of affairs in the East in an unfavorable light while at the same time drawing attention to Antony's private extravagances, such as the use of gold chamber pots.[7] Plancus, for his part, shamelessly recounted the debaucheries of the court at Alexandria, in which he himself had taken part. Tales of this sort were warmly received by the most patriotic Romans, eager to credit anything that helped to sully Antony's reputation. Even the most independent-minded senators, who until then had avoided committing themselves, now closed ranks behind Octavian, overlooking his despotic tendencies. Plancus was rewarded with a suffect consulship for 31, together with the right to share with Agrippa the sumptuous estate in the Carinae district that Antony had seized from Pompey.

That same year, the alternate Senate conferred upon Antony a third consulship and his soldiers, by acclamation, bestowed upon him the title of *imperator* for the fourth time. An army had been marshaled in Greece, where the battle of Actium would take place and the Republic would give way to the Principate. In the months leading up to the battle, Antony, based in Patras, positioned his ships along the western coast of Greece. Octavian had sought to win over local sovereigns and military leaders, such as the Thracian Rhoemetalces. According to an anecdote related by Plutarch, when Rhoemetalces, at a drinking party in which

Octavian was toasting the health of another friendly king, spoke unflatteringly of his new alliance, Octavian replied that "he loved treachery, but hated a traitor."[8]

Others rallied to Octavian out of hatred for Antony, such as Gaius Julius Eurycles of Sparta, son of a certain Lachares, whom he had executed for piracy (Lachares was probably a native of Crete).[9] Eurycles went on to become a warlord, master of the island of Cythera, granted to him by Octavian after Actium.[10] In the meantime Antony could count on a number of oriental allies. In Thrace, Sadalas remained loyal to him. Among the Anatolian kings and chieftains there were Deiotarus Philadelphus, king of Paphlagonia, Mithradates of Commagene, and the Cilician Tarcondimotus. He could also look for support to Bogud, the former king of Mauretania, who had been obliged to flee Africa. These men were at his side. Others could do no more than send him troops: the Pontic ruler Polemon, Amyntas (king of the Galatians and Lycaonians), Artawazd of Media, Herod of Judaea, and, finally, Iamblichus I of Emesa and Malichus, an Arabian chieftain.[11] Additionally, Antony was negotiating with Dicomes, king of the Getae in Thrace, also of the Dacians, "who had before this time sent envoys to Caesar; but when they obtained none of their requests, they went over to Antony."[12] Dellius and Amyntas had been dispatched to Macedonia and Thrace for the purpose of recruiting mercenaries, but Antony did not trust them; his suspicions proved to be well-founded.[13]

Octavian's principal asset was the naval expertise of Marcus Agrippa, who managed to gain control of all the key coastal military posts: Methone (where Bogud was killed), Patras, Corinth, and Leucas.[14] The tide having turned against Antony, he now found himself abandoned by his closest collaborators: Domitius Ahenobarbus (who died shortly afterward), Dellius, and Deiotarus Philadelphus, who fought in Antony's cavalry. Deiotarus, under attack by Titius and Statilius Taurus, was the first to defect, soon followed by Amyntas; Horace later recalled the "two thousand Galatians [who] turned their snorting horses [around], chanting Caesar's name."[15] In the meantime, during a naval battle against Agrippa, the loyal Tarcondimotus met his death.[16]

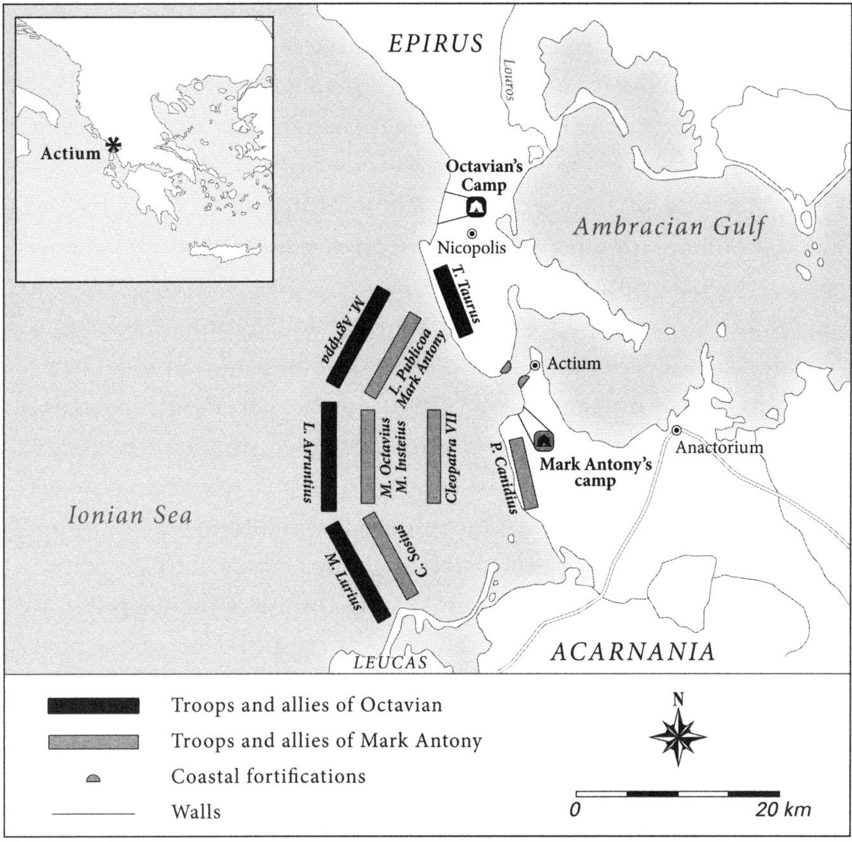

MAP 9. The battle of Actium

Antony commanded his troops more skillfully on land than on sea, but the theater of operations was probably not his to choose; moreover, both his legionaries and his foreign allies must have had grave reservations regarding the wisdom of a new civil war. Be that as it may, the decisive battle took place off the coast, with the majority of his fleet being concentrated near Actium, a promontory of Empirus at the mouth of the Ambracian Gulf, where Antony tried to break through the blockade to reach the open sea. The date was 2 September 31.

On the eve of the battle, addressing his troops, Octavian reminded them that they were going to fight "Alexandrians and Egyptians . . . slaves to a woman and not to a man."[17] When conditions were favorable, the two maritime coalitions engaged and the combat began, while their infantry looked on from the shore. The course of the battle has been recounted by Plutarch and Cassius Dio. Their accounts diverge on certain points; in respect of military tactics, neither one is at all credible. Both authors adhere to the official version promulgated by Augustus long afterward, according to which Antony's great error was to have relied on a fleet of triremes, imposing ships, but slow, and therefore vulnerable to attacks by Agrippa's lighter and faster vessels. Although historians up to the present day have accepted this version, it cannot be accurate. While the two fleets were deployed in much the same fashion, Octavian's was clearly more numerous. This being the case, the Egyptian fleet decided to withdraw—probably a strategic retreat, though according to a particularly subjective source close to Augustus, whose account was transmitted by Cassius Dio, Cleopatra had waited almost until the outcome of the battle was known before giving the signal to her ships.[18] This maneuver threw Antony's forces into confusion, though not many lives were lost as a result. Technically, Antony and Cleopatra actually won the battle of Actium, because they succeeded in breaking through the blockade and escaping unharmed. But this was the only positive aspect of an otherwise disastrous encounter. Octavian had little difficulty transforming 2 September 31 into the pivotal date that modern scholars have considered to mark the end of the Hellenistic period.

Egypt, the last of the Hellenistic kingdoms, did not in fact capitulate until the following year. Octavian welcomed into his own army Antony's surviving soldiers and, by advancing rapidly eastward, was able to take the situation in hand, undoing most of what Antony had done. Then, fearing a military revolt in Italy, he went back to Rome and granted amnesty to those of Antony's supporters who agreed to surrender on his terms. A month later he set sail once more to the East. During this time, in Alexandria, Antony and Cleopatra were taking vengeance against traitors, assassinating Artawazd of Armenia among other prisoners—to no avail. Allied sovereigns such as Herod of Judaea defected. Generals who had remained loyal were killed in action; legions, auxiliaries, and more or less regular troops laid down their arms. A company of gladiators fought valiantly but in vain, first against Amyntas's soldiers in Galatia, then in Cilicia, where Tarcondimotus's sons had changed sides after the death of their father. Earlier these gladiators had been brought to Cyzicus to train for the triumphal games that Antony was expecting to hold after defeating Octavian, but they were unable to join him on his return to Egypt. The governor of Syria, Quintus Didius, a turncoat who wished to avoid having to fight them, arranged for them to be billeted in Daphnis, a wealthy suburb of Antioch, until such time as the matter could be brought to Octavian's attention; later, during his proconsulship in Syria in 28, Messalla promised to enlist them in his legions, and once they had been dispersed to various places, they were killed, "in some convenient manner," as Cassius Dio remarks—a sign that the transfer of power does not always take place smoothly.[19]

Faced with this situation, Cleopatra sought to open negotiations, too late. Her enemies had set out for Egypt, planning to attack on two fronts. One force was led by Octavian, the other by Gaius Cornelius Gallus, a loyal lieutenant since the Perusine War who was also known as an elegiac poet, author of four books celebrating his mistress "Lycoris"—Volumnia Cytheris, the mime actress who some years before had been Antony's mistress. Gallus was to show his strategic talent in taking the Egyptian port of Paraetonium (Marsā Maṭrūḥ), west of Alexandria; Octavian, for his part, landed at Pelusium, at the eastern edge of the Delta, where Pompey, coming ashore from Anatolia, had been dishonorably struck down almost twenty years before.

After a brief resistance, Antony went away to die in Alexandria, the city he had made his home. Ordinarily loud and animated, the capital had fallen silent. But one night the calm was said to have been broken by the sound of music and dance issuing from a Dionysian procession that led out from the center of the city to the gate beyond which the enemy forces had set up an encampment. Although surely untrue, this story reflects the state of mind of the people of Alexandria, who until then had enjoyed the favor of Dionysus and now found themselves, together with Antony himself, forsaken by the god; it has come down to us in more or less fictive versions of Antony's end, and inspired the modern Alexandrian Greek poet Constantine Cavafy to write "The God Abandons Antony" (1911). Antony took his own life on 1 August 30, at the age of fifty-three years. With Octavian's victory, Rome was now the master of Egypt. Cleopatra, unable to turn the course of events in her favor, committed suicide as well, thirty days later.

Antyllus, Antony's son by Fulvia, was betrayed by his tutor Theodorus and decapitated by Roman soldiers, having pleaded in vain for Octavian's mercy at the feet of Caesar's statue. As for Caesarion, the last pharaoh-king Ptolemy XV, "he was sent by his mother, with much treasure, into India, by way of Ethiopia. There Rhodon, another tutor like Theodorus, persuaded him to go back, on the ground that [Octavian, who later usurped his Egyptian title 'Chosen of Ptah' (*Setepenptah*)], invited him to take the kingdom."[20] Instead, Octavian had him put to death. To prevent any compromising writings from being discovered, Octavian ordered that Antony's archives, including Caesar's papers, be burned. Once the news of Antony's death reached Rome, a measure of *damnatio memoriae* was voted by the Senate, and Antony's name erased from official documents and inscriptions. Public activities were prohibited on Antony's birthday (14 January), declared to be a *dies vitiosus*. Later, Antony was rehabilitated by two emperors descended from him, Gaius ("Caligula") and Claudius. At the time of his death, Antony's possessions may have included Seius's infamous and now quite elderly horse, which was part of the spoils of Philippi and seems to have survived for a number of years more, perhaps even until the taking of Alexandria. In that case it may be that Octavian, warned of the unfortunate fate that had befallen the animal's previous owners, declined to claim it as his own. He was already rich enough from so great a triumph.

After having pretended to mourn the death of his enemy (Caesar had done the same with regard to Pompey), Octavian hastened to read to his entourage the letters that they had exchanged, insisting on his own impartiality and fairness in contrast to Antony's tyrannical arrogance. Unlike Caesar, who nonetheless had granted military honors to Pompey, one Roman to another, the future Augustus continued to denigrate Antony even after his death. The defunct triumvir's supporters were driven out of the colonies in Italy and sent to the East, making room for the veterans who had fought alongside Octavian in the hope that painful memories of civil war would soon begin to fade. Antony was reviled as a renegade, devoted to the cause of the East by reason of his haughty nature and, above all, his passion for Cleopatra, on account of which he would go down in history as "him who bore the arms of a Pharian [i.e., Egyptian, from the island of Pharos] consort."[21]

Antony's Roman identity was sacrificed for reasons of state. Actium itself, officially memorialized as a victory over "the Egyptians," was to have a strong and lasting hold on the Roman imagination. Of the three triumphs accorded to Octavian by the Senate and celebrated in 29, the one over Egypt was the most lavish and the most colorful, and gave rise to a sort of Egyptomania in the figurative arts; some fifteen years later, the wealthy senator Gaius Cestius, a former praetor and associate of Agrippa, built a tomb for himself, just outside one of the gates of the city of Rome, in the form of a pyramid.

Egypt became a Roman province with a particular status. Its governor now answered directly to the *princeps* (as Octavian came to be styled in 28); the first holder of this office was Cornelius Gallus, the soldier and poet we met with a moment ago. Another poet, Horace, wrote an ode celebrating the end of the *fatale monstrum*; echoing a poem from the sixth century in which Alcaeus applauded the death of Myrsilus, tyrant of Lesbus, Horace applauded that of the infernal couple with the exclamation, "Now let the drinking begin!" (*nunc est bibendum*)—a toast that was destined to have a long life of its own.[22] He went on at once to call for dancing and the performance of a lectisternium, a propitiatory ceremony in which the gods were offered a meal (*dapes*) spread on a couch (*pulvinar*).

With the conquest of Egypt and the disappearance of the last Hellenistic kingdom, the Mediterranean became a "Roman lake"; the Arabs were later to speak of the "sea of the Romans" (*Baḥr al-Rūm*). For all that Alexandria did not lose its commercial importance. In the minds of right-minded citizens (*boni civi*), however, the victory of "all Italy" meant that the center of the world economy, and indeed of the world itself, was now Rome. In 30, after his final triumph over Antony, Octavian had coinage struck bearing the legend *Asia recepta* ("Asia [has been] recaptured)," where "Asia" generically designated the East, which

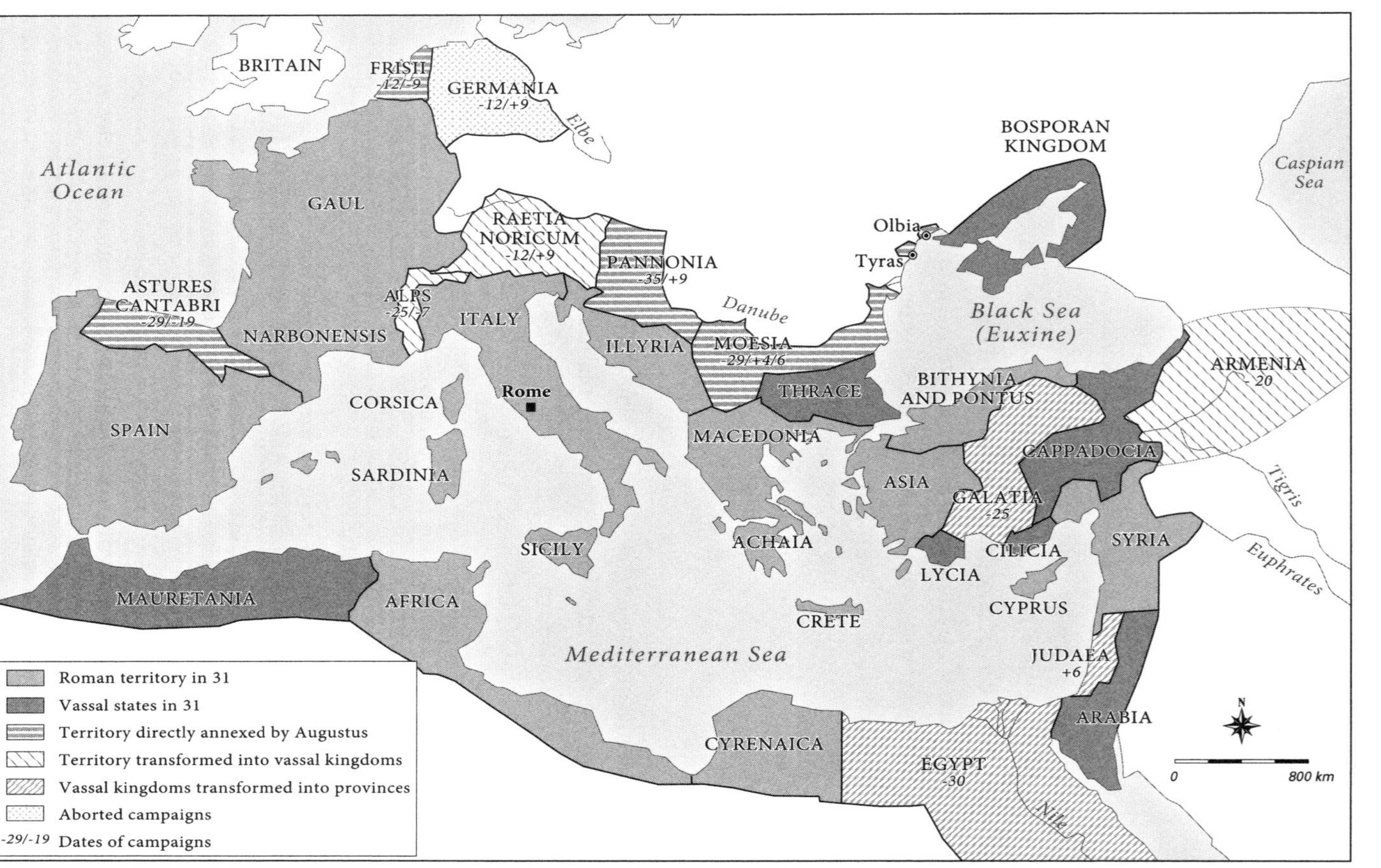

MAP 10. The Roman world under Augustus

is to say all those territories that had been usurped by Antony.[23] For the Greeks and oriental peoples, there was no difference between Antony and Octavian; both were rulers acting on behalf of the same foreign power. Officially, the battle of Actium was the culmination of a foreign war conducted against Egypt. The reality is that it was a mixture of foreign war and civil war—in short, a world war.

TRANSLATOR'S NOTE

UNLESS OTHERWISE INDICATED, for English translations of quoted passages from classical authors and other secondary references I have relied on the most recent versions published in the Loeb Classical Library, without providing further bibliographical information. For the apocryphal letter of Brutus at p. 66, I used the translation by Christopher P. Jones, "The Greek letters ascribed to Brutus," *Harvard Studies in Classical Philology* 108 (2015): 239–40; for the passage of Tacitus's *Annals* at p. 146, Anthony J. Woodman's translation (Hackett, 2004).

NOTES

Preface

1. Ampelius, *Liber memorialis*, 40.

2. John Reed, *Ten Days That Shook the World* (New York: Boni and Liveright, 1919).

3. This conception, no doubt borrowed from Livy, is found in Florus, *Epitome of Roman History* 21.12.

4. Thucydides, at the outset of the *History of the Peloponnesian War* (1.1), went so far as to speak of his subject as "great and noteworthy above all the wars that had gone before." See Luciano Canfora, *La grande guerra del Peloponneso: 447–394 a.C* (Rome: Laterza, 2024). An echo of Thucydides's phrase is found in Livy, *History of Rome* 21.21.6, in connection with the Second Punic War.

5. Florus, *Epitome of Roman History* 2.13.4. This line recalls the first verse of Lucan's poem on the war between Caesar and Pompey, where one encounters the rather odd phrase "war worse than civil" (*The Civil War* 1.1).

6. See Ronald Syme, *The Roman Revolution* (Oxford: Clarendon Press, 1939); also Giusto Traina, "Introduzione alla seconda edizione italiana," in Ronald Syme, *La rivoluzione romana* (Turin: Einaudi, 2014), vii–xxii.

7. Syme, *Roman Revolution*, 223.

8. Syme, *Roman Revolution*, 275. For Syme's judgement on Antony see Gustavo García Vivas, *Ronald Syme: El camino hasta "La Revolución Romana" (1928–1929)* (Barcelona: Edicions de la Universitat de Barcelona, 2016), 116, 125.

9. See Phiroze Vasunia, "Edward Said's *Orientalism*: A Reappraisal," in *The Routledge Handbook of Classics, Colonialism, and Postcolonial Theory*, ed. Katherine Blouin and Ben Akrigg (London: Routledge, 2025), 43.

10. See Sailakshmi Ramgopal, "Connectivity and Disconnectivity in the Roman Empire," *Journal of Roman Studies* 112 (2022): 215–35. For a broader discussion of the limits of ancient history, see Walter Scheidel, *What Is Ancient History?* (Princeton: Princeton University Press, 2025).

11. See Kristina Sessa, "Keep Late Antiquity Weird," *Studies in Late Antiquity* 6, no. 2 (2022): 213–16; also Mark Humphries, "Late Antiquity and World History: Challenging Conventional Narratives and Analyses," *Studies in Late Antiquity* 1, no. 1 (2017): 8–37.

12. See Giusto Traina, "Post-Scriptum," in *Connected Histories of the Roman Civil Wars (88–30 BCE)*, ed. David García Domínguez, Juan García González, and Federico Santangelo (Berlin: De Gruyter, 2024), 267–74.

13. See Giusto Traina, *428 AD: An Ordinary Year at the End of the Roman Empire* (Princeton: Princeton University Press, 2009); also the updated French edition, *428, une année ordinaire à la fin de l'Empire romain* (Paris: Fayard, 2020).

14. See Sanjay Subrahmanyam, "Connected Histories: Notes Towards a Reconfiguration of Early Modern Eurasia," *Modern Asian Studies* 31, no. 3 (1997): 735–62; also idem, *Connected History: Essays and Arguments*, expanded ed. (London: Verso Books, 2022). See too Romain Bertrand, "Histoire globale, histoires connectées: Un 'tournant' historiographique?" in *Le "tournant global" des sciences sociales*, ed. Alan Caillé and Stéphane Dufoix (Paris: La Découverte, 2013), 44–66.

Introduction: Caesar's Last Campaign

1. Nicolaus of Damascus, *Life of Augustus* 95 [= M 101 XXVI]. [Here and below at n. 62, English version from the volume edited and translated by Mark Toher (Cambridge: Cambridge University Press, 2017).—Trans.]

2. See Plutarch, *Life of Crassus* 33.1–7.

3. See Cassius Dio, *Roman History* 40.28.4.

4. See Caesar, *The Gallic War* 8.54–55.

5. Justin, *Epitome of the Philippic History of Pompeius Trogus* 42.4.6.

6. See Cassius Dio, *Roman History* 41.55.3.

7. See Cassius Dio, *Roman History* 42.2.5.

8. See Quintilian, *Institutes of Oratory* 5.8.33.

9. See Cassius Dio, *Roman History* 41.63.1.

10. See Pseudo-Caesar, *The Alexandrian War* 65.

11. See Caesar, *Civil War* 3.31–33 (Metellus Scipio continued to hold sway in the province of Asia) and Appian, *The Civil Wars* 3.77.312, 4.58.250.

12. Quoted in Cassius Dio, *Roman History* 45.29.4. Earlier (at 44.46.3) Dio had said that the expedition of 47 was postponed on account of the disorder in Rome, but he attributed the idea to Antony, who had mentioned it, implicitly accusing Dolabella, in his speech at Caesar's funeral.

13. See Suetonius, *Life of Julius Caesar* 37.4; also Florus, *Epitome of Roman History* 2.13.88.

14. Caesar refrained from celebrating his victories in the civil wars, limiting the depiction of his Roman adversaries to statues and paintings, while avoiding all reference to Pompey. See Appian, *The Civil Wars* 2.101.418–19.

15. Suetonius, *Life of Julius Caesar* 39.1, 39.4.

16. See Pliny, *Natural History* 8.22; also Suetonius, *Life of Julius Caesar*, 39.2–3.

17. Cassius Dio, *Roman History* 43.23.1–2; regarding Pompey's entertainments, see Pliny, *Natural History* 8.71–72.

18. See Cassius Dio, *Roman History* 47.26.6.

19. See Sallust, *Fragments of the Histories* 1.5.2.

20. See Cicero, *Letters to Atticus* 14.9.3.

21. Cassius Dio, *Roman History* 43.51.1.

22. Plutarch, *Life of Crassus*, 16.2.

23. See Cornelius Nepos, cited by Pomponius Mela 3.45; also Pliny, *Natural History* 2.170.

24. Strabo, *Geography* 3.5.3.

25. Suetonius, *Life of Julius Caesar* 7.1.

26. See Suetonius, *Life of Julius Caesar* 47.

27. See Pliny, *Natural History* 37.12.

28. Artemidorus devotes an entire chapter to this subject in the *Oneirocritica* (1.79).

29. Suetonius, *Life of Julius Caesar* 7.2, and Cassius Dio, *Roman History* 37.52.2. According to Plutarch, *Life of Julius Caesar* 32.4, he had the same dream before crossing the Rubicon in early 49.

30. See Suetonius, *Life of Julius Caesar* 52.1; also Appian, *The Civil Wars* 2.90.378–79 (where he promised to recount the episode in a book on Egypt that he never got around to writing).

31. See Nicolaus of Damascus, *Life of Augustus* 68 [= M 101 XX]; also Suetonius, *Life of Julius Caesar* 79.3.

32. See Suetonius, *Life of Julius Caesar* 52.2.

33. See Cicero, *Letters to Atticus* 14.8.

34. See Suetonius, *Life of Julius Caesar* 52.1.

35. See Velleius Paterculus, *Compendium of the History of Rome* 2.59.4; also Suetonius, *Life of Augustus* 8.2 and Cassius Dio, *Roman History* 45.3.1 (who mentions only the Parthians).

36. See Appian, *The Civil Wars* 2.110.460.

37. Appian, *The Civil Wars* 3.24.92.

38. *Prologues to the Philippic History of Trogus* 3.

39. See Strabo, *Geography* 7.3.11.

40. See Strabo, *Geography* 7.3.13.

41. See Cassius Dio, *Roman History* 38.10.2–3.

42. See Strabo, *Geography* 7.3.5.

43. Jordanes, *Getica* 67–68.

44. See *Inscriptiones Graecae in Bulgaria repertae* 1.13.

45. Appian, *The Civil Wars* 2.51.211.

46. Cassius Dio, *Roman History* 44.44.1.

47. Lucan, *Civil War* 7:272–73.

48. See Caesar, *Civil War* 3.4.3, 3.95. On the pardoning of Sadalas see Cassius Dio, *Roman History* 43.61.1.

49. Appian, *The Civil Wars* 2.74.308.

50. See Cicero, *Letters to Friends* 5.10a.3.

51. Caesar, *The Alexandrian War* 78.2.

52. See Strabo, *Geography* 13.4.3; also 11.2.11. See too Appian, *Mithridatic Wars* 120 and Cassius Dio, *Roman History* 42.48.4.

53. Suetonius, *Life of Julius Caesar* 44.4.

54. See Strabo, *Geography* 7.5.9 [= Theopompus, BNJ 115 F129].

55. Appian, *The Civil Wars* 2.110.459.

56. Suetonius, *Life of Julius Caesar* 44.1, 44.3.

57. Plutarch, *Life of Caesar* 58.6–7. It is difficult to say whether we are dealing here with Caesar's own propagandistic propensity to exaggeration, or the flattering assurances of his entourage, or an a posteriori manipulation of the ideology subsequently associated with the

conquests of Trajan, who was making plans for his own eastern campaign around 110 CE, when Plutarch was composing his *Parallel Lives*.

58. See Cicero, *Letters to Atticus* 15.4.3.

59. Nicolaus of Damascus, *Life of Augustus* 80 [= M 101 XXII].

60. See Suetonius, *Life of Julius Caesar* 79.4; also Appian, *The Civil Wars* 2.110.460 and Cassius Dio, *Roman History* 44.15.3.

61. See Plutarch, *Life of Caesar* 64.3.

Chapter One: Apollo vs Dionysus

1. See Julius Honorius, *Cosmographia*, 1*. Didymus, not to be confused with the celebrated Greek scholar to whom the epithet *chalkenteros* ("bronze guts") was attached, was the author of a work on metrology, the few fragments of which are known to us show the influence of the manuscript tradition of Hero, the famous Alexandrian mathematician and engineer of the first century BCE.

2. See Plutarch, *Life of Pompey* 45.5.

3. See Cicero, *On the Responses of the Haruspices* 14.31.

4. See Varro, *On Agriculture* 1.2.1–3.

5. See Velleius Paterculus, *Compendium of Roman History* 2.59.4; also Suetonius, *Life of Augustus* 8.2 and Cassius Dio, *Roman History* 45.3.1.

6. See Strabo, *Geography* 14.1.48.

7. Cicero, *Philippics* 11.11.2.

8. See Suetonius, *Life of Augustus* 89.1; also Nicolaus of Damascus, *Life of Augustus* 37 [= M 101 XVI].

9. See Velleius Paterculus, *Compendium of Roman History* 2.59.

10. As a consequence, Cratippus had taken the *nomen* of his sponsor, Tullius; a certain M. Tullius Cratippus, no doubt his son, is mentioned by a Latin inscription from Pergamum (*Corpus inscriptionum Latinarum* 3.399).

11. See Plutarch, *Life of Cicero* 24.7.

12. On the early military exploits of Marcus junior, see Cicero, *On Duties* 2.45.

13. See Nicolaus of Damascus, *Life of Augustus* 41 [= M 101 XVI].

14. The lines of demarcation among provinces in the eastern Balkans during this period were rather flexible, all the more as the term *provincia*, applied to territories that had yet to be pacified, retained the sense of a zone of military operations.

15. See Cicero, *Letters to Friends* 5.10a.3.

16. See Cicero, *On Divination* 2.89.

17. Suetonius, *Life of Augustus* 94.5.

18. Suetonius, *Life of Augustus*, 94.12.

19. See Nicolaus of Damascus, *Life of Augustus* 40 [= M 101 XVI].

20. See Velleius Paterculus, *Compendium of Roman History* 2.59.5; also Nicolaus of Damascus, *Life of Augustus* 41 [= M 101 XVI].

21. Augustus, *Res Gestae Divi Augusti* 1.1.

22. See Suetonius, *Life of Augustus* 89.1.

23. Cicero, *Philippics* 1.1.

24. See Josephus, *The Jewish War* 1.180–82.

25. See Frontinus, *Stratagems* 2.5.35.

26. See Cicero, *Letters to Atticus* 5.20.3. In this letter Cicero congratulates himself on having terrorized the Parthians, thereby giving encouragement to Cassius.

27. See Cicero, *Letters to Atticus* 15.11.1.

28. See Suetonius, *Life of Julius Caesar* 72.3; also Cassius Dio, *Roman History* 44.19.5. There is no ancient evidence of a Latin rendering; the famous "et tu, Brute?" is due to Shakespeare, *Julius Caesar* 3.1.77.

29. Pliny, *Natural History* 2.23.6.

30. Cicero, *Letters to Friends* 10.1.1.

31. See Cicero, *Philippics* 2.58.

32. Cicero, *Philippics* 2.112; see also 2.6 and 13.18.

33. See Cicero, *Philippics* 8.24.

34. Probably it was Cicero himself who chose to publish the speeches under the title by which they came to be known, echoing Demosthenes, author of four speeches (later named *Philippikà* by Alexandrian grammarians) in which the great orator, between 351 and 340, had exhorted the Greeks to rebel against the imperialist ambitions of Philip of Macedon.

35. Athenaeus, *The Learned Banqueters* 152f–53b [= Posidonius, *FGrHist* 87 f.5 = EK 57 = Theiler 114].

36. See Cicero, *Letters to Atticus* 14.12.1; also *Philippics* 2.95.

37. See Cicero, *Letters to Atticus* 6.1.14; also *Philippics* 11.33.

38. See Varro, *On Agriculture* 1.1.10 and Cicero, *Pro rege Deiotaro* 27.

39. See Appian, *The Civil Wars* 3.24.92.

40. See Cassius Dio, *Roman History* 45.9.3.

41. See Appian, *The Civil Wars* 3.25.96.

42. See Velleius Paterculus, *Compendium of Roman History* 2.69.3.

43. See Suetonius, *Life of Augustus* 86.5; also Plutarch, *Life of Antony* 1.2.

44. Cassius Dio, *Roman History* 45.11.1; see also Thucydides, *History of the Peloponnesian War* 1.66.

45. See Cicero, *Letters to Atticus* 16.15.3.

46. Cicero, *Letters to Friends* 11.4; on the Inalpini, see Pliny, *Natural History* 3.47.

47. Cicero, *Letters to Friends* 11.5.

Chapter Two: Western Warlords

1. See Pseudo-Caesar, *The Spanish War* 39.3.

2. See Appian, *The Civil Wars* 5.143.596.

3. Cicero, *De provinciis consularibus* 31.

4. Velleius Paterculus, *Compendium of Roman History* 2.73.1.

5. Florus, *Epitome of Roman History* 2.18.2.

6. See Appian, *The Civil Wars* 2.105.439–106.440.

7. See Cicero, *Letters to Friends* 11.1.4.

8. Cicero, *Letters to Atticus* 15.29.1 and 16.1.4; see also Appian, *The Civil Wars* 3.4.11.

9. See Cicero, *Letters to Atticus* 14.13.2.

10. See Cicero, *Letters to Atticus* 16.4.2.

11. See Appian, *The Civil Wars* 4.8.34; also Cicero, *Letters to Atticus* 15.17.1.

12. See Cicero, *Letters to Atticus* 14.1.2, 14.9.6.

13. Strabo, *Geography* 4.1.5.

14. Valerius Maximus, *Memorable Doings and Sayings* 2.6.7.

15. See Justin, *Epitome of Pompeius Trogus* 43.5.11; also Caesar, *Gallic War* 5.36.1.

16. See Appian, *The Civil Wars* 4.84.353.

17. See Cassius Dio, *Roman History* 45.10.6.

18. See Cassius Dio, *Roman History* 46.50.4–5.

19. See Appian, *The Civil Wars* 4.54.234.

20. On the rebuilding of Carthage see Appian, *Roman History* 8.1.36; also Solinus, *Collectanea Rerum Mirabilium* 27.11.

21. See Suetonius, *Life of Julius Caesar* 24.2.

22. See *Corpus inscriptionum Latinarum,* 9.1460. Valerius's Iranian cognomen, recalling the founder of the Parthian royal dynasty of this name, seems to associate him with Antony's campaigns in the East, however.

23. See Cicero, *Philippics* 5.46; also Cassius Dio, *Roman History* 45.13.4, 42.1; 46.37.2.

24. Ovid, *Tristia* 4.10.6.

25. See Frontinus, *Stratagems* 1.7.5.

26. Cicero, *Letters to Friends* 10.28, 12.4.

27. Letter from Decimus Brutus dated 5 May 43, in Cicero, *Letters to Friends* 11.10.

28. See Suetonius, *Life of Augustus* 12.

29. See Cicero, *Philippics* 14.10.28.

30. See Nicolaus of Damascus, *Life of Augustus* 112 [= M 101 XXVIII].

31. Cicero, *Letters to Brutus* 1.10.3 (mid-June 43).

32. See Livy, *History of Rome: Summaries* 120.2; also Orosius, *Histories Against the Pagans* 6.18. Livy says that Camilus was a Sequanus, a tribal name that is attested chiefly among the Helvetians; see *Corpus inscriptionum Latinarum,* 13. 5063, 5093, 5094, 5110.

33. See Appian, *The Civil Wars* 3:98.405–7.

34. See Cicero, *Letters to Friends* 10.33.4.

35. See Cassius Dio, *Roman History* 47.8.3.

36. See Plutarch, *Life of Crassus* 31.6; and 32.1.

37. See Xenophon, *Anabasis* 1.10.1.

Chapter Three: The Wars of the Tyrannicides

1. See Cicero, *Letters to Atticus* 15.11.2.

2. See Florus, *Epitome of Roman History* 2.17.4, and Appian, *The Civil Wars* 3.2.5; also Cassius Dio, *Roman History* 46.39.3.

3. See Cassius Dio, *Roman History* 45.15.2.

4. See Valerius Maximus, *Memorable Sayings and Doings* 2.10, ext.

5. See Plutarch, *Life of Brutus* 2.4; also Quintilian, *The Orator's Education* 10.6.4.

6. Appian, *The Civil Wars* 2.88.368.

7. See Aulus Gellius, *Attic Nights* 3.9.4.

8. See *Supplementum epigraphicum Graecum* 17.75.

9. See *Inscriptions de Délos* 1622; also *Inscriptiones Graecae* 7.383.

10. See Plutarch, *Life of Brutus* 24.3.

11. See Seneca, *Epistles* 95.45; also Priscian, *Institutiones grammaticae* 6.7.

12. See Plutarch, *Life of Brutus* 24.1; also Cassius Dio, *Roman History* 47.21.3.

13. See Caesar, *Civil War* 3.4.2.

14. See Plutarch, *Life of Caesar* 24; also Appian, *Civil Wars* 2.88.368.

15. See Appian, *Civil Wars* 4.88.373.

16. See Cicero, *Philippics* 10.4–6; Appian, *The Illyrian Wars* 13.

17. See Appian, *Civil Wars* 3.79.324, 4.75.318.

18. See Josephus, *The Jewish War* 1.216–17; also *Jewish Antiquities* 14:268–70.

19. See Josephus, *Jewish Antiquities* 14.144, 14.188.

20. See Plutarch, *Life of Antony* 3.1.

21. See Cassius Dio, *Roman History* 40.20.2, 47.27.3.

22. See Lucan, *The Civil War* 7.230.

23. See Caesar, *The African War* 20.1.

24. See Strabo, *Geography* 16.2.10.

25. See Cassius Dio, *Roman History* 47.27.4–5.

26. See Appian, *Civil Wars* 3.77.316.

27. See Appian, *Civil Wars* 3.78.317–18, 4.59.255–56.

28. See Cicero, *Letters to Friends* 12.12.3.

29. Cassius Dio, *Roman History* 47.28.5; Josephus, *The Jewish War* 1.219; also *Jewish Antiquities* 14.271.

30. See Josephus, *Jewish Antiquities* 14.276–80; at *The Jewish War* 1.225 he speaks of all of Syria.

31. See Aulus Gellius, *Attic Nights* 3.9.4.

32. See Cicero, *Philippics* 11.4.

33. See Appian, *Civil Wars* 4.60.258; also the letters from P. Lentulus Spinther in Cicero, *Letters to Friends* 12.14.4, 12.15.7.

34. See Cicero, *Letters to Friends* 12.14.1–2.

35. See Caesar, *Civil War* 3.102.7.

36. Appian, *Civil Wars* 4.64.273.

37. See Cassius Dio, *Roman History* 47.26.2.

38. Cicero, *Letters to Friends* 15.1.2.

39. See Lucan, *The Civil War* 9.219–25.

40. Pseudo-Caesar, *The Alexandrian War* 66.

41. Strabo, *Geography* 15.5.18.

42. See Cassius Dio, *Roman History* 47.31.1–2.

43. See Pliny, *Natural History* 5.18, where it is described as "a free town."

44. See P. Lentulus Spinther in Cicero, *Letters to Friends* 12.15.7; also 12.14.4.

45. See Appian, *Civil Wars* 4.61.261–62.

46. See Appian, *Civil Wars* 4.63; also Cassius Dio, *Roman History* 47.30.3.
47. See Appian, *Civil Wars* 4.62.267.
48. See Aulus Gellius, *Attic Nights* 3.9.5.
49. See Appian, *Civil Wars* 5.7.30.
50. See Josephus, *Jewish Antiquities* 14.304–23.
51. Appian, *Civil Wars* 4.52.224–25.
52. See Cassius Dio, *Roman History* 47.24.3.
53. See Appian, *Civil Wars* 4.75.320.
54. See Cicero, *Letters to Atticus* 6.1, 6.3.
55. See Cassius Dio, *Roman History* 47.37.1.
56. See Cassius Dio, *Roman History*, 47.33.1, 47.33.4.
57. See Plutarch, *Life of Brutus* 28.1.
58. Appian, *Civil Wars* 4.5.18.
59. See Appian, *Civil Wars*, 4.63.269.

Chapter Four: Avenging Caesar

1. See Pliny, *Natural History* 9.116.
2. See Cassius Dio, *Roman History* 46.48.4, 48.17.3.
3. See Appian, *Civil Wars* 4.36.151; also Cassius Dio, *Roman History* 47.12.3.
4. Pliny refers to Menas and Menecrates as freedmen; see *Natural History* 35.43.
5. See Appian, *Civil Wars* 5.67.280.
6. Orosius, *Histories Against the Pagans* 6.18.19.
7. See Appian, *Civil Wars* 4.36.152.
8. See Appian, *Civil Wars*, 4.25.104–6.
9. See Cicero, *Letters to Atticus* 15.17.2; also Cicero, *Pro Ligario* 7.22.
10. See Appian, *Civil Wars* 4.53.226–57.243.
11. See Appian, *Civil Wars*, 4.52.224.
12. See the *Tabula triumphorum Barberiniana* (*Inscriptiones Italiae*, 13.36.7): *L*[*ucius*] *Antonius ex Alpibus K*[*alendis*] *Ian*[*uariis*] *triumpavi*[*t*].
13. See Cassius Dio, *Roman History* 48.18.1–19.1. Octavian, suffering from dropsy, did not take part in these operations; see Pliny, *Natural History* 7.148.
14. See *Corpus inscriptionum Latinarum*, 10.8337a–g.
15. See Appian, *Civil Wars* 4.86.362.
16. See Appian, *Civil Wars* 4.70.288.
17. See Appian, *Civil Wars* 4.66.279–74.313; also Cassius Dio, *Roman History* 47.33.3–4.
18. See Plutarch, *Life of Brutus* 30.4–32.4; also Appian, *Civil Wars* 4.80.335–37.
19. See Plutarch, *Life of Brutus* 33; also Appian, *Civil Wars* 2.90.377.
20. Appian, *Civil Wars* 2.82.346; on the death of L. Domitius Ahenobarbus, see Cicero, *Philippics* 2.29.2.
21. Cicero, *Philippics* 11.12; see also 13.27 and 14.10.
22. See Appian, *Civil Wars* 4.87.369.
23. Appian, *Civil Wars*, 4.104.437.

24. Appian, *Civil Wars,* 4.8.35.

25. See Aulus Gellius, *Attic Nights* 3.9.6.

26. See Cassius Dio, *Roman History* 48.24.5–6.

27. See Appian, *Civil Wars* 4.88.373.

28. See Plutarch, *Life of Brutus* 49.4.

29. See Appian, *Civil Wars* 4.82.345.

30. See Appian, *Civil Wars* 4.90.379.

31. See Appian, *Civil Wars* 4.134.566; also Plutarch, *Life of Brutus* 48.5.

32. See Plutarch, *Life of Brutus* 46.1–2; also Appian, *Civil Wars* 4.118.498.

33. See Augustus, *Res Gestae Divi Augusti* 2.1.

34. See Suetonius, *Life of Augustus* 13.1–2; also Cassius Dio, *Roman History* 47.49.2.

35. Suetonius, *Life of Augustus* 27.4.

36. See Appian, *Civil Wars* 4.38.160, 136.575.

37. See Appian, *Civil Wars,* 4.138.580.

38. Appian, *Civil Wars* 4.136.573.

Chapter Five: Between Concord and Discord

1. Cassius Dio, *Roman History* 48.1.2–3.

2. See Aulus Gellius, *Attic Nights* 14.7.5.

3. The part of Gaul lying to the north of the Alps was also known as Gallia Comata in view of the fact that most of its inhabitants let their hair grow long; see Cassius Dio, *Roman History* 46.55.4.

4. Cassius Dio, *Roman History,* 48.4.2–6.

5. See Appian, *Civil Wars* 5.12.47; also Cassius Dio, *Roman History* 48.1.3.

6. See Appian, *Civil Wars* 4.115.480.

7. Plutarch, *Life of Pompey* 70.1–3.

8. See Appian, *Civil Wars* 4.36.151; also Cassius Dio, *Roman History* 47.12.3.

9. See Velleius Paterculus, *Compendium of Roman History* 2.72.3.

10. Cassius Dio, *Roman History* 48.24.1–2.

11. See Josephus, *The Jewish War* 1.244; also Plutarch, *Life of Antony* 3.

12. Mario Attilio Levi, *Ottaviano capoparte: Storia politica di Roma durante le ultime lotte di supremazia,* 2 vols. (Florence: La Nuova Italia, 1933), 1:147–48.

13. See *Inscriptiones Graecae* 2.1039.57.

14. See Seneca the Elder, *Suasoriae* 1.6–7.

15. See Appian, *Civil Wars* 5.7.29–30.

16. See *Supplementum Epigraphicum Graecum* 38.856.

17. See Cassius Dio, *Roman History* 48.43.3.

18. See Appian, *Civil Wars* 5.4.15.

19. See Josephus, *Jewish Antiquities* 15.89; also Appian, *Civil Wars* 5.9.35–36 (though here the temple is said to have been in Miletus).

20. Pliny, *Natural History* 5.111; see also Barclay V. Head, *Historia numorum: A Manual of Greek Numismatics* (Oxford: Oxford University Press, 1911), 564.

21. See Socrates of Rhodes, BNJ 192, fr. 2 [= Athenaeus, *Learned Banqueters* 4.29.148b–c].
22. See Plutarch, *Life of Antony* 33.4.
23. See *Inscriptiones Graecae* 2.1043.
24. See Pliny, *Natural History* 35.200.
25. Plutarch, *Life of Antony* 24.1–2.
26. See Appian, *Civil Wars* 5.7.31.
27. See Plutarch, *Life of Antony* 61.1.
28. Quoted in Martial, *Epigrams* 11.20.
29. Plutarch, *Life of Antony* 25.1.
30. See Appian, *Civil Wars* 5.7.30.
31. Plutarch, *Life of Antony* 27.1, 26.1–3.
32. See Socrates of Rhodes, BNJ 192, fr. 2 [= Athenaeus, *Learned Banqueters* 4.29.147e–148b].
33. Lucan, *The Civil War* 10.169.
34. See Appian, *Civil Wars* 5.9.36; also Josephus, *Jewish Antiquities* 15.89.
35. Josephus, *Jewish Antiquities* 14.320–23.
36. See Appian, *Civil Wars* 5.9.37–38.

Chapter Six: The Advent of a Golden Age

1. Ennius, *Annals* 7, fr. 24 Skutch; see also Livy, *History of Rome* 22.10.9–10.
2. See Varro, *On Agriculture* 1.1.4.
3. See Suetonius, *Life of Augustus* 70.1–2.
4. See Appian, *Civil Wars* 5.3.12.
5. See Appian, *Civil Wars* 5.20.80.
6. Strabo, *Geography* 17.3.5.
7. See Appian, *Civil Wars* 5.26.103.
8. See Strabo, *Geography* 3.5.3; also Porphyry, *On Abstinence* 1.25.
9. Appian, *Civil Wars* 5.26.102.
10. See Cassius Dio, *Roman History* 48.23.3.
11. Appian, *Civil Wars* 5.11.43–44.
12. Plutarch, *Life of Antony* 27.3–4.
13. See Valerius Maximus, *Memorable Doings and Sayings* 8.7, ext. 16.
14. See Appian, *Civil Wars* 5.52.217; also Cassius Dio, *Roman History* 48.15.2.
15. See Appian, *Civil Wars* 5.52.218.
16. See Appian, *Civil Wars* 5.55.230.
17. See Appian, *Civil Wars* 5.66.277; also Cassius Dio, *Roman History* 48.30.7–8.
18. See Appian, *Civil Wars* 5.60.255.
19. See Appian, *Civil Wars* 5.66.278–79.
20. See Servius Danielis, *Commentary on Virgil's "Bucolics"* 8.12; and Appian, *Civil Wars* 5.55.234.
21. Cassius Dio, *Roman History* 48.30.1.
22. See Josephus, *Jewish Antiquities* 14.376–83, and *The Jewish War* 1.279–83.

23. See Appian, *Civil Wars* 5.65.274; also Cassius Dio, *Roman History* 48.20.3–4.

24. Appian, *Civil Wars* 5.92.386.

25. See Plutarch, *Life of Antony* 31.3.

26. See Josephus, *Jewish Antiquities* 14.385–89, and *The Jewish War* 1.284–85.

27. Josephus, *Jewish Antiquities* 14.384.

28. See Velleius Paterculus, *Compendium of Roman History* 2.78.3.

29. See Appian, *Civil Wars* 5.75.321; also 140.584.

30. See Cassius Dio, *Roman History* 48.31.1–3; also Appian, *Civil Wars* 5.67.280.

31. See Cassius Dio, *Roman History* 48.30.3.

32. Appian, *Civil Wars* 5.72.304–5.

33. See Appian, *Civil Wars* 5.77.336–27.

34. See Horace, *Epodes* 4.18–19.

35. See Appian, *Civil Wars* 5.75.318.

36. Cassius Dio, *Roman History* 48.39.1.

37. See Appian, *Civil Wars* 5.75.320; also Cassius Dio, *Roman History* 48.41.7.

38. See Jeanne Robert and Louis Robert, *Bulletin épigraphique* 1948, nos. 284–85.

39. See Cassius Dio, *Roman History* 48.39.2.

40. Appian, *Civil Wars* 5.76.322–23

Chapter Seven: The *Imperium* Strikes Back

1. See Cassius Dio, *Roman History* 48.33.5.

2. See Appian, *Civil Wars* 5.75.319.

3. See Cassius Dio, *Roman History* 48.40.6.

4. See Cassius Dio, *Roman History* 48.41.5.

5. See Plutarch, *Life of Crassus* 33.2.

6. See Plutarch, *Life of Crassus* 33.3.

7. See Cicero, *Letters to Atticus* 5.21.2.

8. Cassius Dio, *Roman History* 48.24.7–8. The term *ethnos* is used ambiguously, signifying both "people" and "Roman province."

9. See Josephus, *Jewish Antiquities* 14.358–59; also *The Jewish War* 1.265.

10. See Josephus, *Jewish Antiquities* 14.372.

11. See Cassius Dio, *Roman History* 48.25.2–4.

12. See Plutarch, *Life of Antony* 28.1.

13. Cassius Dio, *Roman History* 48.26.5.

14. Horace, *Odes* 3.5.5–8.

15. Justin, *Epitome of Pompeius Trogus* 42.4.7.

16. Strabo, *Geography* 14.2.24. On Hybreas's origins, see Valerius Maximus, *Memorable Doings and Sayings* 9.14.12, ext. 2.

17. See Strabo, *Geography* 12.8.9.

18. See Cassius Dio, *Roman History* 48.39.3.

19. See Josephus, *Jewish Antiquities* 14.469.

20. See Florus, *Epitome of Roman History* 1.46.2, and Plutarch, *Life of Crassus* 20.1.1.

21. See Josephus, *Jewish Antiquities* 14.434–436.

22. See Cassius Dio, *Roman History* 48.39.3.

23. See Cassius Dio, *Roman History* 48.40.1–5.

24. Frontinus, *Stratagems* 2.5.36.

25. See Cassius Dio, *Roman History* 48.40.6.

26. See Plutarch, *Life of Antony* 33.4. Velleius Paterculus, in his summary of various episodes of this conflict, says that Labienus was killed along with Pacorus and the Parthian army, but that does not necessarily mean that he died during the course of a battle, as Velleius claims; see *Compendium of Roman History* 2.78.1.

27. See Cassius Dio, *Roman History* 48.41.1–4; also Strabo, *Geography* 16.2.8 (who calls the Parthian general Phranicates); and Frontinus, *Stratagems* 2.5.37 (who calls him Pharnastanes).

28. See Josephus, *Jewish Antiquities* 15.394.

29. See Appian, *Civil Wars* 5.75.319.

30. See Cassius Dio, *Roman History* 49.19.3–4; also Strabo, *Geography* 16.2.8.

31. See Frontinus, *Stratagems* 1.1.1; also Cassius Dio, *Roman History* 49.19.2–3.

32. See Plutarch, *Life of Antony* 34.1–2; Florus, *Epitome of Roman History* 2.19.5–7; Gellius, *Attic Nights* 15.4.4 [= Suetonius, fr. 210 Reifferscheid]; Cassius Dio, *Roman History* 49.19–20; Justin, *Epitome of Pompeius Trogus* 42.4.11–16, 5.1–2; and Eutropius, *Summary of Roman History* 7.5.

33. See Florus, *Epitome of Roman History* 2.19.5–7; on Ventidius's wonderful career see also Juvenal, *Satires* 7.199, where he is compared to the sixth king of Rome, Servius Tullius.

34. See Plutarch, *Life of Antony* 34.4–5.

35. See the *Fasti triumphales* (*Inscriptiones Italiae*, 13.1b.7, ll. 716–717): *P[ublius] Ventidius P[ubli] f[ilius] pro co[n]s[ule] ex Tauro an[no] DCCX[V] / monte et Partheis V K[alendas]*.

36. See Gellius, *Attic Nights* 15.4.3–4.

37. See Fronto, *Letters to Verus Caesar* 2.9.

Chapter Eight: *Mare Nostrum*

1. See Cassius Dio, *Roman History* 48.42.1–4

2. See *Corpus inscriptionum Latinarum* 6.1301: *Inscriptiones Latinae liberae rei publicae* 429.

3. See Cassius Dio, *Roman History* 48.42.4. In the *Fasti triumphales Capitolini* (*Inscriptiones Italiae*, 13.1b., l.7) we read: *Cn[aeus] Domitius M[arci] f[ilius] M[arci] n[epos] Calvinus an[no] DCCXVII / pro co[n]s[ule] ex Hispania XVI K[alendas] Sextil[es]*; the *Fasti triumphales Barberiniani* (*Inscriptiones Italiae*, 13. l. 36) add the formula *palmam dedit* ("he dedicated the palm [of victory]").

4. See Suetonius, *Life of Augustus* 49.1.

5. See Cassius Dio, *Roman History* 48.49.3.

6. See Caesar, *Gallic War* 4.17–18.

7. See Virgil, *Bucolics* 10.46–48, and *Georgics* 1.509.

8. See Cassius Dio, *Roman History* 48.49.3–4.

9. See Appian, *The Civil Wars* 5.92.386.

10. See Cassius Dio, *Roman History* 48.50.1–3; also Virgil, *Georgics* 2.161–62.

11. See *Année épigraphique* (1959), 77: *Inscriptiones Latinae liberae rei publicae*, 1276.

12. See Cassius Dio, *Roman History* 48.45.3.

13. See Appian, *The Civil Wars* 5.98.406.

14. See Andrea Raggi and Pierangelo Buongiorno, eds. and trans., *Il "senatus consultum de Plarasensibus et Aphrodisiensibus" del 39 a. C.* (Stuttgart: Franz Steiner, 2020).

15. See Orosius, *Histories Against the Pagans* 6.18.23; also Plutarch, *Life of Antony* 34.2–4, and Cassius Dio, *Roman History* 49.20.5.

16. Strabo, *FGrHist* 91, F 11 [=Josephus, *Jewish Antiquities* 15.9–10].

17. See Cassius Dio, *Roman History* 49.32.5.

18. See Appian, *The Civil Wars* 5.93.387.

19. See Plutarch, *Life of Antony* 35.1.

20. See Appian, *The Civil Wars* 5.93.388–95.

21. Appian, *The Civil Wars* 5.118.491.

22. See Appian, *The Civil Wars* 5.133.550.

23. Appian, *The Civil Wars* 5.127.525.

24. See Strabo, *Geography* 6.2.6.

25. See Cassius Dio, *Roman History* 49.8.3–4.

26. Appian, *The Civil Wars* 5.130.542.

27. Augustus, *Res Gestae Divi Augusti* 25.1.

Chapter Nine: Antony's Eastern Campaign

1. Strabo, *Geography* 11.2.12.

2. See Strabo, *Geography* 7.4.6.

3. See Strabo, *Geography* 12.3.38, where Strabo speaks of more than one king.

4. See Cassius Dio, *Roman History* 49.32.3 (where Amyntas is mentioned only after Antony's eastern campaign); also Strabo, *Geography* 12.3.42.

5. See Strabo, *Geography* 14.1.23.

6. See Strabo, *Geography*, 14.1.41.

7. Plutarch, *Life of Antony* 24.2. Neither Metrodorus nor Xanthus is attested in other sources.

8. See Strabo, *Geography* 12.3.6.

9. Memnon of Heracleia, *Excerpta* 40.4.

10. See Cassius Dio, *Roman History* 49.23.1–2; also 22.3.

11. See Plutarch, *Life of Antony* 36.

12. See Strabo, *Geography* 14.5.14.

13. See *Supplementum epigraphicum Graecum* 54 (2008): 1625, and 58 (2012): 1733.

14. See Appian, *Civil Wars* 5.139.577; Cassius Dio (*Roman History* 49.14.6) says more vaguely that Octavian sent back to Antony "ships equal in number to those which had been lost."

15. See Plutarch, *Life of Antony* 72.2. A Christian author of the seventh century, Sophronius of Damascus, speaks also of Nicolaus of Damascus (*The Miracles of Saints Cyrus and John* [= *FGrHist* 90 T1]), but Nicolaus probably was tutor to the twins in Rome, after the death of their parents.

16. See Cassius Dio, *Roman History* 47.15.4.

17. Justin, *Epitome of Pompeius Trogus* 42.5.1–4. Cassius Dio (*Roman History* 49.23.3–5) confirms these massacres, dating them to 37. See also Plutarch, *Life of Antony* 37.1.

18. See Plutarch, *Life of Antony* 37.2; also Cassius Dio, *Roman History* 49.24.2.

19. See Cassius Dio, *Roman History* 49.24.2.

20. Tacitus, *Annals* 2.56.1.

21. Plutarch, *Life of Antony* 34.6.

22. *Life of Antony* 42.4.

23. See Cassius Dio, *Roman History* 49.24.1. Zober, unlike the Iberian king, did not bear an Iranian name.

24. See Strabo, *Geography* 11.13.4, 14.9; also Plutarch, *Life of Crassus* 19.1.

25. See Plutarch, *Life of Antony* 37.3–4.

26. See Cassius Dio, *Roman History* 49.25.1–2.

27. See Livy, *Summaries* 130.1.

28. See Plutarch, *Life of Antony* 37.3.

29. Florus, *Epitome of Roman History* 2.20.2.

30. See Plutarch, *Life of Antony* 38.1–2.

31. See Strabo, *Geography* 11.13.3.

32. See Strabo, *Geography* [Here again I use the rule of conversion standardly applied in the English-language literature (one mile = eight stadia); the French text calculates the distance to be 430 kilometers, or about 267 miles.—Trans.].

33. See Plutarch, *Life of Antony* 38.3, 39.6, 50.1; also Cassius Dio, *Roman History* 49.25.3.

34. Justin, *Epitome of Pompeius Trogus* 42.2.6.

35. See Plutarch, *Life of Antony* 38.2–3, 39.1; also Cassius Dio, *Roman History* 49.25.

36. See Plutarch, *Life of Antony* 39.5–7; also Cassius Dio, *Roman History* 49.26.

37. See Plutarch, *Life of Antony* 39.7; also Frontinus, *Stratagems* 1.37.

38. Cassius Dio, *Roman History* 49.27.5.

39. Cassius Dio, *Roman History* 49.29.4.

40. See Velleius Paterculus, *Compendium of Roman History* 2.82.2–3; also Florus, *Epitome of Roman History* 2.20.3–6.

41. Florus, *Epitome of Roman History* 2.20.4–5.

42. Plutarch, *Life of Antony* 43.2.

43. See Cassius Dio, *Roman History* 49.31.4.

Chapter Ten: End of the Young Pompey, Wars of the Young Caesar

1. Appian, *The Civil Wars* 5.133.551.

2. Appian, *The Civil Wars* 5.133.554.

3. See Plutarch, *Life of Antony* 42.2–3.

4. Cassius Dio, *Roman History* 48.30.5.

5. See Appian, *The Civil Wars* 5.138.572–75.

6. See Appian, *The Civil Wars* 5.140.580.

7. Appian, *The Civil Wars* 5.141.585–142.595; see also Velleius Paterculus, *Compendium of Roman History* 2.79.

8. Appian, *The Civil Wars* 5.145.601.

9. Hyginus Gromaticus, *De Constitutione* [*Limitum*], in Carl Olof Thulin, ed., *Corpus Agrimensorum Romanorum*, vol. 1 (Leipzig: Teubner, 1913), 142.

10. See Suetonius, *Life of Augustus* 47; Appian, *The Civil Wars* 5.129.537; Cassius Dio, *Roman History* 49.34.1. On Statilius Taurus's triumph, see *Inscriptiones Italiae* 13.1.569.

11. See Florus, *Epitome of Roman History* 2.25; also Cassius Dio, *History* 48.41.7.

12. See Appian, *Illyrian Wars* 14.40.

13. See Suetonius, *Life of Augustus* 85.1; also *Suda*, s.v. *Augoustos Kaisar*.

14. See Appian, *Illyrian Wars* 16.46.

15. Augustus, *Res Gestae Divi Augusti* 29.

16. See Appian, *Illyrian Wars* 25.71.

17. See Cassius Dio, *Roman History* 48.45.7; on Menodorus's recognition as a freeman born free (*ingenuitas*), see Suetonius, *Life of Augustus* 74.1 [= M. Valerius Messalla, fr. 4 Cornell].

18. Appian, *Illyrian Wars* 15.42–43.

19. Strabo, *Geography* 7.3.11.

20. See Appian, *Illyrian Wars* 22.62–63.

21. See Livy, *Summaries* 131.

22. Appian, *Illyrian Wars* 17.49–50.

23. Strabo, *Geography* 4.6.7.

24. Strabo, *Geography* 4.6.7.

25. Appian, *Illyrian Wars* 17.50–51.

26. Caesar, *Gallic War* 8.24.3.

27. *Inscriptiones Latinae liberae rei publicae* 418.

28. See *Inscriptiones Italiae* 10.4.31.

29. See Appian, *Illyrian Wars* 19.54.

30. See Appian, *Illyrian Wars* 20.57; also Cassius Dio, *Roman History* 49.38.1.

31. See Appian, *Illyrian Wars* 19.54–21.61.

32. See Cicero, *Letters to Atticus* 5.20.1.

33. Appian, *Illyrian Wars* 20.58.

34. Strabo, *Geography* 7.5.4.

35. See Appian, *Illyrian Wars* 22.63–64.

36. Cassius Dio, *Roman History* 49.36.2–4.

37. Cassius Dio, *Roman History* 49.38.1.

38. On account of the priority attached to Dalmatia, military operations beyond the Danube were postponed indefinitely. Thus Appian concludes the Illyrian book with an account of the victories of L. Licinius Lucullus's younger brother, M. Terentius Varro Lucullus. In 71, while Lucullus was pressing on with the war against Mithradates, Varro Lucullus crushed the Mysians, bringing under Roman control six Greek cities on the western coast of the Black Sea. See Appian, *Illyrian Wars* 30.85.

39. See *Inscriptiones Latinae selectae* 8893 [= *Inscriptiones Latinae liberae rei publicae*, 417].

40. See the *Fasti Capitolini Triumphales* (*Inscriptiones Italiae*, 13.1b.7.1, ll. 343–44, 559–60).

41. Appian, *Illyrian Wars* 25.72.

42. Appian, *Illyrian Wars* 28.82.

43. See Cassius Dio, *Roman History* 49.43.7.

Chapter Eleven: The Inimitable Life of Alexandria

1. See Plutarch, *Life of Antony* 28.2.

2. Pliny, *Natural History* 14.148.

3. Plutarch (*Life of Antony* 58.5) attributes this report to a certain Calvisius, a "companion of Caesar"; he seems not to have been G. Calvisius Sabinus, consul in 39, never so far as we know posted to the East.

4. See Nicolaus of Damascus, *Life of Augustus* 44 [= M 101 XVII]. Apollodorus died a little more than twenty years later, in 23.

5. See Strabo, *Geography* 14.1.14.

6. See Joyce Reynolds, *Aphrodisias and Rome* (London: Society for the Promotion of Roman Studies, 1982), pl. 13.

7. See Cassius Dio, *Roman History* 50.5.2.

8. Cited in Georges Daux, *Fouilles de Delphes*, vol. 3 (Paris: Éditions de Boccard, 1943), 4.58.

9. See Plutarch, *Life of Antony* 1.1–3 and 28.4–7.

10. See Plutarch, *Life of Antony* 71.1–3.

11. See Cassius Dio, *Roman History* 49.39.1–3.

12. See Plutarch, *Life of Antony* 53.2–3; also Cassius Dio, *Roman History* 49.33.3–4.

13. See Cassius Dio, *Roman History* 49.31.1. One of these territories was Symbakē, mentioned by Strabo, *Geography* 11.13.2.

14. Cassius Dio, *Roman History* 49.39.5–6.

15. See Cassius Dio, *Roman History* 49.40.2–3.

16. See Cassius Dio, *Roman History* 36.53, 5; also Plutarch, *Life of Pompey* 24.4–5.

17. See Pliny, *Natural History* 33.24.82–83.

18. See Movsēs Khorenatsʻi, *History of Armenia* 2.22–23. The last passage is borrowed from Josephus, *The Jewish War* 1.363, which mistakenly calls Artawazd (Artabazēs) "the Parthian."

19. Cassius Dio, *Roman History* 49.40.3.

20. Plutarch, *Life of Antony* 55.2.

21. See Cassius Dio, *Roman History* 49.41.5.

22. Cassius Dio, *Roman History* 50.1.1–2.

23. Plutarch, *Life of Antony* 50.4.

24. See Cassius Dio, *Roman History* 49.40.3–4.

25. See *British Museum Coins*, 701 var.; *Roman Imperial Coins*, 492.

26. See Cassius Dio, *Roman History* 50.1.4–5.

27. See Movsēs Khorenatsʻi, *History of Armenia* 2.24.

28. Plutarch, *Life of Antony* 54.4–6; see also Cassius Dio, *Roman History* 49.41.1–4.

29. Suetonius, *Life of Augustus* 69.3.

30. Anthony Pagden, *Worlds at War: The 2,500-Year Struggle Between East and West* (New York: Random House, 2008), 94.

31. See Cassius Dio, *Roman History* 50.8.6.

Chapter Twelve: The Oath of All Italy

1. See *Sibylline Oracles*, 3.350–80.

2. Plutarch, *Life of Antony* 56.4.

3. Augustus, *Res Gestae Divi Augusti* 25.12.

4. Virgil, *Georgics* 2.136.

5. See Appian, *The Civil Wars* 1.25.107–13.

6. See, for example, Cassius Dio, *Roman History* 50.4.1–4, and Augustus, *Res Gestae Divi Augusti* 34.1.

7. See Pliny, *Natural History* 33.50.

8. Plutarch, *Life of Romulus* 17.3.

9. See Plutarch, *Life of Antony* 67.2–3.

10. See Plutarch, *Sayings of Kings and Commanders* 8.5.1.

11. See Plutarch, *Life of Antony* 61.2–3; on Iamblichus, see Cassius Dio, *Roman History* 50.13.7.

12. Cassius Dio, *Roman History* 51.22.8; see also Plutarch, *Life of Antony* 63.4.

13. See Cassius Dio, *Roman History* 50.13.8.

14. See Cassius Dio, *Roman History* 50.11.3, 13.5.

15. See Plutarch, *Life of Antony* 63.2–3; Cassius Dio, *Roman History* 50.13.5–8; Horace, *Epodes* 9.17–18.

16. See Cassius Dio, *Roman History* 50.14.2.

17. Cassius Dio, *Roman History* 50.24.6–7.

18. See Cassius Dio, *Roman History* 50.33.1–2.

19. Cassius Dio, *Roman History* 51.7.2–7.

20. Plutarch, *Life of Antony* 81.2.

21. Martial, *Epigrams* 4.11.4.

22. Horace, *Odes* 1.37.1; see also Alcaeus, fr. 332 Lobel-Page.

23. See *Roman Imperial Coinage* I (2nd ed.), Augustus 276.

SELECT BIBLIOGRAPHY

General Works and Major Topics

Alston, Richard. *Rome's Revolution: Death of the Republic and Birth of the Empire.* Oxford: Oxford University Press, 2015.

Börm, Henning, Ulrich Gotter, and Wolfgang Havener, eds. *A Culture of Civil War? "Bellum civile" and Political Communication in Late Republican Rome.* Berlin: De Gruyter, 2023.

Cadiou, François. *L'Armée imaginaire: Les soldats prolétaires dans les légions romaines au dernier siècle de la République.* Paris: Les Belles Lettres, 2018.

Canfora, Luciano. *Augusto, figlio di dio.* Rome: Laterza, 2015.

Canfora, Luciano. *La prima marcia su Roma.* Rome: Laterza, 2007.

Cosme, Pierre. *Auguste, maître du monde: Actium, 2 septembre 31 av. J.-C.* Paris: Tallandier, 2014.

Eramo, Immacolata. "L'Italia delle guerre civili: Dalla tarda repubblica ai Severi." In *Guerre ed eserciti nell'Antichità,* edited by Marco Bettalli and Giovanni Brizzi. Bologna: Il Mulino, 2019.

Ferrary, Jean-Louis. "L''oikoumène', l'Orient et l'Occident d'Alexandre le Grand à Auguste: Histoire et historiographie." In *Convegno per Santo Mazzarino (Roma, 9–11 maggio 1991),* edited by Augusto Fraschetti, Andrea Giardina, and Elio Lo Cascio. Rome: L'Erma di Bretschneider, 1998. Reprinted in *Rome et le monde grec: Choix d'écrits,* edited by Jean-Louis Ferrary and Denis Rousset. Paris: Les Belles Lettres, 2017.

Gara, Alessandra, and Daniele Foraboschi, eds. *Il triumvirato costituente alla fine della Repubblica romana.* Como: Edizioni New Press, 1993.

García Domínguez, David, Juan García González, and Federico Santangelo, eds. *Connected Histories of the Roman Civil Wars (88–30 BCE).* Berlin: De Gruyter, 2024.

Gowing, Alain M. *The Triumviral Narratives of Appian and Cassius Dio.* Ann Arbor: University of Michigan Press, 1992.

Gotter, Ulrich. *Der Diktator ist tot! Politik in Rom zwischen den Iden des März und der Begründung des Zweiten Triumvirats.* Stuttgart: Franz Steiner, 1996.

Gruen, Erich S. *The Last Generation of the Roman Republic.* Berkeley: University of California Press, 1974.

Hölkeskamp, Karl-Joachim. *Libera Res Publica. Die politische Kultur des antiken Rom—Positionen und Perspektiven.* Stuttgart: Franz Steiner, 2017.

Hölkeskamp, Karl-Joachim. *Reconstructing the Roman Republic: An Ancient Political Culture and Modern Research.* Princeton: Princeton University Press, 2010.

Hölkeskamp, Karl-Joachim. *Roman Republican Reflections: Studies in Politics, Power, and Pageantry.* Stuttgart: Franz Steiner, 2020.

Holmes, Thomas Rice. *The Architect of the Roman Empire (44–27 B.C.)*. Oxford: Clarendon Press, 1928.

Hurlet, Frédéric. "De Pompée à Auguste: Les mutations de l'*imperium militiae*. 1. Les réalités institutionnelles." In *Cassius Dion: Nouvelles lectures*, vol. 2, edited by Valérie Fromentin, Estelle Bertrand, Michèle Coltelloni-Trannoy, et al. Bordeaux: Ausonius, 2016.

Jal, Paul. *La Guerre civile à Rome: Étude littéraire et morale de Cicéron à Tacite*. Paris: Presses universitaires de France, 1963.

Lange, Carsten Hjort. *Res Publica Constituta: Actium, Apollo and the Accomplishment of the Triumviral Assignment*. Leiden: Brill, 2009.

Lange, Carsten Hjort. *Triumphs in the Age of Civil War: The Late Republic and the Adaptability of Triumphal Tradition*. London: Bloomsbury Academic, 2016.

Lange, Carsten Hjort, and Frederik JuliaanVervaet, eds. *The Historiography of Late Republican Civil War*. Leiden: Brill, 2019.

Levi, Mario Attilio. *Ottaviano capoparte: Storia politica di Roma durante le ultime lotte di supremazia*. Florence: La Nuova Italia, 1933.

Millar, Fergus. "The Mediterranean and the Roman Revolution: Politics, War, and the Economy." *Past and Present* 102, no. 1 (1984): 3–24. Reprinted in *Rome, the Greek World, and the East*, vol. 1, edited by Hannah M. Cotton and Guy M. Rogers. Chapel Hill: University of North Carolina Press, 2002.

Osgood, Josiah. *Caesar's Legacy: Civil War and the Emergence of the Roman Empire*. Cambridge: Cambridge University Press, 2006.

Osgood, Josiah, and Christopher Baron, eds. *Cassius Dio and the Late Roman Republic*. Leiden: Brill, 2019.

Pelling, Christopher. *Plutarch, Life of Antony*. Cambridge: Cambridge University Press, 1988.

Pelling, Christopher. "The Triumviral Period." In *The Cambridge Ancient History*, vol. 10, *The Augustan Empire, 43 B.C.–A.D. 69*, 2nd ed., edited by Alan K. Bowman, Edward Champlin, and Andrew Lintott. Cambridge: Cambridge University Press, 1996.

Pina Polo, Francisco, ed. *The Triumviral Period: Civil War, Political Crisis and Socioeconomic Transformations*. Seville: Editorial Universidad de Sevilla, 2020.

The Roman Civil Wars: A House Divided. Double issue of *Hermathena*, 196/197 (2014).

Rosillo-López, Cristina. *Political Conversations in Late Republican Rome*. Oxford: Oxford University Press, 2022.

Rosillo-López, Cristina. *Public Opinion and Politics in the Late Roman Republic*. Cambridge: Cambridge University Press, 2017.

Santangelo, Federico. *Divination, Prediction and the End of the Roman Republic*. Cambridge: Cambridge University Press, 2013.

Steel, Catherine. *The End of the Roman Republic, 146–44 B.C.: Conquest and Crisis*. Edinburgh: Edinburgh University Press, 2013.

Sumi, Geoffrey S. *Ceremony and Power: Performing Politics in Rome Between Republic and Empire*. Ann Arbor: University of Michigan Press, 2005.

Syme, Ronald. *Approaching the Roman Revolution: Papers on Republican History*, edited by Federico Santangelo. Oxford: Oxford University Press, 2016.

Syme, Ronald. *The Roman Revolution*. Oxford: Oxford University Press, 1939; corrected editions 1952, 1956.

Tatum, W. Jeffrey. *A Noble Ruin: Mark Antony, Civil War, and the Collapse of the Roman Republic.* Oxford: Oxford University Press, 2024.

Traina, Giusto. "La battaglia di Nauloco." In *Storia mondiale della Sicilia,* edited by Giuseppe Barone. Rome: Laterza, 2018.

Traina, Giusto. "Mark Antony's Arrangements in the Roman East, 41–37 BCE." In *Eski Çağda Savaş ve Diplomasi—War and Diplomacy in Ancient Times,* edited by Gülgüney Masalcı Şahin and Alican Doğan. Istanbul: Ege Yayınları, 2021.

Traina, Giusto. "Sesto Pompeo nel giudizio di Mario Attilio Levi." In *Segmenti della ricerca antichistica e giusantichistica degli anni Trenta,* edited by Pierangelo Buongiorno, Annaroso Gallo, and Laura Mecella. Naples: Editoriale scientifica, 2022.

Traina, Giusto, ed. *Studi sull'età di Marco Antonio.* Galatina: Congedo, 2006.

Vervaet, Frederik J. *The High Command in the Roman Republic: The Principle of the summum imperium auspiciumque from 509 to 19 BCE.* Stuttgart: Franz Steiner, 2014.

Vervaet, Frederik J., and Christopher James Dart. "On the Military Crowns Awarded After Naulochus: Historical Circumstances and Wider Significance." *Historia* 67 (2018): 313–45.

Vivas García, Gustavo A. "El Ottaviano capoparte de Mario Atilio Levi y su influencia en *The Roman Revolution* de Ronald Syme." *Gerión* 35 (2017): 277–95.

Vivas García, Gustavo A. *Ronald Syme: El camino hasta "La Revolución Romana" (1928–1939).* Barcelona: Universitat de Barcelona Edicions, 2016.

Vivas García, Gustavo A. "'That Sickly and Sinister Youth': The First Considerations of Syme on Octavian as a Historical Figure." *Cadmo* 24 (2015): 87–110.

Welch, Kathryn, ed. *Appian's Roman History: Empire and Civil War.* Swansea: Classical Press of Wales, 2015.

Wienand, Johannes, Henning Börm, and Carsten Hjort Lange, eds. *Ancient Cultures of Civil War: Polarisation, Conflict, and Reconciliation.* Berlin: De Gruyter, 2025.

Zack, Andreas. *Das Ende des Zweiten Triumvirates und die Amtsgewalten des Imperator Caesar Divi filius (Octavianus) in der politischen Ordnung Roms (43–27 v. Chr.) Übersehene, vergessene und neue Überlegungen zur Deutung von Augustus,* Res Gestae *7,1; 25,2 und 34,1.* Norderstedt: PubliQation, 2022.

Zerndl, Andreas. *Generationenbewusstsein, Generationenwechsel und Generationenkonflikte in der Aristokratie des spätrepublikanischen Roms.* Hamburg: Verlag Dr. Kovač, 2012.

The Protagonists

Broughton, Thomas Robert Shannon. *The Magistrates of the Roman Republic.* Vol. 2, *99 B.C.–31 B.C.* New York: American Philological Association, 1952.

Ferriès, Marie-Claire. *Les partisans d'Antoine.* Bordeaux: Ausonius, 2007.

Grattarola, Pio. *I cesariani dalle Idi di marzo alla costituzione del secondo triumvirato.* Turin: Tirrenia Stampatori, 1990.

Julius Caesar

Canfora, Luciano. *Julius Caesar: The Life and Times of the People's Dictator.* Translated by Marian Hill and Kevin Dwindle. Edinburgh: Edinburgh University Press, 2009.

The Four Surveyors Sent by Caesar

Nicolet, Claude. *Space, Geography, and Politics in the Early Roman Empire*. Ann Arbor: University of Michigan Press, 1991.

Nicolet, Claude, and Patrick Gautier-Dalché. "Les 'quatre sages' de Jules César et la 'mesure du monde' selon Julius Honorius: Réalité antique et tradition médiévale." *Journal des Savants* 4 (1986): 157–218.

Mark Antony

Cresci Marrone, Giovannella. *Marco Antonio*. Rome: Salerno editrice, 2020.

Huzar, Eleanor G. *Mark Antony: A Biography*. Minneapolis: University of Minnesota Press, 1978.

Traina, Giusto. *Marco Antonio*. Rome: Laterza, 2022.

Octavius > Octavian > Caesar the Younger > Augustus

Bleicken, Jochen. *Augustus: The Biography*. Translated by Anthea Bell. London: Allen Lane for Penguin, 2015.

Borgies, Loïc. *Le conflit propagandiste entre Octavien et Marc Antoine: De l'usage politique de la vituperatio entre 44 et 30 a.C.n.* Brussels: Latomus, 2016.

Fraschetti, Augusto. *Augusto*. Rome: Laterza, 2013.

Lewis, Anne-Marie. "Augustus and His Horoscope Reconsidered." *Phoenix* 62 (2008): 308–37.

Brutus and Cassius

Cristofoli, Roberto. *Marco Giunio Bruto*. Rome: Salerno editrice, 2022.

Tempest, Kathryn. *Brutus: The Noble Conspirator*. New Haven: Yale University Press, 2017.

Cicero

Grangé, Ninon. "Cicéron contre Antoine: La désignation de l'ennemi dans la guerre civile." *Mots: Le langage du politique* 73 (2003): 9–23.

Lintott, Andrew. *Cicero as Evidence: A Historian's Companion*. Oxford: Oxford University Press, 2008.

Narducci, Emanuele. *Cicerone: La parola e la politica*. Rome: Laterza, 2009.

Sextus Pompey

Kersten, Laura, and Christian Wendt, eds. *Rector Maris: Sextus Pompeius und das Meer*. Bonn: Habelt, 2020.

Welch, Kathryn. *Magnus Pius: Sextus Pompeius and the Transformation of the Roman Republic*. Swansea: Classical Press of Wales, 2012.

Seius's Horse

Traina, Giusto. "*Equus Seianus*: Un cavallo nel corso delle guerre civili (Gell. 3.9)." In *Aulo Gellio tra diritto e antiquaria*, edited by Aniello Atorino, Gaetana Balestra, and Raffaele D'Alession. Lecce: Edizioni del Grifo, 2023.

Dolabella

Rohr Vio, Francesca. "Publio Cornelio Dolabella, *ultor Caesaris primus*: L'assassinio di Gaio Trebonio nella polemica politica del post cesaricidio." *Aevum* 80 (2006): 105–19.

Lepidus

Allély, Annie. *Lépide, le triumvir*. Bordeaux: Ausonius, 2004.

Weigel, Richard D. *Lepidus: The Tarnished Triumvir*. London: Routledge, 1992.

Munatius Plancus

Borgna, Alice. "Note filologiche all'epistolario tra Cicerone e Lucio Munazio Planco (*fam.* 10, 1–24)." In *Tanti affetti in tal momento: Studi in onore di Giovanna Garbarino*, edited by Andrea Balbo, Federica Bessone, and Ermanno Malaspina. Alessandria: Edizioni dell'Orso, 2012.

Valentini, Alessandra. "Gli Antoniani nelle *Historiae* di Velleio Patercolo: Il caso di Lucio Munazio Planco." *Rivista di cultura classica e medioevale* 50 (2008): 71–96.

Watkins, Thomas H. *Munatius Plancus: Serving and Surviving in the Roman Revolution*. London: Routledge, 2018.

Domitius Ahenobarbus

Etcheto, Henri, and François Jougleux. "Les ressorts politiques d'une falsification historique: Cn. Domitius Ahenobarbus et les Ides de Mars." *Historia* 64 (2015): 106–30.

Decidius Saxa

Syme, Ronald. "Who Was Decidius Saxa?" *Journal of Roman Studies* 27, no. 1 (1937): 127–37. Reprinted in *Roman Papers*, edited by E. Badian and Anthony R. Birley, vol. 1. Oxford: Clarendon Press, 1979.

Lucius Antonius

Livadiotti, Umberto. "Lucio Antonio, Appiano e la propaganda augustea." *Seminari romani di letteratura greca* n.s., no. 2 (2013): 65–91.

Roddaz, Jean-Michel. "Lucius Antonius." *Historia* 37 (1988): 317–46.

Balbus

Pina Polo, Francisco. "Les Cornelii Balbi de Gadès: Un exemple de clientélisme provincial?" In *Les gouverneurs et les provinciaux sous la République romaine*, edited by Nathalie Barrandon and François Kirbihler. Rennes: Presses universitaires de Rennes, 2011.

Agrippa

Roddaz, Jean-Michel. *Marcus Agrippa*. Rome: École française de Rome, 1984.

Romeo, Ilaria. Ingenuus Leo*: L'immagine di Agrippa*. Rome: L'Erma di Bretschneider, 1998.

Salvidienus Rufus

Vivas García, Gustavo. "Quinto Salvidieno Rufo: Algunos apuntes sobre su biografía política." *Studia histórica, Historia antigua* 39 (2021): 237–51.

Octavia

Vivas García, Gustavo. *Octavia contra Cleopatra: El papel de la mujer en la propaganda política del Triunvirato, 44–30 a. C.* Madrid: Liceus Ediciones, 2013.

Domitius Calvinus

Bonneville, Jean-Noël. "Les patrons du municipe d'*Emporiae* (Ampurias, Espagne)." *Revue des Études Anciennes* 88, nos. 1–4 (1986): 181–200.

Carlsen, Jesper. "Cn. Domitius Calvinus: A Noble Caesarian." *Latomus* 67, no. 1 (2008): 72–81.

Quintus Labienus

Curran, John. "The Ambitions of Quintus Labienus 'Parthicus'." *Antichthon* 41 (2007): 33–53.

Lerouge-Cohen, Charlotte. "Entre légende monétaire et légende noire: De nouveau sur *Q. Labienus Parthicus Imp.*" *Historia* 59 (2010): 176–88.

Maecenas

Le Doze, Philippe. *Mécène: Ombres et flamboyances*. Paris: Les Belles Lettres, 2014.

Messalla

Tansey, Patrick. "Messalla Corvinus and the 'Bellum Siculum'." *Latomus* 66, no. 4 (2007): 882–90.

Ventidius

Rohr Vio, Francesca. *Publio Ventidio Basso: "Fautor Caesaris," tra storia e memoria*. Rome: L'Erma di Breschneider, 2009.

Q. Dellius

Nicolai, Roberto. "Strabone e la campagna partica di Antonio: Critica delle fonti e critica del testo." In Giusto Traina, *Studi sull'XI libro dei "Geographika" di Strabone*, edited by Giusto Traina. Galatina: Congedo.

L. Plinius Rufus

Silvestrini, Marina. "Nuove epigrafi da Lilibeo." *Antichità altoadriatiche* 79 (2014): 207–26.

Cleopatra

Capponi, Livia. *Cleopatra*. Rome: Laterza, 2021.

Legras, Bernard. *Cléopâtre l'Égyptienne*. Paris: Les Belles Lettres, 2021.

Sartre, Maurice. *Cléopâtre: Un rêve de puissance*. Paris: Tallandier, 2018.

Caesarion ("Little Caesar")

Capponi, Livia. "Osservazioni su Cesarione." *Quaderni di storia* 95 (2022): 31–59.

Quaegebeur, Jan. "Cléopâtre VII et le temple de Dendara." *Göttinger Miszellen* 120 (1991): 49–72.

Deiotarus

Parker, Victor. "Deiotarus: Zur Karriere eines römischen Klientelkönigs." *Electrum* 25 (2018): 187–208.

Herod

Parmentier, Edith. *Le roi Hérode: De la légende à l'histoire*. Paris: Les Belles Lettres, 2022.

Roddaz, Jean-Michel. *Hérode le roi architecte*. Paris: Actes Sud/Errance, 2014.

Hybreas of Mylasa

Delrieux, Fabrice, and Marie-Claire Ferriès. "Euthydème, Hybréas et Mylasa: Une cité grecque de Carie dans les conflits romains de la fin du Ier siècle a.C." *Revue des études anciennes* 106, no. 1 (2004): 49–71 and 499–519.

Seleucus of Rhosus

Raggi, Andrea. *Seleuco di Rhosos: Cittadinanza e privilegi nell'Oriente greco in età tardo-repubblicana*. Pisa: Giardini, 2006.

Tarcondimotus

Andrade, Nathanael. "Local Authority and Civic Hellenism: Tarcondimotus, Hierapolis-Castabala and the Cult of Perasia." *Anatolian Studies* 61 (2011): 123–32.

Wright, Nicholas L. "The House of Tarkondimotos: A Late Hellenistic Dynasty Between Rome and the East." *Anatolian Studies* 62 (2012): 69–88.

Peoples and Their Lands

North Africa

Hobson, Matthew S. "Africa Under the Roman Republic." In *A Companion to North Africa in Antiquity*, edited by R. Bruce Hitchner. Oxford: Blackwell, 2022.

The Iberian Peninsula

Cadiou, François. *Hibera in terra miles: Les armées romaines et la conquête de l'Hispanie sous la République (218–45 av. J.-C.)*. Madrid: Casa de Velázquez, 2008.

Rico, Christian. *Pyrénées romaines: Essai sur un pays de frontière (IIIe siècle av. J.-C.-IVe siècle ap. J.-C.)*. Madrid: Casa de Velázquez, 1997.

Gades

Gagé, Jean. "Hercule-Melqart: Alexandre et les Romains à Gadès." *Revue des Études Anciennes* 42, nos. 1–4 (1940): 425–38.

Pina Polo, Francisco. "Les *Cornelii Balbi* de Gadès: Un exemple de clientélisme provincial?" In Barrandon and Kirbihler, eds., *Les gouverneurs et les provinciaux sous la République romaine*.

The Gauls

Ouzoulias, Pierre, and Laurence Tranoy, eds. *Comment les Gaules devinrent romaines*. Paris: La Découverte, 2010.

Woolf, Greg. *Becoming Roman: The Origins of Provincial Civilization in Gaul*. Cambridge: Cambridge University Press, 1998.

The Alps

Giorcelli Bersani, Silvia. *L'impero in quota: I romani e le Alpi*. Turin: Einaudi, 2019.

Sicily

Caliò, Luigi Maria et al., eds.. *La Sicilia fra le guerre civili e l'epoca giulio-claudia: Atti del I° Convegno Internazionale.* Rome: Quasar, 2024.

Illyricum

Dzino (Džino), Danijel. *Illyricum in Roman Politics, 229 BC–AD 68.* Cambridge: Cambridge University Press, 2010.

Šašel Kos, Marjeta. "The Role of the Navy in Octavian's Illyrian War." *Histria Antiqua* 21 (2012): 93–104.

Dacia

Lica, Vasile. *The Coming of Rome in the Dacian World.* Konstanz: Universitätsverlag, 2000.

Oltean, Ioana A. *Dacia: Landscape, Colonization and Romanization.* London: Routledge, 2007.

Thrace

Sullivan, Richard D. "Thrace in the Eastern Dynastic Network." In *Aufstieg und Niedergang der römischen Welt,* 2.7.1 (1979): 186–211.

Greece

Ernst, Paul. "Le logement des particuliers romains dans la Grèce égéenne aux IIe et Ier siècles av. J.-C." *Bulletin de correspondance hellénique* 141 (2017): 313–36.

Ferrary, Jean-Louis. "Les Grecs des cités et l'obtention de la *ciuitas Romana.*" In *Citoyenneté et participation à la basse époque hellénistique: Actes de la table ronde des 22 et 23 mai 2004,* edited by Pierre Fröhlich and Christel Müller. Geneva: Droz, 2005. Reprinted in *Rome et le monde grec: Choix d'écrits,* edited by Jean-Louis Ferrary and Denis Rousset. Paris: Les Belles Lettres, 2017.

Athens

Tatum, W. Jeffrey. "Antonius and Athens." In Pina Polo, ed., *Triumviral Period,* 459–73.

Peloponnese

Balzat, Jean-Sebastien. "Les Euryclides en Laconie." In *Le Péloponnèse d'Épaminondas à Hadrien,* edited by Catherine Grandjean. Bordeaux: Ausonius, 2008.

Balzat, Jean-Sebastien, and Benjamin W. Millis. "Provincial Involvement with Roman Power in the Late 1st Century B.C." *Hesperia* 82 (2013): 651–72.

Rhodes

Delrieux, Fabrice, and Marie-Claire Ferriès. "Le siège de Rhodes par C. Cassius Longinus en 42 av. J.-C., de la bataille de Myndos à la prise de la ville." In *Les sièges de Rhodes*, edited by Nicolas Faucherre and Isabelle Pimouguet-Pédarros. Rennes: Presses universitaires de Rennes, 2010.

The Near East

Fisher, Greg. *Rome, Persia, and Arabia: Shaping the Middle East from Pompey to Muhammad.* London: Routledge, 2020.

Marciak, Michał. *Sophene, Gordyene, and Adiabene: The Three Regna Minora of Northern Mesopotamia Between East and West.* Leiden: Brill, 2017.

Sartre, Maurice. *D'Alexandre à Zénobie: Histoire du Levant antique, IVe siècle avant Jésus-Christ-IIIe siècle après Jésus-Christ.* 2nd ed. Paris: Fayard, 2003. An abridged version is available in English as *The Middle East Under Rome*, translated by Catherine Porter and Elizabeth Rawlings. Cambridge, MA: Belknap Press of Harvard University Press, 2005.

Van Wijlick, Hendrikus A. M. *Rome and the Near Eastern Kingdoms and Principalities.* Leiden: Brill, 2021.

Asia Minor

Jordan, Bradley. *Imperial Power, Provincial Government, and the Emergence of Roman Asia, 133 BCE–14 CE.* Oxford: Oxford University Press, 2023.

Laignoux, Raphaëlle. "Reconnaître Octavien et ses concurrents en Anatolie: Les allégeances asiatiques durant les guerres civiles de la fin de la République." In *Auguste et l'Asie Mineure*, edited by Laurence Cavalier, Marie-Claire Ferriès, and Fabrice Delrieux. Bordeaux: Ausonius, 2017.

Sartre, Maurice. *L'Asie Mineure et l'Anatolie d'Alexandre à Dioclétien (IVe siècle av. J.-C.–IIIe siècle).* Paris: Armand Colin, 1995.

Ephesus

Kirbihler, François. *Des Grecs et des Italiens à Éphèse: Histoire d'une intégration croisée (133 a.C.–48 p.C.).* Bordeaux: Ausonius, 2016.

Pontus, Cappadocia

Mitchell, Stephen. "In Search of the Pontic Community in Antiquity?" In *Representations of Empire: Rome and the Mediterranean World*, edited by Alan Bowman, Hannah M. Cotton, Martin Goodman, et al. Oxford: Oxford University Press, 2002.

Cilicia

Jordan, Bradley. "Political Authority and Local Agency: Cilicia Pedias and Syria Between the Seleucid Empire and the Roman Republic." *Mnemosyne* 75 (2021): 483–513.

Tarsus

Franco, Carlo. "Tarso tra Antonio e Ottaviano (Strabone 14, 5, 14)." In Traina, ed., *Studi sull'età di Marco Antonio.*

Commagene

Blömer, Michael, Stefan Reidel, Miguel John Versluys, et al., eds. *Common Dwelling Place of All the Gods: Commagene in Its Local, Regional and Global Hellenistic Context.* Stuttgart: Franz Steiner, 2021.

Facella, Margherita. *La dinastia degli Orontidi nella Commagene ellenistico-Romana.* Pisa: Giardini, 2006.

Coele-Syria

Sartre, Maurice. "Retour vers la Cœlé-Syrie." *Syria* 95 (2018): 447–60.

Ituraeans

Aliquot, Julien. "Les Ituréens et la présence arabe au Liban du IIe s. a.C. au IVe s. p.C." *Mélanges de l'Université Saint-Joseph* 56 (1999–2003): 161–290.

Hoffmann-Salz, Julia. "The Ituraeans as a Hellenistic Dynasty: Working the Middle Ground in Hellenistic Syria." In *The Middle East as Middle Ground? Cultural Interaction in the Ancient Middle East Revisited,* edited by Julia Hoffman-Salz. Vienna: Holzhausen, 2021.

Myers, Elaine A. *The Ituraeans and the Roman Near East: Reassessing the Sources.* Cambridge: Cambridge University Press, 2010.

Palmyra

Hekster, Olivier, and Ted Kaizer. "Mark Antony and the Raid on Palmyra: Reflections on Appian, *Bella Civilia* V, 9." *Latomus* 63, no. 1 (2004): 70–80.

Raja, Rubina. *Pearl of the Desert: A History of Palmyra.* Oxford: Oxford University Press, 2022.

Raja, Rubina, ed. *The Oxford Handbook of Palmyra.* Oxford: Oxford University Press, 2024.

Sartre, Annie, and Maurice Sartre. *Palmyre: Vérités et légendes.* Paris: Perrin, 2016.

Arabs

Retsö, Jan. *The Arabs in Antiquity: Their History from the Assyrians to the Umayyads.* London: RoutledgeCurzon, 2003.

Judaea

Dąbrowa, Edward. "The Hasmoneans and Their State: A Study in History, Ideology, and the Institutions." *Electrum* 16 (2010): 7–212.

Rocca, Samuel. *Herod's Judaea: A Mediterranean State in the Classical World*. Tübingen: Mohr Siebeck, 2008.

Parthians

Bivar, David. "The Political History of Iran Under the Arsacids." In *The Cambridge History of Iran, 3(1): The Seleucid, Parthian and Sasanian Periods*, edited by Ehsan Yarshater. Cambridge: Cambridge University Press, 1983.

Dąbrowa, Edward. *Studia Graeco-Parthica: Political and Cultural Relations Between Greeks and Parthians*. Wiesbaden: Harrassowitz, 2014.

Ellerbrock, Uwe. *The Parthians: The Forgotten Empire*. London: Routledge, 2021.

Lerouge, Charlotte. *L'image des Parthes dans le monde gréco-romain: Du début du Ier siècle av. J. C. jusqu'à la fin du Haut-Empire romain*. Stuttgart: Franz Steiner, 2007.

Olbrycht, Marek J. Parthia et ulteriores gentes: *Die politischen Beziehungen zwischen dem arsakidischen Iran und den Nomaden der eurasischen Steppen*. Munich: Utzverlag, 1998.

Traina, Giusto. *Carrhes, 9 juin 53 av. J.-C.: Anatomie d'une bataille*. Paris: Les Belles Lettres, 2011. Originally published as *La resa di Roma: Battaglia a Carre, 9 giugno 53 a.*C. Rome: Laterza, 2010.

Visonà, Lucia. *La guerre contre l'autre: Les campagnes parthiques dans l'oeuvre de Plutarque*. Alessandria: Edizioni dell'Orso, 2023.

Armenia

Ferrari, Aldo, and Giusto Traina. *Storia degli Armeni*. Bologna: Il Mulino, 2020.

Patterson, Lee E. "Antony and Armenia." *Transactions of the American Philological Association* 145, no. 1 (2015): 77–105.

Traina, Giusto. "*Ambigua gens*? Methodological Problems in the Ancient Armenian History." In *Reflections of Armenian Identity in History and Historiography*, edited by Houri Berberian and Touraj Daryaee. Irvine, CA: Jordan Center for Persian Studies, 2018.

Caucasian Albania

Traina, Giusto. "Strabo and the Caucasian Albanians: Some Preliminary Remarks." In *Constructions identitaires en Asie Mineure (VIIIe siècle avant J.-C–IIIe siècle après J.-C.)*, edited by Lauriane Locatelli, Émilie Piguet, and Simone Podestà. Besançon: Presses universitaires de Franche-Comté, 2021.

Media Atropatene

Schottky, Martin. *Media Atropatene und Gross-Armenien in hellenistischer Zeit*. Bonn: Habelt, 1989.

INDEX

Achaemenid Empire, 8
Africa, 43–45, 71, 101–102, 109; Lepidus in, 127–128
Agrasius, Publius, 22, 23
Agrippa, Marcus Vipsanius, 24, 26, 126–127, 180, 182; honored by Octavian, 135; victory over Sextus Pompey, 131–134
Agrius, Gaius, 22
Ahenobarbus, Domitius, 74, 100–101, 105–106, 139
Alchaidamus, 59
Alexander the Great, 5, 8–9, 94, 150
Alexandria: Antony's life in, 167–168; banquets and wine in life of, 167–169; plunder of art in, 168. *See also* Greece
Alpine territories, 160–163
Antigonus II, 106, 108
Antioch, 62–63
Antonius, Gaius, 12, 28, 34, 52, 56; ordered killed by Brutus, 66
Antonius, Lucius, 84–85, 92–93, 99; Perusine War and, 101–102
Antony, Mark, 5, 10, 12, 27–28, 66–67; Armenia and, 147–151, 155, 169–172; attack on Media Atropatene, 148–149; attack on Palmyra, 98–99; attack on the Balkans, 74; attack on Vera, 149; attitude toward political situation in Italy, 93; Canidus Crassus and, 147; children of, 108; Cicero's writings on, 34; conferred third consulship, 179–180; criticisms of, 175–176; death of, 76; Egypt and, 93–94; first eastern campaign of, 139–140; floggings ordered by, 31–32; friends and freeloaders of, 32–33; in Greece, 90–94, 102, 103–104; Hyrcanus II and, 57; imitation of Alexander the Great, 150; last will and testament of, 178–179; legions in Gaul and, 45–46; marriage to Cleopatra, 143–144; marriage to Octavia, 106, 107, 112–113, 144; military leadership of, 30–31, 33, 94, 181; Mutina and, 46–49; naval blockade against, 74; officials in the East appointed by, 140–141; Parthian problem and, 93–94, 120–124; Perusine War and, 104–105; Philippi campaign and, 76–78, 88; policy towards Hebrews, 130; proclaimed a new Dionysus, 92–93; relationship with Cleopatra, 93–97, 169, 172–175, 177–178; relationship with Octavian, 34–36, 85, 130–131; responsibility for running operations in East, 88–89, 93; restructuring of provincial appointments by, 30–31; second eastern campaign of, 169–170; seizure of army in Macedonia by, 33–34; successful campaigns in the east, 128–130, 172–175; in Syria, 142–143
Antyllus, 168–169
Apollonia, 24–26
Appian, 64, 66–67, 102, 113, 153
Arabio, 43–45, 71
Ariobarzanes III, 15, 66, 74
Aristodemus of Nysa, 24
Armenia: conspiracy between Octavian and, 171; first campaign in, 146–151, 155; second campaign in, 169–172; temple of Anahit in, 170
Arsinoë IV, 5, 91, 97, 140

Artavasdes. *See* Artawazd II
Artawazd II, xiii, 15, 116–117
Artawazd I of Armenia, 147–150, 167, 169, 171; as prisoner of Rome, 172
Asander, 14
Asia Minor, 1, 5, 24, 52; Antony's marriage to Cleopatra and, 144; Antony's plans for, after defeat of Sextus Pompey, 139–140; Ariobarzanes killed in, 66; Brutus in, 29, 64; Caesar's successes in, 16; Cassius in, 73–74; Dolabella as governor of, 60–61, 63; Gaius Antonius sent to, 28; Gaius Furnius in control of, 140; Labienus driven out of, 121–122; punishment of cities in, 141; tribal systems in, 33; tribute and requisition troops taken from, 72–73, 74; triumvir artists and musicians in, 91; triumvir taxation of, 66–67; united with Europe by king of Macedon, 8
astrology, 26
Athens, 53–54; support for Brutus, 55–56
Atticus, Titus Pomponius, 54

Balbus, Lucius Cornelius, 107, 108
Balkans, the, 13–14; Censorinus put in charge of, 90; Roman order imposed on, 87; Roman victories and political organization of, 156–160
Bassus, Publius Ventidius, 46, 125; support of Alchaidamus for, 59; support of Sampsiceramus of Emesa for, 59
Bassus, Quintus Caecilius, 6–7
Bibulus, Calpurnius, 78–79
Bocchus II, 44
Brutus, Decimus, 17, 24, 28–29, 39, 45; amnesty granted to, 37; awarded province by Caesar, 29; in Cilicia, 65; Crete granted to, 52–53; departure from Rome, 52; at Mutina, 46–49; operations in Lycia, 73–74; responsibility for Rome's grain supply, 28–29; suicide of, 76, 78; supported in Athens, 55–56; Thessalians and, 56–57
Brutus, Lucius Iunius, 55
Brutus, Marcus Junius, 35, 38, 39, 42, 64–67, 83, 160, 162; amnesty given to, 27, 37; armies and allies of, 90–91, 112, 118–119; in Athens, 24, 53–56; Crete granted to, 52; death of, 85; Octavian and, 48–49, 74; in Macedonia, 64, 74–75; in Mutina, 45–46, 60; in Philippi, 76–79; in Sicily, 28–29; in Syria, 57; triumvirs' price on head of, 69, 72–74, 87
Burebista, 11–12, 13, 14, 158

Caesar, Julius: ambitions of, 15–16; assassins of, 17, 24; campaigns in the East, 11; Cleopatra and, 5, 9–10; colonies in Africa under, 45; death of, 1, 17, 25; as dictator, 16–17, 68; divinization of, 68; entertainments and stage plays enjoyed by, 6; exploration of the world under, 21–24; false reports of death of, 6–7; in Gades, 8–9; intent with Gallic Wars, 40; learning under, 24–25; map of civil wars of, 4; military triumphs of, 5–6, 26–27; Nicolaus of Damascus on campaigns of, 1, 7–8, 11; plot against, 17; prominent prisoners taken by, 5; public works in Rome under, 10; relationship with Cleopatra, 9–10, 93, 94; riots in Rome during time of, 3, 5; Roman citizenship granted to soldiers from Spain and Gaul by, 27; rumors circulating prior to assassination of, 9–10; in Syria, 3; war with Pompey, 2–3, 6–7; war with Spain, 37–38; war with the Parthian Empire, 1–3, 14–15
Caesar, Sextus Iulius, 5, 6, 15, 37–38; replaced by Antistius Vetus, 57
Calenus, Quintus Fufius, 101
Calvinus, Domitius, 108, 125–126
Caninus, Marcus Acilius, 25
Cassius Longinus, Gaius, 2, 24, 28–29; Alexander and Mnaseas attack on fleet of, 73; amnesty granted to, 37; awarded province by Caesar, 29; Cyrenaica granted to, 52–53; departure from Rome, 52; in Greece, 60–64; occupation of Syria,

57; Parthian troops and, 77; responsibility for Rome's grain supply, 28–29; suicide of, 76, 78; in Syria, 59–60; in Tarsus, 62; treatment of Jews by, 60
Castor of Rhodes, 116
Censorinus, Lucius Marcius, 90
Cicero, 5, 7, 10, 16; *On Divination* by, 26; execution of, 50–51, 66; Mark Antony and, 34, 35–36
Cicero, Marcus Tullius, 24–25
Circus Maximus, 6
Cleopatra, 5, 9–10, 67, 88, 102; children of, 102–103, 108, 178–179; marriage to Antony, 143–144; relationship with Antony, 93–97, 169, 172–175; relationship with Caesar, 9–10, 93, 94; sinking of fleet of, 74; summoned by Antony, 89; in Syria, 142–143. *See also* Egypt
Corinth, 54–55
Cornificius, Quintus, 71, 86
Corvinus, Lucius Valerius Messalla, 78–79
Cotta, Lucius Aurelius, 16
Cotyla, Lucius Varius, 47
Cotys IV, 13
Cotys VI, 13, 65, 75
Cotys VII, 153
Crassus, Canidius, 147
Crassus, Marcus Licinius, 1, 7, 15, 32
Crassus, Marcus Licinius, Jr., 2

Dacians, 11–15, 34
Dalmatia, 157–160, 165–166
Deiotarus, 32–33
Dio, Cassius, 3, 5, 7, 43; on Cicero's death, 51; comparison of Antony and Octavian, 35; criticism of Antony by, 106, 112; on marriage of Octavia and Antony, 112–113; on negotiations between Sextus and Antony/Octavian, 111; on Quintus Labienus and Syria, 117; on Roman control of the eastern Mediterranean, 83, 88
Dolabella, Publius Cornelius, 33–34, 52; in Greece, 60–64; suicide of, 64

Egypt, 3, 5, 6, 51, 66–67, 74, 77; Antony and, 89, 93–97; Octavian's last war against, 178, 180–187. *See also* Cleopatra
Eratosthenes, 21
Eurycles, Gaius Julius, 180

Figulus, Publius Nigidius, 26
Fulvia (wife of Mark Antony), 32–33, 34, 49, 50, 84, 99; children of, 85; Eumeneia renamed after, 91–92; important social and political role of, 85; Lucius Antonius and, 92–93; marriage to Antony, 97; Perusine War and, 101; responsibility for the Perusine War, 104–105
Fundanius, Gaius, 22
Furnius, Gaius, 153

Gades, 8–9
Gallic Wars, 12, 21, 40–50
Gallius, Quintus, 78
Gaul, 104, 107; Agrippa in, 126–127; Roman citizenship granted to soldiers from, 27, 84–85; Romanization and founding of new towns and cities in, 84
Gorgias, 24
Goths, 13
Greece, 90–91; Antony in, 90–94, 102, 103–104; honors awarded to soldiers of, 141–142; Roman citizenship granted to notables from, 92; Roman soldiers finding asylum in, 91–92. *See also* Alexandria
Gromaticus, Hyginus, 155–156

Helios, Alexander, 108
Herod the Great, 57, 106, 108
Hirtius, Aulus, 46
Horace, 24, 78, 120, 146, 151, 180, 185
Hortensius, Quintus, 25
Hybrida, Gaius Antonius, 72
Hyrcanus II, John, 3, 57

Ides of March, 1, 17
Iphicrates, 101
Isotype, 114

Juba, 5
Judea, 106, 108, 117–118, 130

Labienus, Quintus, 76–77, 117–121; driven out of Asia Minor, 121–122
Lepidus, Marcus Aemilius, 16, 39–40, 72, 99, 100, 108–109; in Africa, 127–128; beginning of the Principate and, 155–156; fall of, 134; marginalization of, 171; relationship with Octavian, 85–86
Levi, Mario Attilio, 89
Livy, 119, 122, 148, 150, 159
Lycia, 73–74

Macedonia, 33–34
Massinissa II, 43
Maximus, Valerius, 41–42
Media Atropatene, 148–149, 153
Mela, Pomponius, 22
Messana (Messina), 70
Metellus, Quintus Caecilius, 3, 8
Metulum, 162–163
Mithradates II, 66
Mithradates III, 15
Mithradates VI, 5, 12, 30, 103, 140
Mithridates of Pergamum, 14
Mithridatic War, 2
Murcus, Lucius Staius, 59, 74
Mutina, 46–49, 64

Nepos, Cornelius, 8
Nerva, Lucius Cocceius, 105
Neurath, Otto, 114
Nicolaus of Damascus, 1, 7–8, 11
Norbanus Flaccus, Gaius, 75–76

Octavia, 106, 107, 112–113, 144, 177
Octavian, 11, 17, 66–67; as adversary of Sextus, 38–39; Africa and, 101–102; after Caesar's assasination, 25; astrology and, 26, 30; attack on the Balkans, 74; birth and education of, 24, 25–27; campaign in Metulum, 162–163; decision to take over for Caesar, 27–28; desire to imitate Caesar, 164–165; entertainments under, 106; Gaul and, 107; last war against Egypt, 178, 180–187; last will and testament of Antony and, 178–179; naval blockade against, 74; negotiations with Sextus, 109–111; Perusine War and, 101–102, 104–105; Philippi campaign and, 76–78; relationship with Antony, 34–36, 85, 130–131, 177–178; relationship with Lepidus, 85–86; return to Rome after Caesar's assasination, 25; secret conspiracy with Armenia, 171; strategy for attacks in the east, 157–158; as successor to Caesar, 29–30; supporters of, 180; victory over Illyria/Dalmatia, 158–159
Octavius, Gaius, 26
Orodes II, 2, 11, 15, 145
Osaces, 28–29
Ovid, 47

Pact of Misenum, 111–112
Palmyra, 98–99
Pansa, Gaius Vibius, 46
Parthian Empire, 1–3, 14–15, 76–77, 93–94; Antony's pretext for attacking, 146–147; aristocratic support for Antony in, 120; armies defeated by, 156–157; Cappadocia and, 116; Judea and, 106; Labienus and, 117–121; prisoners of, 151; unrest in Cappadocia and, 116–117; Ventidius and, 121–124
Paterculus, Velleius, 11, 38
Perusine War, 101–102, 104–105
Pharnaces II, 5
Pharsalus, battle of, 2–3, 13, 25, 29, 37, 54–56, 59–62, 77, 86
Philippi campaign, 74–79, 88, 153
Philotas of Amphissa, 168–169
Phraates, 145–146, 149–150
Plancus, Munatius, 41
Pliny the Elder, 30, 170
Plutarch, 2, 15, 74, 92; on Antony's triumph in Armenia, 172; on Caesar and Pompey,

86–87; on Canidus Crassus, 147; on Cleopatra, 102–103; on Labienus, 119; on life in Alexandria, 168–169; on superiority of the Roman army, 152
Pollio, Gaius Asinius, 37, 43, 49
Pompey the Great, 2–3, 6–7
Posidonius, 31
Principate, the, 155–156
Ptolemy XIII, 74
Ptolemy XIV, 10
Ptolemy XV, 9–10
Punic War, 70

realpolitik, 85–86
Rhascupolis (or Rhescuporis), 13, 75, 76, 79, 153
Rhascus, 75, 76, 79
Rhodes, 73
Roman Republic, the: in Africa, 43–45, 71, 101–102, 109; agricultural study in, 22–23; Apollonia in, 24–26; battle at Pharsalus and, 2–3, 13, 25, 29, 37, 54, 56, 59–62, 86; Caesar's last campaign and, 1–17; control of Judea, 106, 108, 117–118, 130; control of the Mediterranean by, 68–72, 83, 185–187; deterrent power of, 139; education in, 24–25; entertainments in, 6, 32, 106; exploration of the world by, 21–23; fiscal resources provided by eastern provinces to, 65–67; gods of, 100; learning in, 24–25; Philippi campaign and, 74–79, 88; piracy in, 139; realpolitik used in, 85–86; reconfiguration of alliances on eastern borders and, 114–116; survey and world geography and, 21–24; victory in the Alpine region, 160–163

Sadalas II, 13, 65
Salassians, 157, 160–161
Salvidienus Rufus, Quintus, 24, 73, 104, 105; execution of, 105
Sapaean dynasty, 75–76
Saxa, Lucius Decidius, 75
Sertorius, Quintus, 39
Sextus Pompey, 37–38, 53, 64, 79, 99; Agrippa's victory over, 131–134; in Armenia, 155; battle at Pharsalus and, 2–3, 13, 25, 29, 37, 54, 56, 59–62, 86; command at Massalia, 42–43; control of Africa and, 43–44; control of Sicily and, 70–71; eastern campaign and, 153–155; grain intercepted by, 74; hopes for revenge on Rome, 139; influence of, 38–39; Jewish hostility toward, 57; naval successes of, 69–71; negotiations with Antony and Octavian, 109–111; Pact of Misenum and, 111–112; Perusine War and, 103–104; as threat to triumvirs' plans, 70
Sicily, 70–71, 134
Sittius, Publis, 44–45
Socrates of Rhodes, 92
Sosius, 44, 141
Spain, 37–38, 39–40, 72; Roman citizenship granted to soldiers from, 27
Spinther, Publius Lentulus, 61
Statianus, Oppius, 149
Strabo, 12, 139, 150–151
Suetonius, 9, 15
Syria, 117; Bassus' control of troops in, 6–7; Cassius in, 59–60; Cleopatra in, 142–143; restructured by Sosius, 141

Tarcondimotus, 62
Tarsus, 61–62
Taurus, Titus Statilius, 131, 156, 166
Temple of Anahit, 170
Temple of Jerusalem, 3
Thasos, 78–79
Theodotus of Chios, 74
Thessaly, 56
Tigran II, 15, 30
Titius, Marcus, 154
Trajan, 15
Treaty of Tarentum, 140
Trebonius, Gaius, 47, 60–61
triumvirate, first, 50
triumvirate, second, 50

triumvirs: African support for, 71; Appian on activities of, 66–67; appointment of new leaders by, 107; armies assembled by, 71; artists and musicians moved through Asia by, 91; Brutus and Cassius named traitors by, 69, 72, 76; Caesar's former lieutenants and success of, 125–126; Cornificius and, 71; domination of executive organs of the Republic, 72–73; list of major figures in Ides of March plot gathered by, 50; powers of, 50, 83–84; preparations for war against Caesar's murderers, 69, 72; promotion of territorial conquests of Caesar by, 68; Sextus as threat to, 70; success in the Philippi campaign, 74–79

Varius, Lucius, 31
Varro, 22–23
Vatinius, Publius, 14, 25
Ventidius Bassus, Publius: conquest of Perusia and, 101; control of Asia Minor, 121–124, 126–127; retreat to Picenum, 46–49; victory over Labienus and the Parthians, 148
Vera, 149
Vercingetorix, 5
Vetus, Antistius, 57
Virgil, 84, 108, 113, 126, 178

Xanthus, seige of, 73–74

A NOTE ON THE TYPE

This book has been composed in Arno, an Old-style serif typeface in the classic Venetian tradition, designed by Robert Slimbach at Adobe.